SELF MASTERY

OTHER WORK BY BOGDAN JUNCEWICZ

SKILLED SUCCESS

6 DAY PUBLISH

SELF MASTERY

CREATE THE LIFE YOU WANT BY
BECOMING THE PERSON YOU WANT TO BE

BOGDAN JUNCEWICZ
AUTHOR OF SKILLED SUCCESS

SELF MASTERY
Copyright © Bogdan Juncewicz, 2019

All rights reserved. No part of this publication may be reproduced, transmitted, shared or distributed - except for brief quotations in critical book reviews or articles - without prior, written permission. The contents of this publication are the intellectual property of Bogdan Juncewicz. If you are not sure as to what exactly you can and cannot do with the contents of this publication, contact the author and gain written permission first.

www.BogdanJuncewicz.com
ISBN: 9781798730270

CONTENTS

INTRODUCTION:

THE RESULTS YOU WANT...   1
...& the profound, yet forgotten or overlooked, key to creating the health, wealth, love & happiness you want.

CONSTANT STORY OF *VARIED* RESULTS   3
...& the 1 special ingredient that changes everything!

IT ALL STARTS WITH *SELF MASTERY*...   4
If you could become the best version of 'you' - someone who follows through on what matters, kicks butt & makes things happen - how would this impact <u>ALL</u> areas of life?

WHO AM I & WHAT YOU'LL LEARN INSIDE?   6
A mission to elevate, improve & evolve human education, achievement & life experience... (PLUS: how this book will positively impact 'who you are' & results you'll get!)

1 | POTENTIAL:
RECOGNIZING POSSIBILITY

1 | POSSIBILITY STREAMS   13
What makes up the 'future?' What possibilities exist for you? - How our thoughts, feelings, decisions & actions shape our future - Why the past doesn't have to equal the future -'Self-fulfilling prophecies' & how to create powerful forward momentum!

2 | IDENTITY: WHO ARE YOU?   47

Albert Einstein, Nikola Tesla, who we really are & the subjective nature of reality - The 'identity' filter & why people see things differently - Profound insights into why you do what you do - How to seize any opportunity better! - Why 'be yourself' is dangerous advice & the journey of self-mastery...

3 | RADICAL RESPONSIBILITY   74

Viktor Frankl, the Nazi concentration camps & the 'last human freedom' - The true consequences of blame & cultivating an internal 'locus of control' - Gandhi, reducing stress & power of interpretation - Global issues, change & circles of responsibility.

2 | AMBITION:
ALIGNING INTENTIONS

4 | CLARITY: SET & ALIGN INTENTION   103

The correlation between clarity & success - The 'Reticular Activating System,' & how to prime your mind for success - Motivation 1.0, 2.0 & 3.0 - Why the right 'motive' is the key to lasting happiness - Self-transcendence, Map of Consciousness & the meaning of life - Ambition Circles & other practical exercises to help you identify what you really want in life - A new model of thinking that'll help you make the absolute best decisions in life.

5 | HEIGHT: PLAYING A BIGGER GAME   160

Mark Twain, Steve Jobs & their views on playing big, regret & society's 'rules' - Danger of 'comfort' & what separates greatness from mediocrity - Elephant training, chickens in water & 1 question that can radically change the course of your life!

<u>PLUS:</u> *5 biological, psychological & environmental reasons that keep people dreaming small (& how to turn the tables on them to achieve more...)*

1. 'Rules' Of Society

How 'social norms' form & why following all of them is a path to being average & unhappy - Enzo Ferrari, Harley Davidson, challenging the status quo & how to live the life you truly want to live...

2. Survival Instincts

Your '3 brains' & how they affect your decisions - What 1000+ scientific studies say about meditation - How to reduce fear, boost your confidence & 'feed the wolf' of profound thinking & feeling in your life.

3. Current Circumstances

Internet in Kenya, rate of growth & how impossible things get achieved every day - The big danger of basing your goals on the past or present & what to do instead - How to put yourself on a 'trajectory' for success!

4. Opinions Of Others

Walt Disney, Elvis Presley, why opinions of other's hurt & how to handle judgment, rejection, criticism & hate better - What to do when those you love most encourage you to 'dream small' or 'be realistic'...

5. Fear Of Failure

Why 'fear of failure' can be so terrifying - Michael Jordan, J.K. Rowling, startups in Silicon Valley & how to react to failure like the world's highest achievers...

3 | PSYCHOLOGY: MASTERING MINDSET

6 | WHY YOU ARE 'WHO YOU ARE'   241

What drives your decision making? Are our limits self-imposed? How can you create better results at anything you do? - People watching, my deep fascination & how to turn goals into reality...

<u>PLUS:</u> *The groundbreaking framework - the '3 Categories Of Conditioning' - which, better than ever, explains why you are who you are...*

> **1. *Ancestry:* Biological Conditioning**
> *Do genetics shape your destiny? How do our genes impact our health, abilities, IQ & success? - The new science of 'epigenetics' & cutting-edge genetic research - Geniuses, child prodigies & what makes a master?*
>
> **2. *Childhood:* Pre-Consciousness**
> *Why children don't question Santa Claus or the Tooth Fairy early on & why they begin to in later childhood - First 7 years, brain waves & how we get 'conditioned' - Why a bad childhood doesn't doom you for a failed life (& what to do if you had one...)*
>
> **3. *Environmental:* Endless Influence**
> *How people, information & physical things influence what we think, feel & do? - The 'people' phenomenon, 3 proven degrees of influence & how smoking or even obesity spreads - The value of history, why fear is such a strong motivator & how the media uses it to keep you hooked - Veganism, supply & demand & changing the world...*

7 | CONDITIONING A NEW 'YOU' — 328

Is it possible to change something you've done almost every day for 4, 7, 12, 20 or 32 years? Is change really possible? And if so, how?

<u>PLUS:</u> *A powerful 4-step process you can use to change any 'belief' 'habit' or 'behavior' you want...*

1. ### Clarity & Disassociation
   Smoking, drinking, phobias, nail-biting, drugs, limiting beliefs & other changes you make - How to believe a change is possible for you (even if you don't believe it now)...

2. ### A Big Enough 'Why'
   The 2 guiding forces that control our lives & how to make change feel like a 'must' (so you actually follow through & get results!)

3. ### Breaking Old 'Patterns'
   Power of 'interrupting' old habits - Why it's never too late (or early) to change! - Pour water on yourself, strike a yoga pose & other ways to start 'breaking' old habits...'

4. ### Wiring New 'Patterns'
   The importance of 'repetition' & how to 'overwrite' old beliefs, habits or behaviors with new ones that bring you success!

INTRODUCTION

THE RESULTS YOU WANT (& THE PROFOUND, *YET OFTEN FORGOTTEN*, KEY TO ATTAINING THEM...)

We spend a lot of our time thinking, wishing, wondering about & looking for opportunities to make our lives better...

Opportunities that'll bring us better *health & fitness*, more *wealth & freedom*, greater *love, relationships & connection*, as well as more *happiness, joy & fulfillment* in general!

And when we look for these things, similar messages appear:

"This new diet will revolutionize your health" or...

"This new workout & exercise plan will transform your fitness"

"This business opportunity will help you achieve the financial freedom you desire" or...

"Apply this strategy & it'll double your income..."

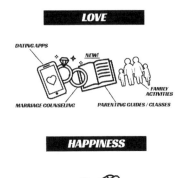

"This dating app will help you find the love you desire" or...

"This guide will help you be a be a better partner & parent..."

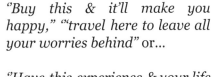

"Buy this & it'll make you happy," "travel here to leave all your worries behind" or...

"Have this experience & your life will be amazing again!"

However, there's just 1 problem will all of these promises...

That there's actually a 2nd, often forgotten or overlooked, side to the story which made these results possible...

See, each of the above statements <u>could</u> be true for us...

We all know people - either personally or just those we've seen online or in the media - who have used a certain diet or workout routine to be healthier, fitter & stronger than before.

In that same way, we all know people who have used some type of business opportunity or investment vehicle to make more money, get out of debt, earn more while working less or tap into more freedom, joy & fulfillment in their work.

We all know people who have found a date - perhaps even the love of their life - through some fancy new dating app or used some guide, course, event or training to become a better lover, spouse, parent, friend, family member & member of society.

However, this was only possible for them *(& therefore is only possible for you)* if you have the 2nd **critical component** (which is too often forgotten or overlooked) in place...

CONSTANT STORY OF *VARIED* RESULTS (& THE 1 SPECIAL INGREDIENT THAT CHANGES *EVERYTHING*)

Take any 2 people, give them the same opportunity, such as a new diet or business opportunity (& even give them the same training on how to get the most out of that opportunity) - yet despite everything, people are going to get *different* results.

And I'm sure you've seen this play out countless time in your life - 2 students in the same class who get different grades, 2 people who start in the same business opportunity yet end up earning vastly different amounts of income from it, 2 people with get themselves a fancy gym membership with the goal of 'losing 20 pounds' yet end up getting different results.

1 of the people succeeds while the other, perhaps, fails. Or, 1 person achieves the goal in 3 months, while the other gets the desired result in only 1 month (a third of the time!).

And the same applies to that new business opportunity, that dating course, those horse-riding lessons, swimming classes or that big goal you set for yourself on New Years...

At first, this may seem odd... *'given the same opportunity, they should produce the same results'* one may even reason. But, rarely (if ever) is that how it works. *This is the 'constant, story of varied results' that we all experience all of the time...*

To explain this though is actually easier than it may seem. While in all these simple, everyday examples everything may seem the same, however, it's not. *1 thing is different (which makes all the difference!) That 1 variant is...* <u>YOU</u>.

Think about it... there was probably a time in your life in which some information was conveyed to you (by a teacher, a driving instructor, an art professor, your boss or someone else) & you quickly understood & followed through on that information, yet someone who also got that <u>same</u> information (a fellow student, employee, etc) didn't understand it *(or if they did, didn't do anything with it & didn't get the results.)*

What made the difference between your success & that other person's failure? Was it the information conveyed (which was the <u>same</u>) or was it the person who got the information?

In this same way, what made the difference between your failed attempts in the past & other's successes?

Just as a skilled craftsman can take the 'tools' & use them to create something extraordinary, an unskilled craftsman - even though they may have the <u>same</u> 'tools' - will get worse results.

And they may even get disheartened, blaming the 'tools' as the reason for the failure instead of their own shortcomings...

In reality, it's the person going into an 'opportunity' - using a particular 'tool' - that makes the biggest difference. Which makes working on yourself - or, **self mastery** - the missing key to creating the health, wealth, love & happiness you want.

Self mastery, simply put, is this simple, profound, yet too often forgotten or overlooked, key to being on the right side of the *constant story of varied results...*

IT ALL STARTS WITH <u>SELF MASTERY</u>...

> *"You will never have a greater or lesser dominion than that over yourself... the height of a man's success is gauged by his self-mastery"*
>
> \- LEONARDO DA VINCI

'Opportunities' (or 'tools') are important, but they're also **step #2** to achieving anything...

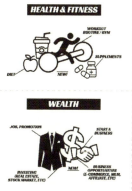

Step #1 you must have in place <u>first</u> is **_self mastery_**.

The perfect business opportunity given to someone who's unclear on their goals, is uninspired, lacks motivation, gets easily distracted, doesn't kick butt & doesn't follow through on what's needed - *isn't* the recipe for success.

The business opportunity may be incredible 'tool,' but unless the 1st step of **_'self mastery'_** is in place, it's rather useless…

Self mastery is <u>step #1</u>. The **_'opportunities'_** are <u>step #2</u>.

Hence, it's by changing, improving & mastering 'who you are' *(including: knowing who you are & what you want, setting goals effectively, mastering mindset, building self-discipline, being productive, not distracted & getting great at following through)* can you fully seize 'opportunities' & get results.

Becoming the best version of yourself really is like a 'big domino' in life. Once that one begins to fall, all other things fall into place much easier too *(great health, vast wealth, amazing relationships, deep happiness & fulfillment, etc)*.

Plus, **_self mastery_** is the 1 thing you have true control over…

You may not be able to change the economy, the government, the industry you work in, the weather or how many fast food restaurants open up near your home, but you can always change, improve & master yourself...

Ultimately, I've found your results do not outweigh your level of *self mastery* (or, if they do, it's temporary - it doesn't last)

So the best, more predictable, controllable & sustainable way to create the life you want is to become the best version of yourself *(which is what this book will help you do...)*

WHO AM I & WHAT YOU'LL LEARN INSIDE?

> *"There is only one corner of the universe you can be certain of improving, and that's your own self"*
>
> - ALDOUS HUXLEY

Hey, before we get into the book, *let me introduce myself...*

My name's Bogdan & when I was about 14 years old, I made probably the smartest decision I've ever made...

It changed my life, led me down my own journey of *self mastery* & ultimately guided me to the mission I've now dedicated my life to - *elevating, improving & evolving human education, achievement & life experience.*

While perhaps sounding a little counterintuitive at first, this 'best decision' of mine was actually choosing to drop out of high school & become, what I now refer to as, a *'voluntary high school dropout.'*

You may have heard of entrepreneurial kids flunking out of college before the last semester as their revolutionary idea just couldn't wait - well, it's like that *(only slightly different...)*

Firstly, it was high school. Secondly, unlike those genius kids in the movies, I didn't yet have a clear idea of what I wanted or what I was going to do after dropping out...

Rather, I just had questions. Questions about success, the world we live in, why people do what they do & life in general.

At the time, I had already been involved in self-help & personal development, going to events with my parents & reading as many books as I could on these topics...

And this initial research (outside of the school curriculum) was enough for me to recognize there was more to life than what my teachers were telling me. *I sensed it, knew it & felt it.*

So, at the end of the school year, after making this decision with my parents, it turned from choice to reality.

Sure, a part of me was terrified at the beginning *(which I had too much pride to admit at the time)* as I had just cut off my backup - the safety of traditional education & employment.

But, the excitement & prospects for my prosperous future far outweighed the fear. *I knew if I didn't do this, I would regret it.* Big time! So I kept my head held high & got to work...

After dropping out, I used the 8, or so, hours I normally would have spent in school to get educated about life...

I spent the next few years reading around 500 books, going through countless articles, videos, online courses as well as in-person events. On topics, from psychology to business, from neuroscience & quantum physics to marketing & sales. From learning, skill development, productivity & performance psychology to economics, relationships & spirituality.

Initially, I never actually intended on sharing these learnings with anyone. It was just a way of quenching my own curiosity & actually learning about life. But, soon after, it became more.

'Why isn't this taught in schools?' I remember thinking to myself over & over again, *'This knowledge is so valuable - many of the world's problems would get solved if only people learned this stuff...'*

And, it was one of the times that my mind went down this rabbit hole of questions that something just 'clicked' for me & I knew this is what I wanted to do with my life. It became my mission; the life purpose I wake up every day to actualize...

This mission is to elevate, improve & evolve human education, achievement & life experience; to provide an alternative to the traditional school curriculum (for people of all ages) that's based on what people actually want in life, as well as what cutting-edge research shows us is possible...

Skipping ahead: since then I've gone on to publish multiple books, travel around the world & speak on stages & platforms across 3 continents now as part of this mission. To teach, coach & work with thousands & thousands of people around the world. Including multi-millionaires, TEDx speakers, gym owners, musicians, school teachers *(that one's a bit ironic...)*, entrepreneurs, health experts, TV producers & more...

My first book, titled, **Skilled Success**: *Learn Faster, Train Like The Best & Become Extraordinary At Anything,* has been ordered from & delivered to 56 countries *(& growing...)*

I started 2 businesses around this mission as well, which now serve fans, readers, customers & clients across 6 continents.

One of which operates like an agency, making me the person behind the content & marketing of other top influencers, businesses & brands too. Ones which share unconventional, yet highly effective, information about health & wellness, personal development, business, finance & more *(all stuff I believe should be taught in school, but largely isn't...)*

And I share all of this with you for 2 fundamental reasons...

Firstly, so you know the mission I'm on, as well as trust that what you're about to read here is highly effective information that has years of research, testing & experience behind it *(it's not stuff that's been put together overnight after watching some motivational videos on the internet for the first time.)*

Secondly, to thank you & acknowledge you for the smart choice you made to pick up & start reading this book - *you're literally about to shortcut years in hours!*

What I mean is that the content in this book has taken me more than half a decade of almost day-in, day-out work to learn, improve, tweak & refine. However, instead of you also having to invest years of your life to get this information, you're getting the best, most effective, curated understandings & strategies in this 1 single book.

This is the content I wish the education system taught me (& others) back when I was in school...

The pages you're about to read also compile some of the latest & most cutting-edge scientific research & discoveries *(across fields such as human psychology, neuroscience, performance psychology, human biology & sociology)* as well as proven, practical strategies you can apply, almost immediately, to become the best version of yourself & create the life you want.

I really look forward to going on this journey with you inside the chapters of this book. *And with that, let's get started...*

1.
POTENTIAL:
RECOGNIZING POSSIBILITY

"A thought, even a possibility, can shatter & transform us."
FRIEDRICH NIETZSCHE

What's possible for you? How much potential is there for you to play within? How high up is the glass ceiling set - or is the glass ceiling just something we've been misled to believe, which in itself is the only limit that could hold us back? Perhaps, it's our belief there are limitations placed on our potential that are the only real limits that exist for us...

Ultimately, it's only through our willingness & courage to explore any limits we may perceive that we can answer these questions. And that's where we start: with the exploration of what's really possible for us. This is because a single insight in this area can change our lives forever. And now's the time to entertain these questions of our true potential...

1 | POSSIBILITY STREAMS: HOW TO SHAPE A BETTER FUTURE

"The best way to predict your future is to create it"

- ABRAHAM LINCOLN

We all have a past. *You. Me. Everybody.* And, as you read this, you're experiencing the present moment. And then, of course, there's the future. We all have a future we're creating, influencing & shaping in some way - whether that's a minute, an hour, a day, week, month, year or decade from now...

The difference between these though is where the insight is found. While the past is *known,* the future is not - it's *unknown*. It exists as pure potential with an infinite number of possibilities - or 'possibility streams' - we can tap into...

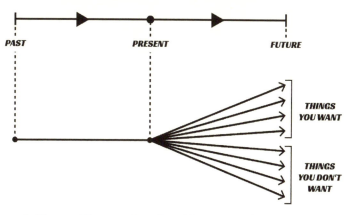

The past is linear. Known. Predictable. Sure, there's room for interpretation. You can learn from the past, heal the past &

use it as fuel or motivation, but the universal understanding is that the past has already happened & cannot be changed.

You can't impact it or go back in time & change it. It's linear. And it's known. Hence, the reason why you can't bet on the score of yesterday's game - that's already in the past.

Now, the present is also known. Predictable. It's happening as we speak. *Right here. Right now.* You can see what's around you. You can experience your current reality - what you see, what you hear & what you feel - it's very linear. Known, but fleading. *Each second to the next...*

The future, on the other hand, is very different. It's not linear. Far from it. It's infinite, holding an endless number of 'possibilities.' Quantum physics shows us this is the case. In the quantum field that governs all matter, all space, time, distance, energies & frequencies co-exist simultaneously. All of this simply means...

| The Future Is Filled With One Thing & One Thing Only: <u>Potential</u>

Not 'matter' (physical "things") but energy. Potential exists & doesn't at the same time, depending on where you place your attention. **Simply put:** at any given moment, our future is nothing more than infinite, untapped potential - an endless number of 'possibility streams.'

To understand this, picture kayaking down a river, & coming to a crossing. A single path splitting into many, many streams of water in the river. Except, there aren't 2, 3 or 5 streams (possibilities) from here, but an infinite amount.

Any mathematics attempted here would, of course, fall short as *infinity* cannot be put in a box like that, but just to help you to scope the true potential that exists for you, me & everybody, let's explore...

Imagine if someone told you that you had to crack a code. Not a hard one, just a 2-digit one. Each digit, 0 - 9.

Mathematically speaking, it's not too difficult. Chances are you would be pretty confident that, with enough time, you could crack this 2 digit code.

Why? Because there are only 100 possible combinations (or, 'possibilities') with just 2 variables (2 digits). Take a look...

X	0	1	2	3	4	5	6	7	8	9
0	0,0	1,0	2,0	3,0	4,0	5,0	6,0	7,0	8,0	9,0
1	0,1	1,1	2,1	3,1	4,1	5,1	6,1	7,1	8,1	9,1
2	0,2	1,2	2,2	3,2	4,2	5,2	6,2	7,2	8,2	9,2
3	0,3	1,3	2,3	3,3	4,3	5,3	6,3	7,3	8,3	9,3
4	0,4	1,4	2,4	3,4	4,4	5,4	6,4	7,4	8,4	9,4
5	0,5	1,5	2,5	3,5	4,5	5,5	6,5	7,5	8,5	9,5
6	0,6	1,6	2,6	3,6	4,6	5,6	6,6	7,6	8,6	9,6
7	0,7	1,7	2,7	3,7	4,7	5,7	6,7	7,7	8,7	9,7
8	0,8	1,8	2,8	3,8	4,8	5,8	6,8	7,8	8,8	9,8
9	0,9	1,9	2,9	3,9	4,9	5,9	6,9	7,9	8,9	9,9

All you would have to do is test each of the combinations (& since there are only 100 of them, it wouldn't take long) & 1 of them will work. Easy, peasy - no problem at all.

But, what if I showed you another lock that was a 3-digit combination? How easy would it be to crack now?

Although you're adding just 1 extra digit, the amount of possible combination ('possibilities') multiplies 10-fold. Not 100 anymore, but now 1000 possible combinations ow.

Now, what about yet if another digit was added? A 4-digit code this time. Again, the number of possible combinations grows 10 times up to 10,000 possible combinations. So, while it's just 2 extra digits, the reality is that a 4 digit code is actually 100 times harder to crack than a 2 digit code.

"Now, what has this got to do with us? With you? With me? With success? With shaping a better future?" you may think. Well, assuming the world had only 2 variables to it, the future would still have 100 'possibilities' for how it *could* unfold.

> *3 variables = **1000** possibility streams*
> *4 variables = **10,000** possibility streams*
> *5 variables = **100,000** possibility streams*
> *6 variables = **1,000,000** possibility streams*
> *7 variables = **10,000,000** possibility streams*
> *8 variables = **100,000,000** possibility streams*
> *9 variables = **1,000,000,000** possibility streams*
> *10 variables = **10,000,000,000** possibility streams*

And that's just 4 variables. Or 6. Or 10. Now, let's look at life...

There are more than 7 billion people, with different beliefs, viewpoints, ambitions, opinions & values. Many different countries, cultures, communities, religions & spiritual beliefs between them. People wanting different things, making different choices & taking different actions.

As a result, people, situations & circumstances change - all the time. The world is never the same, but constantly changing.

This shouldn't come as a surprise when you have billions of people dancing together in this incredible game called life. All different. All unique. All beautiful. All doing the absolute best they can with what they know, understand & believe.

And if, mathematically, 9 variables working together gives you 1 billion different 'possibility streams' for what the world would look like in the future, how many do over 7 billion variables give you?

Mathematically, it gives you a result - a number with 7 billion zeros to it (for context, imagine a library in which every book was filled with nothing but zero's & that would still be far from the 7 billion zeros this number would have).

And remember: this maths here is just to put things into some type of scope that we can understand as no number here could compute this. This is because potential & possibilities don't play by those rules.

And neither does 'energy,' - subatomic particles at the center of all atoms - which is what the greatest physicists have found to be foundational make-up of all 'matter' - everything we can see, touch & feel.

What's important is we recognize *there is an infinite number of 'possibilities' for what the world - & specifically here, what your world - can look like in the future.* **Potential.**

When I tell people in my work *'nearly anything is possible'*, they think I'm just passing along a cliche. Except: I'm not - that what science, mathematics & specifically here, quantum physics shows us about the universe & our future within it. It's real. All too real even.

Knowing this, our job shouldn't be to fear what could happen or to attempt to control it all. But, rather to find meaning to it.

And, if greater success is what we're after (depending on what this means to you) to skew the odds of the 'possibility streams' we want happening, while reducing the odds of the 'possibility streams' we don't want from becoming the reality...

POSSIBILITY / PROBABILITY STREAMS

> *"The best scientist is open to experience and begins with romance - the idea that anything is possible."*
>
> - *RAY BRADBURY*

You could hit by a car tomorrow. You could find a winning lottery ticket on the floor as you exit a shopping mall. You could bump into the love of your life. Or, a loved one could pass. You could meet someone who takes your career to the next level. Or the economy could crash.

You could overhear something that changes how you view someone in your life, or you could read, listen to, or watch something that changes your life forever.

You could decide that you want to become a painter, or a writer, a musician, a teacher or an investor, change your career path & live a completely different life a few years from now than you do today. So much so that your life would be completely unrecognizable from what it looks like today.

You could meet someone, end up moving to the other side of the world & start a whole new life for yourself.

You could encounter an 'opportunity' (for health, for wealth, for fame or influence, for greater spirituality - anything really), go after it & your life could completely change. For better or for worse, but it's all possible.

While there is an infinite number of possibilities that *coexist* at any moment (& each of these represents different things that 'could' happen in the future), they do not all have an equal 'probability' of happening. Far from it. Some are likely to happen - based on us - have low odds of happening. And that's where 'probability' comes in...

POSSIBILITY / PROBABILITY STREAMS

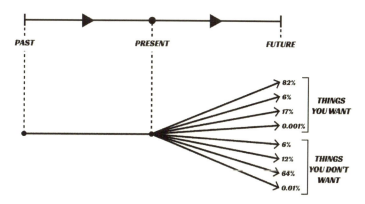

Depending on who you are, what you think, decisions you make, actions you take, who you surround yourself with, or the environment around you, the probability of things you want (or don't want) happening go up or down.

With this understanding, we can begin to skew the odds of success, achievement, freedom, joy & fulfillment in our favor. We can mold, shape & create our future as we freely choose to. *And that's what this book is all about...*

You'll learn how to recognize your potential & then harness your creative power to design the life you want (& create it). You'll learn how to turn possibility into reality & as a result experience a level of success - & most of all, freedom - that few ever experience...

FOUNDATION OF LEARNING, CHOICE & ACTION

> *"It is the small things in life which count; it is the inconsequential leak which empties the biggest reservoir."*
>
> \- CHARLES COMISKEY

Following the advice of *"look left, look right"* before crossing a road, for example, <u>doesn't</u> *guarantee (meaning: 100% chance of success, 0% chance of failure)* that you won't get hit by a car, but it <u>does</u> *radically decrease* the odds of this happening.

Ignoring this advice & crossing a road without precaution on the other hand, mathematically, boosts risk by increasing the probability you'll get hit by a car.

In both examples - precaution or not - you could still get hit by a car, but in one, you've *intentionally* used a piece of knowledge (which aided a new action) to skew your odds of success in your favor. In the other, you did the opposite.

This is a simple example to demonstrate this point, but what's more important though is that all thought, feeling, learning, choice & action has the same impact - it either skews the probability of the things we want turning into reality, or it does the opposite - moving them ever further away from us.

And this is how our future is being shaped by what we do. Not directly, but indirectly. This is how high-achieving people - extraordinary individuals with extraordinary, joy-filled lives - created their future, continue to do so & how you can too...

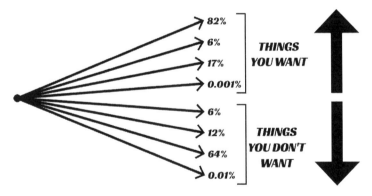

People go to the gym to increase the probability of a future in which they are fit & healthy. It doesn't *guarantee* success. There are plenty of other ways one's health & fitness could disappear - medical condition, struck by lightning, drugged by someone at a party, etc.

Outcomes are not guaranteed, but through our thinking, our choices & our actions we skew the probability of what today, next week, next month & next year will look like for us.

All the possibilities that co-exist for our future (positive & negative) are constantly adjusting based on what we think, feel, decide & do - as well as factors outside of our control.

People meditate, for example, to increase the probability of a future in which they are grounded, peaceful & calm under pressure, while reducing the probability of becoming a stress-out, disconnected & easily annoyed.

Learning about relationships increases the probability of a future in which you're in a happy, loving relationship while decreasing the odds of one in which you're miserable in your relationship or the relationship has ended altogether.

Learning, making decisions & our actions are not accidental, but have motives to them. We do things for a reason - even if we don't realize it consciously.

And the most important foundational understanding is that...

| Every Thought, Feeling, Decision & Action Is Shaping Your Future

Combined & focused, these thoughts, feelings, decisions & actions can create extraordinary things (if we choose) - each little one contributing to the whole.

Each cigarette, beer & stressful situation, for example, contributes to an unhealthy future. While each healthy meal & workout contributes to a healthy future.

"Great things are done by a series of small things brought together" is what Vincent Van Gogh once wrote.

And Mother Teresa said, *"Be faithful in small things because it is in them that your strength lies."*

A magnificent future *(health, wealth, love, fulfillment, joy, freedom)* is created with each small, day-in, day-out, thing that doesn't seem to matter <u>until it does...</u>

RECOGNIZE YOUR TRUE POTENTIAL

> *"It's the possibility that keeps me going, not the guarantee."*
>
> - *NICHOLAS SPARKS*

Does the possibility exist for great health, fitness & vitality? Yes. Absolutely. Although, if you're overweight (or struggling with health problems) right now, you may think, *'No - I'm just destined to struggle in my health. I always have been & always will be...'*

The reality is that while the potential does exist for health & fitness in your future (even if you don't believe it does), it remains pure potential unless you choose to recognize it & do something about it.

When working with customers & client, in situations like this phrasing such as *'If someone put a gun to your head & told you that you have to lose weight & be healthy, could you?'* Or, *"If someone gave you a million bucks to do so, could you lose weight?"*

As simple & even childish as these questions seem, they make us realize that the difference between what we've made up to be possible & what is really possible for us.

So, does the potential for great health, fitness & vitality exist (irrelevant of your current health & fitness)? Yes.

In this work, I've seen this over & over again. I've seen people with health struggles, rising obesity & medical problems turn everything around. They would lose 15 or 20 kg's (sometimes more), reverse their aging (looking younger today than they did 10 or 15 years ago & when examined, seeing their biological age going down, not up) & completely curing themselves of various medical problems that the medical & pharmaceutical industries had considered 'incurable.'

I've seen this work produce theses results. And if it's possible for others, it must mean it's possible for you too...

I've worked with people who were addicted to alcohol, drugs or sex. Some I've worked with personally, while others who told me their story of transformation before we continued doing further work together. These people cleared their lives of these various addictions.

How? By mastering themselves; *self-mastery*. At the core, they decided that their past wasn't going to be their future, that they were going to change things & learned how to master themselves. They did it by aligning their thoughts, feelings, decisions & actions with new potential available in their future. It's possible. Beyond this...

Does the potential for great, connected, friendships, relationships & family bonds exist for you - even if they seem very, very far away? Can you become more confident, more connected, more caring & better socially? Yes, yes & yes. Absolutely. The potential for this all exists...

And I've seen people go from completely closed off, lacking any sense of connection in their lives, abhorring vulnerability & struggling in many social relationships in their lives to becoming entirely new people now surrounded by love.

Family bonds repaired. Friendships transformed. Marriages revolutionized. People who have stepped into a new sense of confidence in their life. These possibilities all exist & people are tapping into them every single day through the intentions of bettering themselves.

And this one here, specifically, is a big one for me personally as I used to be a shy, socially-awkward kid growing up. I was closed off emotionally & found it hard to connect with people. I knew that this was limiting me, but for a long time, I couldn't break out of it. I was in a limiting loop of belief, action & results (as I'll share in a moment) & it kept me stuck.

At a certain point thought - through my personal journey of bettering myself - I recognizing that 1) I wanted to change this & 2) there was a new possibility - different potential - available for me that I can tap into. *And so, I did.*

I tapped into this potential & created this in my life. A shift, crafted through *thought, feeling, choice, decision & action.*

Best part: this personal transformation (in this area) I went through (& am continually improving at) has massively impacted the work I do.

To curate & share content. To work with customers & clients worldwide. To have traveled around the world, speaking on stages & platforms across many countries & continents. To spread my message & support people in their journey's of transformation. *All of this would've been much harder if I remained my 'old self,' who struggled socially - big time!*

I've seen so much transformation in myself, those close to me, my customers, clients, audience & people I've worked with, spoken to & coached over the years, that it's hard to fit all these examples into a book (or anything really).

What's most important is that while all these various changes were made in these people's lives, the way they did it was the same. By deciding to tune into new potential. By believing in something greater. By changing & improving themselves.

Next - Does the potential for vast wealth & abundance exist? Absolutely. No doubt about it. In the infinite potential, each of us can tap into, financial wealth & abundance is part of that.

In my work, study & experimentation of this work for the last 6 years of my life, I've seen people transform their financial outcomes too. Countless times. I've seen people struggling to pay the bills create massive wealth in their lives in reasonably short periods of time through hard work & dedication.

Not overnight. No - it doesn't happen that way. But by changing themselves, their mindset & their thinking, they saw opportunities differently & responded accordingly, which brought them new (better) financial results.

With time, this allowed them to create great wealth in their lives. And greater freedom; as it's not just about the money you make, but *how* you make it. Financial freedom. Financial independence. I've seen people change their work from something they hated to something that they can't wait to do every single day. To a point where their work (like mine) doesn't feel like work, but a calling. A mission.

Imagine waking up Monday morning, excited to 'work' & creating great wealth through it too. It's all possible when you work on yourself.

Lastly, does the potential for happiness, joy & fulfillment exist - even if it may seem the furthest things from you right now? Yes. It does. It's there - <u>but you have to want to see it.</u>

I've seen people go from depression to fulfillment, from ongoing feelings of sadness & struggle in their lives to a life that they love. It's possible. The infinite potential exists in the field for you & you're choosing which potential to tap into.

Now, you may think that this is some type of over-the-top positive thinking, but this is far from that. I don't believe in 'positive thinking' alone as that would perhaps assume that

POTENTIAL | 25

the future is only these bright, beautiful possibilities - great health, vast wealth, blissful love & absolute fulfillment. *This is not the case...*

While the possibility for health exists, so too does the possibility for sickness, poor fitness & medical struggle.

As the possibility for wealth exists, so does the possibility for lack, for struggle & for scarcity.

Love is one possibility which coexists with its opposites of hatred, loneliness & emptiness.

Lastly, while the possibility for total joy, happiness & fulfillment exists for you in your life, so does the path of misery, dissatisfaction & regret.

This is the way of the world & the law of duality states these options all coexist, like 2 sides of a coin. Once again: infinite possibilities for all potential futures you can imagine all exist as potential (as 'energy') for you, & you're choosing which of those possibilities you want to tap into.

The good, the bad, the ugly. The extraordinary. The horrible. And the beautiful. What you want & what you don't. The potential is all these. And it's through your thoughts, feelings, decisions & action that you're skewing the probability of some turning into reality & others not. *Own this & you tap into ultimate freedom & power in your life...*

SKEPTICAL YET?

If you find all of this hard to believe & your mind is filling up with doubt & skepticism, that's ok. That's your biology wanting to take over, as well as your 'survival instincts' & biases bringing you back to the known.

Our internal systems are designed to maintain *homeostasis*.

'Homeostasis' referring to the biological tendency & desire to stay in balance - to stay within what's known & comfortable.

It's the reason we become skeptical when we learn something new that's outside of our current realm of understanding (or challenges our current views of life). Our biology treats this information (even if it's incredibly empowering) as a threat to the 'normal', 'comfortable' state of knowledge & being that we're currently experiencing.

Fortunately, your consciousness can override this impulse. You can choose to keep learning even if you're skeptical, overwhelmed or confused. Just know this skepticism & discomfort is normal when learning or doing something that you haven't done before.

Also know that discomfort isn't a bad thing, but a good thing. Think of your time exercising or being at the gym. Your muscles (when trained) get uncomfortable. They get fatigued. It hurts. But, it's good pain, as - if you keep it up - you'll look at yourself naked in the mirror one day proud of the body that you sculpted. Your muscles grow in that discomfort, as does your mind *(we'll talk more about this later in the book)*.

Our role is to push through this initial resistance, expand knowledge & build skill. Anything is uncomfortable (& seems odd) at first. Like riding a bike, learning a new language or meeting strangers. At first, it's uncomfortable, but becomes incredibly fulfilling & worth it over time.

I remember when I first started my journey within this work; some of the stuff I learned felt a little like a punch in the gut. Not physically, but mentally & emotionally. It was hard. It was uncomfortable. Especially to let go of righteousness & to allow new information, new views & new beliefs into my life. I had to settle my skepticism & develop a new way of thinking about success. *I implore you to do the same...*

Besides our biological desire to maintain 'homeostasis' - to seek comfort & stability - it's also because, as the studies of human psychology show us, we often tie our beliefs & ideas about how the world works into our own identity. We get attached to them.

So, when these are challenged, our 'survival instincts' kick in *(which we'll talk about in the next section)* & it becomes easy to let them take over & fight this new information. To argue with it. To become increasingly righteous - attached to what we believed before instead of investigating this better option.

This can even make us feel good in the short term (as it saves us from feeling 'wrong' about something) however, in the long term, fighting new information is detrimental. We become increasingly closed off. We stop learning & growing. We fall behind. We don't create any new results.

So, in those moments of discomfort & skepticism (perhaps even right now), you also have a choice...

You can let your 'survival instincts' take over & rip you off from greater learning, understanding & success, or you can tune into courage, tell your 'survival instincts' to 'sit & listen,' continue to stay in this possibility & expand your awareness.

Instead of falling into the temptation of sticking with old beliefs, we must expand our thinking & knowledge.

Also, we must remind ourselves that our beliefs are, so often, not even our own. What we believe, so often, is simply passed down to us from our parents, grandparents, friends & family.

Odds are, there are certain things you believed 10 years ago, that today, you don't. It's because you are learning, growing & getting better *(as we'll talk about this more in later chapters).*

What I explore you to do here is simple & will give you profound results over time: be open to new information (even if it contradicts what you previously knew) & be willing...

Remember: what you know now got you to where you are right now. If you want to get somewhere else, it's likely you need some new information, new thinking & new beliefs. That requires openness, but it's ultimately worthwhile...

Important: *keep all this in mind while you read the chapters in this book as it'll make all the difference. This book can either change your life or do nothing for you; it all depends on whether you're open-minded, willing to settle your skepticism, embrace new possibilities & take action...*

CHANGE IS THE WAY OF THE WORLD

> *"In this world you're either growing or you're dying so get in motion and grow."*
>
> - *LOU HOLTZ*

The world is ever-changing, ever-evolving & ever-expanding. Look at nature & you'll see that everything is always in progress. Always growing or dying. Moving up or down. It' the way of nature; the way of the world. *It's said that the only constant in life is* ***'change.'***

So, by blocking change - by resisting it - you're not only blocking the infinite possibilities that exist for you but also you're going against the foundational law of nature.

By clinging to the past, you lose your edge. You fall behind. And you also lose your flexibility as well as your freedom. You become trapped, caged in your own little world that just doesn't exist anymore.

Businesses that resist change go bankrupt, while individuals that resist change, can lose their sense of meaning in life & never embrace true possibility that's available for them.

While fear will always be there - it's hardwired into our biology - we mustn't allow it to make us afraid of change, progress or growth, as change is the path to success.

As Charles Darwin observed, *"It is not the strongest of the species that survives, nor the most intelligent that survives. It is the one that is most adaptable to change"*

Or as Stephen Hawking once wrote, *"Intelligence is the ability to adapt to change."*

Be open to the greatness within you - the infinite potential - that wants to unleash itself by accepting change & being adaptable. When growth opportunities arise, seize them. Be open. Be willing. Be adaptable.

And equally, recognize that change stems from choice. You can choose to be stuck or to change & adapt. To get better. To improve. To grow your capabilities & results. **It's a choice.**

And, as to the first choice, we must all make in each & every moment of our lives…

WHAT ARE YOU CHOOSING TO FOCUS ON?

> *"What you focus on grows, what you think about expands, and what you dwell upon determines your destiny."*
>
> *-   ROBIN SHARMA*

To begin the process of tuning into new possibilities into our reality & creating a truer, more fulfilling future for ourselves, we must explore where we are placing our attention.

See, how we allocate our attention - our focus - will largely dictate the life we live & the future that we create. It's why when I guide people through this first framework - *Possibility Streams* - I follow this up quickly with an observation of what they are paying attention to; what they are 'focusing' on.

When I assess my own life as well & the results I get (those I want & those I *don't* want) I ask myself: *"What am I focusing on?"* as most of the process of change, transformation & shaping of a better future starts right here.

It's with this attentive observation that I find that when people (including myself & those close to me) aren't getting the results they want, it's because they are focusing on what they should not be paying too much attention to...

Most of their energy, attention & focus is spend in either the *'past'* or in *'what they don't want.'* They either complain about a terrible day they had yesterday or spend all their energy hoping they don't have another terrible day today.

We're going to explore the first of these 2 traps - 'the destructive habit of dwelling on the past' - right now & the 2nd - 'focusing on what you don't want' - will be covered in a later chapter of this book...

THE PAST: DWELLING & COMPLAINING

> *"Discontent, blaming, complaining, self-pity cannot serve as a foundation for a good future, no matter how much effort you make."*
>
> - *ECKHART TOLLE*

The first reason people stay the same is that they live in the same, known past that they're looking to move away from. They are stuck - living in the past. And this creates the same behaviors, the same decisions, actions & results as before.

See, we have the power to choose how we place our attention, but most places it primarily in the past. They dwell on what 'would've' 'should've' or 'could've' been, they complain about what happened yesterday or last week.

"Should've. Would've. Could've" That's how a lot of people spend their time & attention; dwelling on what 'should have' or 'could have' been. The challenge of this is that we get attached to a string of the past that <u>didn't</u> happen. We get hooked on it. We get addicted to it. We spend more & more on our attention on it - even though we have absolutely no power to change it (it's the past!). Understand this...

| Every Moment Dwelling On The Past Is A Moment <u>Not Spent</u> Enjoying The Beautiful Present Or Creating A Great Future

Dwelling & complaining - with time - will lead to you living a life filled with regret, rather than potential.

And it's this constant focus on the past that leads us to believe that the best is behind us - 'the good old days' some may say - instead of possibility & potential.

We no longer get out of bed in the morning *excited* for the new day. *Why would you be excited for the new day anyway if you truly believed that it would worse than anything in the past?* You lose that excitement & that sense of meaning for each day, week, month & life as a whole.

We can learn from the past. We can use it as fuel sometimes. We can leverage it. And we should. As Will Durant wrote, *"History is an excellent teacher with few pupils."* But, we must accept it for as it is rather than dwelling on what 'should've,' 'would've' or 'could've' been.

Some people even gather to complain & dwell on past together. They go for coffee to 'catch up' & spend time complaining about the weather, about their boss, about the economy, about the government - the world around them.

Then they wonder why their results stay exactly the same week to week, month to month, year to year *(instead of the lofty goals they set on New Year's).*

Our attention, our energy, our focus is the creative force that can help us create the life we want, but it can't if it's always redirected to the past - the known; the predictable. Instead, we must shift it to focusing on the present & the future.

However, in my work, I've found that merely complaining about the past isn't even the most destructive way we can use the past (although it's a big one!)

What's even more damaging for our potential is when we base our entire future potential on the past.

It's one thing to complain about what happened & it's another to also let yourself (specifically, your future potential) be defined by the efforts & results of your past...

THE PAST ≠ THE FUTURE (UNLESS YOU LET IT)

> *"Yesterday is gone. Tomorrow has not yet come. We have only today. Let us begin"*
>
> *-   MOTHER TERESA*

"...but I've <u>always</u> been overweight" "Everyone in my family has <u>always</u> struggled financially" "I've never been good at relationships" "I've <u>always</u> had difficulty with this" "I would like to meet the right guy, but I <u>always</u> meet the wrong guys" "you don't understand - this is just how it's <u>ALWAYS</u> been"

'If the future is filled with a nearly infinite number of 'possibilities' for us then why do people often stay the same?'

POTENTIAL | 33

you may think, or specifically, you may ask, *"Why do I keep getting the same results over & over again"*

Why do some people (perhaps even yourself) just stay the same, week after week, year after year? The same negative things keep happening, same negative situations occurring & the same future being shaped?

One of the biggest reasons why we don't change & don't harness the true possibilities that are available to us is because we believe that *'the past equals the future.'*

Phrases such as *'but, it's <u>always</u> been this way,'* show that this is how we think about the challenges & struggles in our lives. We think that because something has been this way before it must be that it will always be this way.

We get conditioned to believe that if something has been one way in the past, it will probably be like in the future. This applies to any areas of your life. Health. Career. Love life.

We base our future potential (our ambitions) on our past.

Except, we all know that this is complete nonsense at times.

Even if we hate to admit it sometimes, we know that just because something has seemingly 'always' been one way doesn't necessarily mean it will be that way in the future.

Deep down we know that results can change & those greater things are possible for us. *We must tune into this...*

The past <u>only</u> equals the future *<u>if you let it</u>*. Else, it can change. It can be molded & shaped into something else.

It all comes down to choice & to explore this further, let's deeply consider why people stay the same (as well as how they change). Let's explore how we 'self-prophecize'...

SELF-FULFILLING PROPHECIES: HOW 'BELIEF' SHAPES OUR FUTURE - FOR BETTER OR WORSE...

> *"Believe that life is worth living and your belief will help create the fact."*
>
> — WILLIAM JAMES

"I would like to be fitter & healthier... but it's not going to happen for me. I've <u>always</u> been overweight, so I know it's not going to happen for me" someone might say.

Initially, this thinking is total nonsense.

Does the fact that you're overweight (or broke, or struggling in your relationships, or unhappy with life) <u>right now</u> necessarily mean it'll be that way forever? **Absolutely not.**

It doesn't have to be. It's not guaranteed. It *could* change. Making this thinking initially untrue. It's false. It's a lie.

Except: thinking this way - believing it - makes it so. It becomes a *'self-fulfilling prophecy.'* Allow me to explain...

If you believe that you're not going to lose weight because you've *"always been overweight,"* the statement isn't true, except, because you believe it, it makes it true (over time).

With this thinking in mind, you go on diets knowing that 'they won't work anyway.' You sign up for the gym but don't go consistently. You don't stick to the plan you created for yourself. You never take full, committed action when it comes to your health because deep down you don't believe it would work anyway.

"Why would I bother putting in all this effort, if it's going to fail again" you may have thought to yourself. Your motivation is low. As is your commitment. So your action is 'half-assed.' Which off course shows little to no change in results. Short

term, this little bit of half-assed action can get some small results - they might lose a few kilos or so - but with time, this level of belief that created this half-assed caliber of action doesn't get results. It's the reason that studies show 97% of dieters regain any weight they lose.

And so, 5 years later, you may still be overweight. You didn't believe things would change. You didn't take any committed action to create an alternative reality. Hence, of course, things weren't going to change for you.

Change requires focus, decision, commitment, intensity. However, because you believe that it wasn't going to work out anyway, you didn't have any of those ingredients in place.

It's kinda like when someone goes to look for something that they've lost, but think to themselves, *'I've never going to find it anyway.'* Sure enough, they don't find it. Then a friend, a partner, a parent o a family member goes to look & they find it very quickly. *Why is this?* Is it because your vision is worse than that of your friend, parent or partner? Perhaps. But, the more likely explanation is that your seeking was 'half-assed.' You didn't believe you were going to find it anyway, so you weren't committed in your attempts to look for it. *You looked, but you didn't look as if your life depended on it.*

Same applies to any result we want to get. We often pursue these with the same belief & commitment that got us miserable results in the past. And that's where the really dangerous part kicks in.

'It's no use... I've always been & always will be overweight,' you said to yourself 5 years ago when you were starting. Then after 5 years of the same low belief driving low level of activity, you reinforce your initially-untrue belief to yourself.

'I knew it; I knew that I would always be overweight. I was right,' you might say to yourself. You'll ignore the fact that you skipped key workout days & you didn't follow any of your

meal plans & you'll likely just jump to the conclusion that you were right. Not, just you, this is everybody in part. It's part of human nature. We form assumptions based on recency. And now you've gone & reinforced (reaffirmed to yourself) your belief that you'll *'always be overweight.'*

Let's rewind: The belief that 'because you were overweight before mean you'll overweight in the future too' <u>wasn't</u> true, to begin with. It was false. *Except, you believing it made it so.*

Repeat this cycle & we end up stuck with, not just an opinion or a belief, but a *conviction* (a deep, strong, harder-to-crack belief) that becomes very hard to change.

As the great philosopher, Friedrich Nietzsche, once wrote, *"Convictions are more dangerous enemies of truth than lies."*

You become less likely to question the belief in the first place. You stop wanting to change to begin with. You lose your fighting spirit. Your fire. Your ambition. You end up stuck - trapped in a jail you created through your own mind.

That said, no matter what - as we've established - the possibility still exists for great health & fitness (or another outcome you want to achieve).

The possibility never stops existing; it's always there...

But, to tap into it, you have to approach it in a new way than you've done before...

And that how untrue, false, misconceptions become true. This is how we 'self-prophesize' in our lives.

Robert Merton coined the term *"self-fulfilling prophecy"* in 1948, defining it as, *"A false definition of the situation evoking a new behavior which makes the originally false conception come true"*

Believe that you're not going to amount to anything because of your past failures & that past will become your future. Decide to break out of this downwards cycle & replace it with an upwards cycle to shape the future you want.

SELF-FULFILLING PROPHECIES

WITHOUT OTHERS

WITH OTHERS "PYGMALION EFFECT"

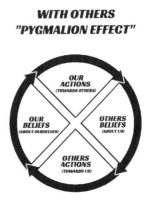

Your level of belief impacts your level of action. Doubt, for example, creates half-assed action. And half-assed action, as you know, tends to turn into half-assed, poor results.

A new belief in the potential that exists for you creates a higher caliber of decision & action.

You believe & now you take committed action. You're all in. Passionate. Inspired. Committed. Willing to do what it takes.

And now - if you keep this going over time - you will get the results you truly want.

These new results, in turn, reinforce your belief. Better results create higher belief in yourself, your efforts & your ability to shape your future & the whole cycle repeats.

This is what the basic cycle for momentum & for *'self-fulfilling prophecies'* looks like; take a look...

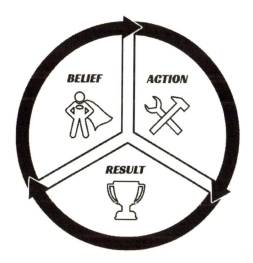

Your level of belief (high, low, in between, etc) affects the action you take. High belief leads to committed action, while doubt (believing something will fail before it even begins) creates half-assed action. Now, if you take different action, you get different results.

Take committed action & you'll much more likely to create the result you want, compared to the contrary. Then, our results reinforce our belief.

Our mind either goes, *"Yes. Great results. This is working. Let me keep going"* (& raises your belief) or it says, *"This isn't working. I told you it wouldn't work"* (your belief drops).

This is how the *law of momentum* affects us. You're either in an upwards spirit of momentum (or a downwards one).

Now, what happens when you add other people into the loop? You get what psychologists call the *'Pygmalion effect.'*

The essence is exactly the same - except the cycle is now even more vicious. A double-edged sword; either gaining positive momentum faster or creating a downwards spiral in even quicker succession.

THE 'PYGMALION EFFECT'

A good example of a self-fulfilling prophecy which includes the beliefs & actions of others - the 'Pygmalion effect' - is that of social anxiety.

For example, beliefs such as *"Nobody like me," "I'm just not good around people,"* or *"I'm unlovable,"* are initially false.

No child is born with a "this baby is unlovable" tattoo. Everybody is lovable & can become good in social situations. So initially, the thinking isn't true. It starts as a lie. There's much greater potential available for you. Except, once again, believing these statements *makes* them true.

Then, beliefs like these shape actions such as avoiding conversations with others & social situations, being alone, doubt themselves in public, etc.

These thoughts then shape the thoughts & beliefs of others. *"What's up with her?" "Why's he so awkward?"* Other begin to form beliefs about us...

Those actions then cause others to disengage from inviting them to social outings or from having conversations with them. This gives the person an excuse not to have to be in social situations. In reality, social skills are trainable. They can be developed. But, to develop these skills you need to put yourself in social situations.

For this individual in this example though, that opportunity is being cut off as others around them are now acting based on their thoughts & beliefs about them. Lastly, those actions (not being invited to social outings, being ignored or avoided, etc) reinforce the individual's initial belief *"Nobody likes me,"* or *"I'm not worthy of friendship & love."* The cycle continues...

WITH OTHERS
"PYGMALION EFFECT"

The belief starts off false but became true because the individual's belief in it made it so. It becomes a *'self-fulfilling prophecy,'* just like before, except this time the cycle included others & helped explain social situations.

1. Our beliefs (about ourselves) shape our actions (towards others).

2. Our outwards actions are then interpreted by others & they form beliefs (about us).

3. Then, just like for us, their beliefs (about us) affect their actions (towards us).

4. This is then interpreted by us, adjusting our belief & refueling the ongoing cycle.

It's important we don't underestimate the power of this as it affects so much more than what you may be able to comprehend right now. In fact, this affects almost everything.

A great example in relationships are the beliefs of *'he's just not marriage material'* or *'yes, she's definitely the one!'*

If a woman starts dating a man with the belief that 'he's not marriage material,' this thinking will drive her to take actions such as not investing time into the deeper conversations, planning the future or taking it seriously. This belief (*about* the partner) affects the actions (*towards* the partner).

Of course, this lack of true emotional investment into this relationship can lead the partner to start believing that she's distant & unavailable, not likely to stick with it long-term. This thinking affects actions. And, when the partner leaves, for example, she might think that she was ultimately proven right - he wasn't 'marriage material.' As you now know, she largely influenced this outcome with her thinking.

On the flip side, if a guy finds someone he believes is *'the one,'* this belief drives his actions. This different thinking creates different actions & with time, the belief - 'the one' - can become true. *That's how our thinking influences our life.*

In the field of education, they conducted multiple studies in which teachers were told that the class of students they were teaching were either 'the best students; destined for the best grades' or 'troublesome students; destined for poor results.'

As you might predict, these teachers beliefs about their students influenced their actions, which were interpreted differently by the students, driving different actions & results.

The results across multiple similar studies of this caliber: the students taught by the teacher who was told these were the 'best students' *(even if they weren't the best ones before)* become the best students with the best results while the opposite was true for those taught by the teachers who were told 'these are the poor, underperforming students.'

Zooming out a little further, stereotypes (over time) are often *'self-fulfilling prophecies,'* as are forms of discrimination, too.

You hear a stereotype so when you interact with someone of that gender, race, country of birth or residence, sexual preference, religion, etc, you're looking for evidence to show you that the stereotype is true.

You act differently & this thinking affects them, their actions & ultimately reinforces your beliefs.

EXERCISE: OBSERVE MOMENTUM
The first step to take charge of *momentum* in your life - the power of 'self-fulfilling prophecies' - is to raise awareness.

This exercise is an opportunity for you to do exactly that; to become aware of how we all 'self-prophecize'...

When have you fallen victim to this cycle of momentum? What was a time in which this cycle worked against you & can you recall a time in which this cycle worked for you?

As you go through your day, observe how others are being affected by this loop, as well as yourself. How is their 'belief' shaping their 'action' & how is that affecting their results? How could they create different results?

By, not just hearing the examples in this chapter, but seeing this play out in real life, you'll be able to better harness this in your own life to create a magnificent reality.

Back to the example in which an individual may say, *"but, I've always been overweight, or broke, or struggling"*...

If you allow yourself to get caught up in this thinking - *that your past equals your future* - then just be aware that you may end up 5 years later re-affirming to yourself the same challenges that you've just 'always' struggled with.

POTENTIAL | 43

Alternatively, you can break free of this cycle (whether it's in your health, your fitness, your career, your business, your relationships, your spirituality or your impact).

Just because you've been living out a certain cycle (or in a downwards spiral) before doesn't mean you have to stay in that hamster wheel.

Just like a car driving on the freeway, at any moment, if you realize you're going in the wrong direction, you can choose to pull off on the next exit & go a different way.

That's the magnificent *power of choice* we have. Simply: if you don't like the direction that you're currently on in various areas of your life, don't continue driving, but pull off & find a direction that's better suited for achieving what you truly want (but no worries, as this book will help you do this.)

| Your Past Only Equals Your Future If You Let It. Else, You Can Choose A New Path

"Choosing a new path - what does that mean & how do I do that?" you may think to yourself...

What it means is changing your *trajectory*. Your past doesn't equal the future, but your *trajectory* (your day-in, day-out, thoughts, feelings, decisions & actions) does.

Think about it with total reason. If you were overweight in the past, but you're on the right trajectory now (you believe, you make new decisions, eat well, exercise, work on your body, treat it like a temple, take action) you'll get the fitness results you want. The past doesn't matter as long as you're on the right path - going in the right direction - now; your trajectory.

I use fitness as an example often as it's very relatable & virtually everybody understands the basics well.

Your path, your trajectory, your direction (or whatever you want to call it) matter more than the past. Focus on those...

TRAJECTORY > CURRENT REALITY

See, the results we have right now (present day) are nothing more than the outcomes (the output) of the beliefs, thought, decisions & actions of the past (the input). This means that the path (trajectory) you used to be on - your thoughts, beliefs & actions (trajectory) of the past created your present-day results. *This ultimately means that new actions (input) will create new results in the future.*

For example, I would much rather be overweight, but be going to the gym consistently, eating well & caring about my health than to be fit & healthy right now but on a downward trajectory, eating unhealthy foods & never exercising.

Meaning: I would rather be in a poor *current reality*, but on a positive, upwards *trajectory*, than the other way around. *I'm sure, thinking long-term, you would choose the same.*

| Focus Less On Where You Stand Today & More On The Path (Trajectory) You're On

Instead of dwelling on the past (which you cannot change), we could better use our energy by following the worlds of the poet, Emily Dickinson, *"I dwell in possibility."* Don't dwell on what has already been, but in what you can become. Focus on possibility & your path to get there.

And, in doubt, always remember Buckminster Fuller's wise analogy, *"There is nothing in a caterpillar that tells you it's going to be a butterfly."*

There may be nothing about you, me or anyone else that indicates we're going to do, become, experience or achieve something a certain thing, but that doesn't mean we won't.

Like a caterpillar, you could have absolutely nothing going for you right now, but that doesn't matter because the past doesn't equal the future.

It doesn't matter what has happened in the past. *What matters is the trajectory - the path - that you're on right now.*

Assuming you're on the right trajectory, you can create the results you want.

As to how you do that - *change your trajectory* - & start making new decisions & taking new actions, this is the result of understanding & improving *'who we are.'* And that's exactly what we're going to cover in the next chapter...

For now - from this chapter - it's important you remember that the future is nothing more than an infinite set of 'possibility streams' that you can *choose* to tap into through your thoughts, decisions & actions.

Don't let your past keep you from dreaming big & creating an extraordinary life for yourself.

We all have a past - me, you, everybody - but it shouldn't define the future - that's for us to *freely choose*...

2 | IDENTITY: WHO ARE YOU?
A NEW 'YOU' = NEW RESULTS

"The key to growth is the introduction of higher dimensions of consciousness into our awareness"

- *LAO TZU*

"Who are we?" It's a question which has been pondered, questioned & studied by people of all walks of life.

Philosophers. Scientists. Physicists. Psychologists. Teachers. Masters. Individuals as well as groups. Even *you* - at one point or anyone, I'm sure you've asked yourself, *"who are we?"* or individually, *"who am I?"*

"Who am I really & why am I am who I am & not someone or something else?" or *"How can I be a different (better) version of whoever or whatever I am?"* you may have thought...

These are big-picture, higher-level questions & the answers influence everything. Our answers to the question, 'Who are we?' or 'Who am I?' shape our meaning of life, our sense of purpose, our thoughts, our decisions, our actions, as well as anything & everything in between.

From how we choose to dress, what study & work we choose to pursue, what we eat, where we live, who we spend time with. Everything is influenced by our answer. Who we date & marry, our bonds with our family, the friends with make, the wealth we accumulate & how we spend our time - all of it.

Like a pair of tinted sunglasses, what we see, situations we encounter, challenges we face & opportunities around us (various forms of 'information') are *filtered* through this lens of how we see ourselves *('who we are' - our 'identity.')*

Our self-esteem, self-worth & our emotional reality, as you'll learn, depend on this sense of self & are dictated by it.

Knowing this, we know the question of *'who I am?'* is not asked out of boredom, but out of curiosity & ambition. As you'll learn, the more we can learn about ourselves, not only the more can we can achieve, but the more magnificent possibilities we can tap into.

In this chapter, we're going to explore various aspects of this, including, how we view opportunities *(for health, for wealth, for love, for happiness, for joy & for success)* in our lives, how our beliefs shape our actions, who we really are, as well as well as the surest, most proven, way to set yourself to tap any of the infinite possibilities you choose to. *Let's begin...*

A SUBJECTIVE REALITY: HOW POSSIBILITIES & OPPORTUNITIES ARE INFLUENCED BY 'WHO WE ARE'

> *"Your big opportunity may be right where you are now"*
>
> - *NAPOLEON HILL*

Just as there are an infinite number of *possibilities* that exist for your future, there are also an incalculable, ever-growing number (if not an infinite amount) of *'opportunities'* for us to seize to get there.

'Possibilities' refers to the end results we want to attain (such as health, wealth, love, joy, freedom). *'Opportunities'* refer to the means of making 'possibilities' happen.

For example, 'financial success' is a <u>*possibility*</u> that exists for you (& your future). Meanwhile, a new job, business venture, business model, investment strategy, education & training are all <u>opportunities</u> that can bring you to that *possibility*.

A 'possibility' is like a destination, while an 'opportunity' is the transport - vehicle; method - that will bring you there.

Opportunities for: health, wealth, love, connection, joy, happiness, fulfillment - they're all there, co-existing...

However, with that said, we do not recognize & truly value all these opportunities, but rather, we only see & seize selective ones, based on *'who we are.'*

In his book, *Opportunity*, Eben Pagan, wrote an example that best illustrates this...

> *A LUMBERJACK, A BOTANIST, and a monk walk into a forest. What do they see? The botanist sees plants to study, the lumberjack sees trees to chop down, and the monk sees the miracle of existence.*
>
> *Three people, three different perspectives on reality. Each of us moves through the world perceiving things through our own unique prisms of personality and experience.*
>
> *We are born with similar senses, but we each live in our own version of reality, and the way we see reality impacts the way we perceive opportunity.*
>
> *Now imagine three people walking into a grocery store. One might see an opportunity to buy tomatoes on sale, another sees an opportunity to socialize, and the third sees an opportunity to start a better grocery store down the street. Each of us is naturally on the lookout for an opportunity in our own unique way, but we can train ourselves to see the world - and opportunity - in new ways.*

POTENTIAL | 49

Everything that comes into our lives (*information*) is filtered through 'who we are' (our *identity*) to form *interpretations*.

A SUBJECTIVE REALITY

2 people can receive the same *message*, experience the same situation or encounter the same stimulus (various forms of *information*) yet *interpret* them in very different ways & form a different *meanings* (based on, once again, *our 'identity'*).

The lumberjack, for example, may not even recognize the opportunity to study the plants in the forest. The opportunity is there but goes unrecognized. For him, the forest is seen as merely a place to cut trees & get wood. The *information* for the lumberjack, botanist & monk is the same (a forest) yet the *interpretation* (specifically, which co-existing 'opportunities' are recognized & which are overlooked) is very different.

You've probably seen this in your own life - for example, you see something (a watch, a car, a new app, new idea, someone, a business venture, vacation spot, new restaurant, etc) & while you get super excited about it, someone else says to you *"Why are you so excited about this? What's the big deal?"*

For you, this is like the coolest new discovery in the world, yet for someone else, it brings them no excitement. *"Don't you understand? Look how awesome this is?"* you might say, but they reply with, *"I understand, I just <u>don't</u> find it exciting."*

This is because we all see things (information & opportunity) differently based on 'who we are.' And for 'opportunities' specifically, it's only when an opportunity is a match with our 'identity,' are we drawn to it & likely to seize it. So, while an 'opportunity' may be available to many, only those whose 'identity' is truly aligned with it will recognize it & tap into it.

See, the *possibilities* we want to attain (goals; end results), as well as the incalculable number of opportunities we can pursue to achieve those goals (means; methods), are a bit like barcodes. And our *'identity'* is like a barcode scanner.

As items with barcodes (*opportunities*) go down the checkout line of life, the barcode scanner is either going to recognize the barcode (& process the encoded information) or not.

To continue the metaphor, if you got items (with barcodes) from 1 supermarket & scanned them with a barcode scanner from a <u>*different*</u> supermarket chain, while the barcode would be the same as before, that barcode scanner <u>*wouldn't*</u> register those items (& interpret the information within the barcodes).

Why? It's simply because this barcode scanner hasn't been 'programmed' to recognize those specific barcodes, but only those from within its own supermarket chain.

Like it or not, we (human beings) operate in a similar way. We interpret *information* (& recognize opportunities) based on 'who we are.' Things outside of that - which we haven't been primed & programmed to recognize - are likely to be misinterpreted or discarded completely...

| Like A Barcode Scanner, We Only Recognize, Effectively Interpret & Act Upon That Which We've Been Primed & Programmed To See

So, as these opportunities for health, wealth, love & happiness present themselves (which are all around us), our 'identity' (our barcode scanner) doesn't register them properly & we either overlooked them completely or aren't mentally set up to take full advantage of them. We miss out...

Knowing this we also know, to begin to see the extraordinary opportunities that could change our lives forever (which we may be overlooking right now) we must become the type of people (align our 'identity') who are primed to recognize, value & seize those opportunities.

A successful entrepreneur sees opportunities to make money everywhere. A successful influencer finds new exciting things to photo, video, write about & share anywhere & everywhere.

A great architect or designer always finds inspiration to scope out & design new things. Musicians see lyrics, rhythm & beats in seemingly-everything. Great painters see beauty & artistry everywhere that inspires their next paintings.

A wine enthusiast can describe different wines in dozens of different ways, while the average person only sees wine as 'good,' or 'bad' wine. Same with the coffee fan or car fanatic.

While the input (information) is the same for them as the average individual (same glass of wine, blend of coffee or sports car) the output (interpretation) is very different. *Why?* Because they've primed, programmed & trained themselves to see what others can't; to see nuances. As the quote goes...

"Life is about the gray areas. Things are seldom black and white, even when we wish they were and think they should be, and I like exploring this nuanced terrain" - Emily Giffin

All of this information (specifically, 'opportunity') technically co-exist for all of the people, yet most don't see them.

The architect may overlook the business opportunity that the successful entrepreneur may seize, while the entrepreneur may miss the opportunity for an incredible relationship that a romantic will easily recognize & seize. *Reality is 'filtered' - by us.* Or, put in other words…

| Reality Is Subjective

Subjective: *based on or influenced by personal feelings, tastes, or opinions.*

Information comes in, but is interpreted very differently based on our 'identity.' Therefore, only by changing parts of our 'identity,' can we interpret the same information differently, recognize opportunities you may have previously overlooked & tap into new streams of the infinite potential that's available to us.

And this, of all the reasons, is one of the biggest & most foundational one for why we don't create the life we want: we haven't primed, programmed & conditioned ourselves to spot the possibilities & opportunities to get the things we want.

We're blind to them because of who we believe we are, as well as who we believe we are <u>not</u> (our 'identity.') *Change this & you change your life…*

HOW WE SEIZE OPPORTUNITIES IS 'FILTERED'

Not only do we recognize (or overlook) opportunities around us, but what we do with those opportunities once we see them is also 'filtered' by our *identity* (by 'who we are.')

Winston Churchill put it best when he said, *"A pessimist sees the difficulty in every opportunity; an optimist sees the opportunity in every difficulty."*

We all know someone who no matter how bad the situation may appear finds a way to spin it into the positive; *"Yes, I know it may seem bad, but look at this silver lining... it's actually a very good thing. And here's why..."*

Equally, we all know someone who does the opposite; no matter how good the situation may appear, they find a way to turn it into something negative. The best, most amazing opportunities for success & fulfillment may be available (& even recognized by them), but they don't do anything about it because they find a way to turn themselves against it. They find every possible excuse <u>not</u> to do it.

You've probably known, have seen or at least heard of some people who have seemed to have nothing yet are love with life & others who seem to have everything, yet are miserable.

Or people who seem to have everything given to them - every possible opportunity is there, waiting for them - yet they do nothing with it & others, who seem to have the odds stacked against them, fully seize an opportunity & get amazing results.

This is, once again, your 'identity' ('who you are') is filtering what you see, what decisions you make & what actions you take outside of yourself based on what's inside of you; you see the world around us through the filter of what's inside. *As a result, the inner world of 'who you are' shapes your outer world of reality.*

If you're a loving person - if that's a belief that's part of your identity - you're likely to see love, connection & heart in all various types of situations.

If you're a clinically depressed person, on the other hand, it's not that all beauty & joy in the world suddenly disappears - woosh; vanished - no, it's simply that you can't recognize or seize those opportunities for wonder & joy.

You may even acknowledge that something looks nice, but you do it half-heartedly - you don't feel it. You recognize this opportunity for experiencing beauty or joy, but based on 'who you think you are,' you don't do anything about it.

If you're a resilient or determined person, you're more likely to seize *any* opportunity that comes your way fully.

These traits are part of our identity (as we'll talk about) & influence how we seize the opportunities that we recognize.

How we interpret information & opportunity (based on *'who we are,'* how we see ourselves & our 'identity' in general) also goes on to shape our thoughts & feelings...

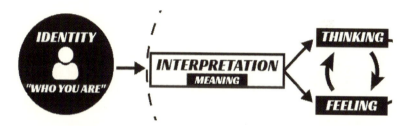

First, information comes in ('opportunities' are also forms of information) & is interpreted by us, *subjectively*. Next, our *interpretation* shapes our thinking & feeling.

Imagine, after some good early growth, progress halts & now the startup is seemingly going backward. For someone who believes they aren't worthy of success, has a negative relationship with failure (as we'll talk about in later chapters), who's bad at 'sticking things out' & in general, isn't generally self-disciplined, determined or committed, this incoming information may be interpreted as: *'It's a sign: it's not going to work. We should close up shop & do something else.'*

That interpretation drives our thinking & feeling. It may drive thinking such as *'I knew it was going to fail anyway,' 'I'm a failure,'* or *'I should just lower my goals & play small.'* It also may drive feelings of shame, guilt, pain or anger.

And people can stay in that thinking & feeling for weeks, month or years...

Their thinking about business, aiming high & going after your dreams tainted...

Thinking & feeling. Feeling & thinking. They can become stuck in this certain 'state of mind.'

On the flip side, in that same situation, someone who's motivated, self-disciplined, resilient, determined, committed, passionate, willing to 'stick it out' & believes that 'failure is a part of success, an opportunity to learn & chance to improve,' might interpret this same information as a sign to change something, to re-assess the strategy, to keep going & to keep testing new things to make this startup successful.

Same information, but interpreted very differently (a new 'meaning' assigned to the 'message') based on 'who we are.'

This interpretation, once again, drives our *thinking & feeling*.

In this case though, it's thinking such as, *'It's just a fork in the road, let's get back on track,' 'What can we do to keep making progress & make this startup a success?'* or *'Let's double-down & do all we can to improve this...'*

As well, feelings of courage, determination & excitement come from this interpretation.

Thinking & feeling. Feelings & thinking. Now, you're **thinking & feeling** in a very different way.

Again: *the same information, interpreted very differently drives very different thinking & feeling.*

When we understand how these pieces work both individually (as well as together) we don't just become more much aware of how we're creating our current results, but it opens us up to great opportunities for us to tap into for new, better results going forward...

HOW IT ALL COMES TOGETHER...

You already know how we 'self-prophesize' & now you know what drives that cycle - your *thoughts & feelings*...

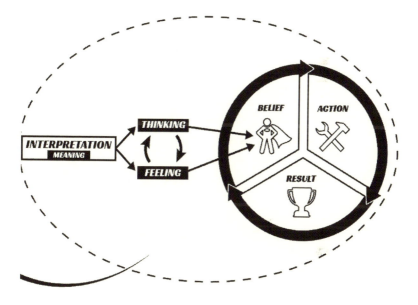

Our thoughts & feelings come from our interpretations.

Which are formed as *information* is filtered through *'who we are,'* how we see ourselves & our 'identity' in general.

Putting it all together, this is <u>why we do what we do</u> (the big picture framework of understanding):

WHY WE DO WHAT WE DO?

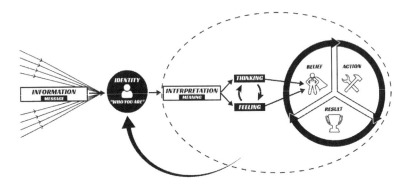

Now, to get different results (tune into new possibilities available to us in the quantum field), let's reverse-engineer...

The results we get in our lives come primarily from our proactive actions *(more on this in the next chapter)*.

Those *actions* (through your decisions) come from your level of *belief*. Believe something will work out & you'll make decisions & take actions very different than if you think something is going to fail.

That *belief* (high or low) is driven by our *thinking & feeling (which we'll explore in the 'Psychology' section of the book.)*

And that *thinking & feeling* is a result of our interpretations of incoming information. How this information is interpreted of course depends on *'who we are,'* - our *'identity.'*

So to change your results (change your life) the most foundational & powerful way to do it from the beginning.

By changing 'who you are,' (your beliefs & views about yourself & the world) you change the root of every problem & most critical part of every solution. At the core...

| Your 'Identity' Creates Your Reality

Or in other words...

| 'Who You Are' = What You Create

Knowing this allows us to also know that...

FOR THINGS TO CHANGE, WE MUST CHANGE

Albert Einstein famously said, *"No problem can be solved from the same level of consciousness that created it."*

Meaning: to fix a problem, or change an outcome in your life, you must first change your level of consciousness.

Short term, this means changing how you think & feel in the moment *(which we'll talk about in a later chapter).*

However, this means to fix problems in your life (not just short term, but long term), you must change *'who you are.'*

Your beliefs. Your thoughts. Your views about the world. These form your level of consciousness & are responsible for the problems, success & results (positive or negative) that you've gotten so far. And the only way to change these results - long term - is to change *'who you are.'*

Just under a century later, Jim Rohn summarized it perfectly:

"For things to change, you have to change. For things to get better, you have to get better. For things to improve, you have to improve. When you grow, everything in your life grows with you."

Your identity - who you are, what you believe, your views on the world & things within it - create the possibilities that you tap into & the results that you get. Hence, to tap into new possibilities, you must actually change *'who you are.'*

We have been misled to believe that we can get new results while remaining exactly the same, but we can't as you'll just continue to see things the same way, make the same decisions, take the same actions & get the same results. *For things to change, you must change.* You must be willing to change yourself - become a new 'you', a better 'you,' an expanded 'you' to get new results...

Simply put: change 'who you are' & suddenly you spot new potential, new possibilities, new ways of thinking arise & as a result of this all, you achieve new results.

Stay the same on the other hand & you continue to get the same results as before. You continue to repeat the same past, bringing it into the future. The same challenges, the same struggles, the same results, continue to repeat (despite the near-infinite potential that exists for you at any moment) because 'who you are,' (the filter of all information; possibility & opportunity) is the same as before.

Fortunately, as you change 'who you are,' so bare in mind that there is always a completely different reality (the one you would prefer to the one you're existing right now) waiting for you. The door is always open...

The catch: you can't walk through that door as the same person as you are right now. You must train yourself to think, feel & do differently.

If this metaphorical door was in front of you, the sign on it would read, *'Come in, but only as a better version of yourself, which isn't going to be easy, but will definitely be worth it'*

To do this though, you must know what you're dealing with, hence we must explore the initial question...

WHO ARE 'YOU?' REALLY? TRULY?

> *"Unlike a drop of water which loses its identity when it joins the ocean, man does not lose his being in the society in which he lives. Man's life is independent. He is born not for the development of the society alone, but for the development of him self."*
>
> - *B. R. AMBEDKAR*

"If you want to find the secrets of the universe, think in terms of energy, frequency, and vibration," Nikola Tesla once said.

Albert Einstein also reportedly said, *"Everything is energy and that's all there is to it,"* based on his studies of the forces that govern the universe & human existence.

To answer the question of *'who are we?'* the best, highest understanding we have right now is that we are *energy*. The greatest physicists have shown us this is the case, as does quantum physics (the most successful & accepted theory & study topic in all of science, to date.)

The world is made of off atoms - which used to be considered the smallest things in the universe. Later on though, scientists found that atoms can also be divided up - that there was something smaller. These are subatomic particles: protons, neutrons, & electrons. These make-up atoms, which are the building blocks of everything we can see, feel & touch.

Except, these subatomic particles are made up of primarily nothing, but *energy*. Tiny part mass & majority energy. What this means is everything seemingly-physical - this includes your body - is actually made of *energy*.

The in-depth scientific explanations of this would add a couple of hundred pages to this book, so are omitted here, but I do urge you to further your exploration by, at least gaining a

POTENTIAL | 61

basic understanding of physics, quantum physics, quantum mechanics & in general, what makes up the world we live in.

And in case you're skeptical to the idea & understanding that everything around you (including your body, your house, car, laptop, cell phone, etc) is made up of - at the subatomic level - mostly nothing but energy, firstly, go & research it & secondly, you're not alone. I used to be skeptical too...

I found it incredibly hard to believe this because energy is invisible. We can't see it. Nor can we touch it, hear it, taste it or smell it. We can't process this with our 5 basic sense, but it's there. This made me doubtful. That's until I also realized that many of the best, most amazing, most magnificent things in this world are also invisible & operate beyond the senses.

Can you see the mobile phone frequencies your phone uses to receive & give out information? Can you see the radio waves (the frequencies of energy) that send radio signals & allow you to tune into different radio stations as you drive? Can you see, hear, touch, smell or taste the internet frequencies (energy) in the air that allow you to connect to the internet, search social media, browse or stream content?

We can't recognize these through our 5 basic senses, yet we don't dispute them because we see the results. Realize this & you start to question existence, *'Maybe there's more to this world than what meets the eye?'* or *'Maybe Einstein or Nikola Tesla (amongst others) knew something about how the world works, that we may not know or fully accept yet...?*

So, to answer the question of *'who are we?'* the first answer (based on the latest research) is *energy. We are energy.*

Beyond this, we are a *species*. And as we briefly touched on so far, the main thing which separates the results of 1 member of our species from another (& as a result, forms the core of our 'identity') is our *'beliefs.'*

We are our 'beliefs' (our views, subjective opinions & perspectives of ourselves, others & the world around us.).

IDENTITY: 'WHO YOU ARE'

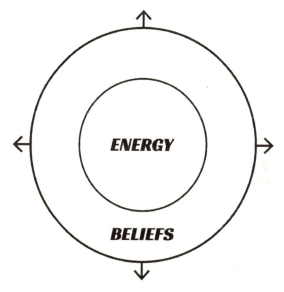

"Under all that we think, lives all we believe, like the ultimate veil of our spirits" Antonio Machado once said.

And, like it not, our *'beliefs'* (about ourselves, our place in the universe, what's right or wrong & how the world works) are what makes us *'who we are'* & influence everything in life.

These *'beliefs,'* of course, are a form of *information*, which in turn, are energy - *it's all connected.*

Knowing this we also know, to change your 'identity' (so you can change your reality) you must change your <u>beliefs</u> (as they are what make us 'who we are.')

'What do you mean by 'beliefs?' or *'what kind of beliefs?'* you may be thinking... A good first rule of thumb for the 'beliefs' in your life that are shaping your reality is whatever words come up after you think to yourself, *'I am...'*

This includes everything from generally-neutral *'I am'* identity statements such as...

> *I am a human being*
> *I am male/female*
> *I am 34 years old*
> *I am an American citizen*

Through to identity statements that align with the things you want. Of course, what's a good identity trait depends on the individual & the ambitions of that individual, but generally things such as these are positive *'I am'* identity statements...

> *I am... a loving & caring person.*
> *I am... great with people.*
> *I am... a self-disciplined person.*
> *I am... an ambitious person.*
> *I am... willing to do whatever it takes.*
> *I am... a person destined for big things.*
> *I am... knowledgeable & skilled.*
> *I am... open-minded, always open to learning.*
> *I am... good person; kind-hearted & caring.*

If you examine everything great that you've ever created in your life (any great experience, situation or circumstance) & trace it back, you'll find that you were able to recognize & seize that opportunity (interpret that incoming information well) because of 1 or many of these well-aligned *'beliefs.'*

Had you not believed those things & been that person, you probably wouldn't have recognized that same opportunity that you did - you would have seen something else instead.

With this said, any experience, situation or circumstance that you really didn't like, you created because of your 'identity' as well. Things worked out the way they did because of the 'beliefs' you did (or didn't) have. *Often, the areas of struggle in our lives come from negative beliefs about yourself...*

I am... not good around people.
I am... bad at relationships.
I am... always stressed.
I am... an angry person.
I am... bad at mathematics.
I am... a slow learner.
I am... not good with money.
I am... not worthy of love.
I am... not worthy of happiness.
I am... a stubborn person.
I am... a failure.

The principle behind this first rule of thumb is simple...

| 'I Am...'s' Make-Up Our *Identity*

The 'beliefs' make up our identity. And, as you already know, our identity acts as a filter for everything that comes into our lives, dictating our decisions, actions & results.

Beyond this first rule of thumb of 'I am...' there are also other beliefs that form our identity & either positively or negatively influence our lives...

I like... (this).
I don't like... (that).
I don't do... (this) or (that).
When (this) happens, I always react (this way).
I always... (do this).
I sometimes... (do that).
I'm good at... (this).
I'm bad at... (this).
The world is... (this).
People are... (that).

And then, of course, we form specific views, opinions & even convictions around specific areas of our lives.

Note: viewpoints, opinions & convictions all fall under this category of *'beliefs,'* but just operate with a higher or lower level of <u>certainty</u>. For example, an *'opinion'* is a reasonable weak *'belief'* that operates with a lower level of <u>certainty</u>. We think this way, but we aren't willing to defend it very strongly. Opinions change often & easily.

'Convictions,' on the other hand, are firm, deeply-ingrained, *'beliefs.'* Convictions run deep & become very hard to change - not impossible, but harder. This is what makes convictions dangerous - we lose our openness to anything else. If you remember the Friedrich Nietzsche quote shared in chapter 1, *"Convictions are more dangerous enemies of truth than lies,"* well, now you have the better understanding of it.

Specific *beliefs* based around areas of our lives may include:

> *My job, career or business is... (this).*
> *Money is... (this).*
> *Wealthy people are... (that).*
> *My friends are... (that).*
> *My family is... (this way).*
> *My family always... (do this).*
> *My partner is... (this).*
> *When my partner does... (this), I do (that).*
> *Healthy people do... (this).*

These beliefs *('who we are')* shape our life either positively or negatively. To change your reality, you must change *'who you are,'* which means changing your *'beliefs'* about yourself & the world around you *(more on this in later sections.)* Do this & your results change to map your new outlook on life...

In summary, *'who we are,'* is firstly, *energy* (we're more nothing than something; not physical mass, but mostly *energy*). Like we talked about in the 1st chapter, we are endless potential. *Energy is potential & potential is energy.*

Secondly, 'who we are' is a series of *'beliefs'* about ourselves, those around us & how the world works. And it's this series of *'beliefs'* that form our *identity* & create our *reality*.

As we change these *'beliefs'* we change *'who we are,'* & we're able to interpret the information from the world in a new way, recognize new opportunities & get new results...

HOW 1 BELIEF CAN SHAPE YOUR LIFE (& ARE MONEY, FAME OR POWER THE ROOT OF ALL EVIL?)

If you believe that 'money is the root of all evil,' for example, you're going to sabotage your financial success because deep down, you don't want to be 'evil' which, based on your beliefs, having lots of money supposedly makes you.

So as opportunities for wealth present themselves, you either overlook them completely or even if you seize them, with time, you find a way to lose any money you made.

You may have set a big financial goal for yourself this year, but subconsciously (because of this 1 belief), you're likely to sabotage your financial upside. Your subconscious mind repeats to itself something a little like:

'Money is the root of all evil,' which means that wealthy people - those with lots of money - are terrible people. And I don't want him to be a bad person so I'll just make sure he finds a way to never obtain lots of money. Or, if he does, to make sure he loses the money to ensure he stays broke & is, therefore, a good person.'

Self-sabotage or any short *(a category of behavior including things such as the widely recognized 'procrastination')* comes from exactly this: **inner-conflicts**.

One part of you is pulling in one direction while another part of you is pulling in another. Like having one foot pressed down on the accelerator pedal, while the other firmly locked down on the brake. You ended up going nowhere. And if you do start to progress, for every step forward, you take 2 back.

Financially, this is a good example. You want to make more money (to pay the bills, to buy something you want, to not have to worry about money, to save for the future, etc) & this is pulling you forward. You set goals, plan & take action.

Yet, beliefs such as *'money is the root of all evil,'* or *'people who make a lot of money are bad people,'* (amongst others) are simultaneously pulling you back.

You want to move forward, but you don't want to be a 'wealthy pig,' so you either procrastinate & never make more money in the first place, or if you do make more, you find a way to blow it so you never have much money left (because you don't want to be a 'bad person,' - as you told yourself people with money all are.)

Then, instead of confronting & resolving these *inner-conflicts* we'll often just blame things around us for our problems. All because we have some limiting beliefs around the areas of our life that are holding us back.

In actuality, money is just a tool. It can be used for good or for bad - it's not the money itself that is good or bad, but those who use it. You can't blame a hammer if someone uses it to bash in someone's skull - the hammer is neutral, neither good or bad, but merely a tool.

The same is for money. Just as it can be used for bad, it can be (& is) used to fund project, foundations & organizations that change the world. *Money is neither good nor bad, but how you use it makes it so.*

Money doesn't make you a good or bad person, but merely amplifies who you already were, so if anything an evil identity is the root of all evil & money, fame or power are merely fuel that turn sparks of evil into full-fledged flames of evil.

If you were a bad person before you amassed money, fame & power, it'll amplify that & make you even worse. If you're a good person though, more money, fame or power will just make you an even better person than before...

Do you think if you had given Gandhi or Mother Teresa a billion bucks, they would suddenly change & become bad people? No. If anything, they would find a way to use the money to do even more good in the world.

Secondly, it's actually the 'lack of money' that statistically is the 'root of all evil' as most theft, hate & crime is committed by people living in lack or poverty.

When people don't have money & are desperate - thinking purely with their 'survival instincts' - they often become the worst versions of themselves, willing to do anything (even if it's immoral & illegal) just to survive. **Meaning:** *money can actually be the antidote for evil, not the cause of it.*

Logically, you may understand this, but if you find yourself hating people purely because they have money (or fame & power) you may not understand this emotionally & again, you have an *internal conflict* in which logically you know 1 thing, but emotionally, you believe another.

Fortunately, you can emotionally believe this too & one of the best ways to experience the positive effects money can have.

Study philanthropy & great charitable acts. Watch what the lack of money does in the world. Go visit those places. And, go see the difference for yourself.

Use your own money in a positive way (give, support causes you care about, etc) & you'll quickly emotionally reprogram yourself to see money as the tool it is.

The big idea here is that you want to resolve these *'inner conflicts'* by aligning your 'beliefs' with your desired outcome, as well as align both the logic & emotion to work together (as we'll talk about later; the different parts of the brain responsible for various roles & how to change any 'belief.')

And this is just an example of how 1 *belief* is influencing your results. In actuality, we have a lifetime of learned & stored 'beliefs' influencing our thoughts, feelings, decisions & actions in any given moment.

They make up our 'identity,' & guide us to do what we do & achieve what we achieve - *change just a few of these core beliefs in each area of your life & you'll get radically different (better) results.* **New beliefs, a new life.**

STOP 'BEING YOURSELF'

> *"The only true voyage would be not to travel through a hundred different lands with the same pair of eyes, but to see the same land through a hundred different pairs of eyes."*
>
> \- MARCEL PROUST

Throughout life we get told to 'be ourselves' (or to 'find ourselves') as if 'who we are' is some fixed, stable thing that we must find, become & stick with for the rest of our lives.

We get told that the past equals the future & that who we are is who we'll always be - that our 'identity' is a constant.

We get conditioned into this *fixed* view of our 'identity' from very early on & it's the reason you may be finding it hard to accept some of the understandings shared so far - because you believe 'who you are' is fixed.

Throughout life, we are told to 'be yourself' & not to, 'be our ever-changing, ever-expanding, best self,' as if our *identity* is something that doesn't change.

In my research, I've found this thinking to be flawed. I've found this to be, not only not how the world works, what creates success & happiness, but also not the way nature intended us to be...

And I've found the best answer to the question, *'Can I really change my identity?'* is not to just say *'Yes!'* followed by an explanation (although that's part of it), but, *'Yes - as you've already changed your identity - 'who you are' - dozens of times with thousands of little adjustments in your lifetime.'*

We are born & from that point we change 'who we are' all the time. Who you were when you were 1 or 2, or 5, or 8 years old was vastly different to who you were when you were 12, 15 or 19 years old. You weren't the same person, but a new person based on all the extra years of learning, watching things around you, 'growing up' & improving.

Then, you didn't continue living your life when you were 18, 25 or 44 years old in the same way as you did when you were 4, 9 or 12 years of age - that'd be weird. You changed. Your 'identity,' evolved over & over again, adapting & improving.

Your *beliefs* about yourself & the world around you changed (& as, outside of pure energy, our 'beliefs' are what make up our identity, 'who you are' changed as a result.)

Each time you learned & applied something new, breaking old habits & creating new ones, thinking differently about the world around you, you become different than before..

You didn't find some 'fixed' version of yourself & just stick there, *'Yepp, who I am right now is me; I'm done changing & growing - that's it, this is me now & until the end of time'* No. You keep changing who you are. You grew; you improved.

"The self is not something ready-made," the American philosopher, John Dewey once said, *"but something in continuous formation through choice of action."*

Your *'identity,'* is not some fixed thing that remains the same, but an ever-changing, ever-expanding thing that grows as you go through life, learn, adapt & change.

And if you've already changed your identity so many times, why not change it again & continue changing it (but, from now on, do it with more intention & clarity to create the results you <u>really</u> want in life?)

Be yourself & stick to your most positive 'beliefs,' but equally be radically open-minded & constantly seek to test your 'beliefs' (& your thinking), to learn & to grow - to become the best version of 'who you are.' As the quote goes...

"Life isn't about finding yourself. Life is about creating yourself." - George Bernard Shaw

'Who you really, truly, are,' as I've found in my work, is much greater than what you can comprehend right now...

Like driving in the dark, you can only see the next few dozen meters in front of you, but that doesn't mean that the road ends there. The road keeps going on & on, and the more you grow, the more you see you can grow further. *That's living!*

PATH OF SELF-MASTERY: AN EVER-CHANGING, EVER-GROWING & EVER-EXPANDING 'YOU'

> *"What you get by achieving your goals is not as important as what you become by achieving your goals."*
>
> - *HENRY DAVID THOREAU*

'You' are not 'who you are' right now - that's just 1 small part of *who you are*; 'the present day you.' And this 'you,' - the 'you' of today - may end up very different than the 'you' of tomorrow, next week or next year.

That's the path of self-mastery: *the infinite, exciting, never-ending & fulfilling journey of, not 'finding yourself,' but 'creating yourself.' Growing. Changing. Expanding. Tapping into higher & higher dimensions of consciousness.*

Despite this, people write in yearbooks, say in their wedding vows or tell members of their family, *"don't change,"* or *"stay exactly as you are."* Unfortunately, this often comes from a place of security more than it comes from a place of love.

When we want someone to 'stay the same,' we're often doing that selfishly; we don't want them to change as it affects us.

In my experience though, true care, love & support is acceptance of someone as an ever-changing, ever-expanding individual. That's not just love, but unconditional love (love without the conditions). True love. True care. True support.

Embrace this path of *self-mastery* (& for those around you). Embrace the ever-changing, ever-expanding 'you' & you'll, not just get *great results*, but experience an *incredible existence!*

3 | RADICAL RESPONSIBILITY: THE ARCHITECT OF YOUR FUTURE

"The price of greatness is responsibility"

- *WINSTON CHURCHILL*

Either you're behind the steering wheel of your life deciding where you want to go & driving there, or you're in the passenger seat watching life just "happen" to you.

The principle of 'responsibility' has been passed around by the greatest philosophers, thinkers & thought leaders for generations. From ancient wisdom to modern research, 'full responsibility,' 'proactiveness' & 'total ownership' are big underlying parts of it.

And that's what this principle (& this chapter) is about: taking charge of what happens in your life, owning your mistakes, avoiding blaming or finger-pointing, being proactive & going through your life as the architect of it (& not the victim)...

VICTIM THINKING

From an early age, we are conditioned that responsibility is a scary, painful or hurtful thing. The words, *"who's a fault is this?"* said by a parent, guardian or teacher are rarely said in a happy tone of voice, but in an angry or frustrated way. So when a parent or teachers tell us off - *"who did this?"* - as kids, our 1st response can be to point the finger at someone else. To avoid getting into trouble, we just pass the buck to someone else, taking ourselves out of the firing line.

"It was him," "It was her fault," "He did it, not me - blame him." Trouble averted. Or more accurately, 're-directed.' We quickly learn to blame other people & things for our mistakes, as a method of avoiding conflict & survival. And it pays off, hence the reason we stick with it & continue to blame.

Repeat this over many times & now we form strong beliefs: *'Responsibility hurts,' 'Owning up to my mistakes is painful.' 'Blaming is easy, responsibility is hard.'* And then we spend our whole lives thinking (& acting) in this way.

When this behavior is challenged & we are told to take responsibility (instead of blaming) we are reluctant. The reason for this is two-fold...

Firstly, we've done it so many times growing up (avoided responsibility) that it's become our 'norm.'

Secondly, we tell ourselves that it's an innocent lie. That it doesn't matter & doesn't do any harm. *This is not the case.* It affects us mentally & emotionally over the long term, taking away our personal power - bit by bit - until we're left with nothing but our 'victim' status (& poor results.)

When we're in this mindset of blame & finger-pointing & we have some financial challenges, for example, we don't take responsibility, but rather blame our boss, job, economy, the government - anything (besides ourselves).

We don't stop to look inwards. Sure, we work 9 - 5 & not a minute more. Sure, we haven't read a book, educated ourselves further & expanded our skills since leaving college all those years ago. Sure, we have many business & income opportunities around us that we haven't done anything with for months. But, we ignore this. Hide it. Or suppress it.

Why do we do this? Because, just like those child all those years ago, it's easy to point the finger at someone else than to take ownership & full responsibility.

POTENTIAL | 75

We ignore the facts that these are people in the same economy - good or bad - & with the same government that are succeeding financially. Deep down, we know that these aren't fully viable excuses, but we push that thinking down. We don't want to hear that. We like our alibi's; our excuses. They make us feel better (short term). We hit "snooze" on our problems, failing to account the true consequences...

THE LONG-TERM CONSEQUENCES OF BLAME

While this way of thinking & acting - blaming, finger pointing, being a 'victim' of life - gets us off the hook & allows us to avoid embarrassment, in the long term, it also makes us completely powerless.

Being a 'victim' - not taking responsibility - strips you of your personal power. Makes you weak. Helpless.

Every time you point the finger & blame someone (or something) besides yourself, you're mentally reinforcing to yourself that your results are _not_ within your control. You're reinforcing that you cannot change the outcome. So, of course, you don't do anything about the situation (this is because we, human beings, are not motivated to do things we feel are outside of our control). It all becomes a *'self-fulfilling prophecy.'* And a rather destructive one to say the least...

As soon as we blame our failure, challenge or problem on a co-worker, a friend or something else, our mind says to itself: *"I'm off the hook. It's their fault, meaning we can't do anything about it & we can't change it, so why to bother attempting to do anything."*

In essence, when we put the blame on somebody else we are giving them the power over that situation, reinforcing to ourselves that we have no power to influence that outcome any longer. *Hence we don't.*

By taking responsibility - full ownership - on the other hand, for all the failures, mistakes & challenges that you created or contributed to, you regain power to modify the outcome.

When you say to yourself, *"I create this in some way. I'm responsible for it"* you have the power to do something. And you're highly motivated to do so as you feel in control - responsible - for that result.

In other words, you want things to be *'your responsibility'* - because that means that you have control over that situation to respond effectively & make it better.

It may cause a little pain at first (until it becomes normal) but in the long term, it causes you massive relief. Plus, it gives you freedom. Mental freedom. True freedom.

As Stephen R. Covey best put it in the hit book, *7 Habits Of Highly Effective People*:

"Look at the word responsibility - "response-ability" - the ability to respond. Highly proactive people recognize that responsibility. They do not blame circumstances, conditions or conditioning for their behavior. Their behavior is a product of their own conscious choice, based on values, rather than a product of their conditions, based on feeling"

| Responsibility Gives You Personal Power

As you take responsibility, you gain the power to change things; to make things better & create the life you choose. That's how we become powerful, filled with strength & with the capacity to make extraordinary things happen...

LOCUS OF CONTROL

Do you believe you have the power to influence your results; to make things happen in your life as you choose?

Do you believe that you have internal power to shape life as you want to, or do you merely believe that life is happening to you? Or, at the least, can you control your thoughts & feelings or do they control you?

'Taking responsibility for your life,' while a bit philosophical, also has a strong grounding in psychology, where this is referred to as your *'Locus of Control.'* Which is divided into:

- *INTERNAL Locus Of Control*
- *EXTERNAL Locus Of Control*

To better explain this, picture a student about to go in for an exam. They complete the exam & later get back the results...

Individuals with a strong *'internal locus of control'* (those who believe they largely influence & create their results) will tend to praise (or blame) themselves & their own capabilities.

If they did badly in the exam, for example, they'll say, *"I need to study harder," "I need to get more help with this topic," "If I study harder & better remember the information, I can get better results next time."* They may still get disappointed, but they are likely to take responsibility - to blame themselves (not others) for their results, which in the long term often brings them results the want.

People with a strong *'external locus of control'* on the other hand, in this same situation, will tend to praise or blame external factors such as the teacher or the exam itself. They don't take personal responsibility for the good or bad results they got. *Which is often sabotaging in both cases.*

If the exam results were good, they'll often *downplay their success* by saying it was the teacher or that the exam was easy.

Over time this can cause low self-esteem, self-efficacy & self-confidence. *Why?* It teaches you that your efforts didn't matter to the outcome. These attributes (self-esteem, self-efficacy, self-confidence) grow when you 'integrate wins.'

Integrating wins: *As we learn, tick of to-do's, complete projects, overcome challenges, attain goals, turn efforts into outcomes <u>& then proceed to pat ourselves on the back for it</u> - praising our efforts - we gain confidence for future tasks.*

That's one of the biggest ways that confidence & esteem grows; through 'integrating wins' & experiences we have into 'who we are.' But, this can only be done with an *'internal locus of control'* as those with an 'external' one will often give themselves no credit for their results.

While it may seem heroic - to never give yourself credit - for over-doing this can sabotage your own self-belief. You need to strike that right balance here...

Of course, your every achievement *can* be attributed to your parents, friends, mentors, co-workers, teachers, etc, but not *all* of the credit. For example, while an author might write an 'acknowledgments' page thanking everyone for helping make this book possible, they equally understand that it was their own effort, time & attention that made the book possible.

The forces work together. We have to <u>both</u> give credit to those around us (as we should), but also give *ourselves* a pat on the back when we've done a good job & 'integrate our wins.' Doing so is rocket fuel for your soul (& confidence)!

On the flip side, if the exam results were bad, those with a *'external locus of control'* will often blame the teacher, the difficulty of the exam or anything else (besides themselves).

This is even more sabotaging as now you're stripping yourself of your personal power. Do this repeatedly & you begin to doubt that your study, your efforts or your actions have any influence on the results you get & as a result, you stop putting in the work that gets you results in the first place.

POTENTIAL | 79

It begins a spiral that gets harder & harder to break out off. You study less, put in less effort & now, as a result, your belief that you're 'not smart enough to pass this test' is reinforced.

You're in a downward spiral with ever less personal power & ever more likelihood of continuing to blame, point fingers & see yourself as a 'victim' in the future.

And then, of course, you have the 3rd variation, in which people attribute all their failures to things outside themselves, but attribute all successes to their own efforts...

If the result is good, it thanks to me and my good work, dedication and intelligence, but when the result is bad it's not my fault, but rather the bad market, the tough competition, the bad training, the employees or the economy.

Not only is this inauthentic, incongruent & when heard by others will cause distrust, but is also very confusing for your brain. Your mind gets confused not knowing who to blame or give credit to, which also strips you of your personal power.

This all moves us back to the ideal for high levels of achievement & fulfillment: *an 'internal locus of control.'*

In fact, if you've ever wondered about the goal of therapy & work of therapist's, one of the biggest things they focus on is this. Many people who go into therapy, for example, believing that they are a product of everything that has happened to them - that's an *'external locus of control'* (as you now know.)

And the goal of therapy is for patients to realize & begin to tap into an *'internal locus of control'* - to realize how they are influencing their future through their beliefs, thoughts, feelings, decisions & actions.

High achieving individuals take radical responsibility for the situations in their lives; they view their results as largely their creation. Their outcomes are on them. Everything great they create is as a result of their effort, hand work, skills & determination & everything that goes wrong is their fault too.

They didn't do enough. Be enough. They need to get better to make the results happen. There is no blaming here. No complaining. No finger pointing. Those are all signs that you believe someone else is in control of your results - that your outcomes of the doing of someone else & you're not in the driver's seat creating life how you want it.

Attribute credit to your efforts (as well as others). Give yourself a pat on the back for the focus, time, energy & attention you put into creating that outcome. And when things go wrong, it's on you too. Own your failures & take true responsibility for them...

You created that result, that situation, that feeling, that reality in some way. Which, while painful to accept, is beautiful news as it gives you the personal power to change things as you go along...

FAULT & RESPONSIBILITY

It's also important to understand that 'fault' & 'responsibility' do not always go together...

For example, it may not have been your 'fault' that you were parented in a certain way, that you had a bad childhood or things outside of your control happen to you.

They wasn't your 'fault,' but it's definitely your 'responsibility' to gain awareness of, understand, change, reshape, discard (if need be), adapt things that happened in your life in order to live the life you want to live. *To find a way; that's your 'responsibility' - even if something wasn't your 'fault'.*

Did your partner cheat on you? Visa got rejected? Did a law change? Did someone destroy something of yours?

Even if these things weren't your *'fault,'* that doesn't mean you don't have to do anything about them. Far from it. More often than not, it's your 'responsibility' to find how to best deal with these things; to change & adapt to the new circumstances.

That may sound harsh, but it has to be said - *as it's your life that it's affecting...*

| *'Fault'* is about who created the problem. *'Responsibility'* is whose job it is to fix it.

We covered the *'why'* - now let's cover the *'how...'*

How do you start to take greater responsibility for things in your life? Well - it all starts with this 1 question...

A QUESTION FOR RADICAL RESPONSIBILITY

> *"You must take personal responsibility. You cannot change the circumstances, the seasons, or the wind, but you can change yourself. That is something you have charge of."*
>
> — *JIM ROHN*

An early mentor of mine taught me this profound question for taking radical responsibility. It's simple, but don't let this simplicity allow you to you discard its power. Here it is:

| How did I create this?

Did someone steal from you? Got scammed? Lost your life savings in a bad business deal? Did someone betray you? Diagnosed with a life-threatening condition? Whatever happens, ask yourself, *'How did I create this?'*

Now, I must warn you, asking yourself this question can be very painful. Your mind will probably come up with a million reasons, excuses & distractions not to think about it.

As you read this, you may have even gotten a little offended. *'Bogdan, you've gone too far!'* you may think, *'How is someone betraying me something that I created?'*

Remember: it's not your 'fault,' but it is your 'responsibility' to create the best, most fulfilling life for yourself. And holding onto these events with blame is probably not serving you.

Maybe you were too gullible during the sales pitch for that business opportunity? You thought you could 'get rich quick. Your thinking was in the wrong place - greed was running your mind - when you jointed that suspicious business opportunity that turned out to be a scam?

If your mind was in the right place, you would have seen right through it & you wouldn't have contributed to getting scammed? It wasn't your 'fault,' but you contributed towards it happening through your state of mind at that moment.

Maybe you didn't do all the research when investing your life savings into that investment opportunity? Maybe your intuition was giving you a bad feeling about this business partner but you ignored it - as well as warning signs - which ended up contributing to you getting scammed?

I've been scammed & stolen from before - perhaps you have too - & while these were not my direct 'fault,' looking back I can see how I created these situations; how I contributed to it happening. And how, had I acted differently, perhaps they could have been avoided...

Maybe your diet & exercise hadn't been the best the last few years before you got diagnosed with that life-threatening health condition? This, for example, is my parent's story...

My mom was diagnosed with early-stage breast cancer & my dad with testicular cancer. They were terrified, but instead of blaming & falling into victimhood (despite this hard situation some would say 'wasn't their fault'), they took *responsibility*.

The began to research health & wellbeing solutions day-in, day-out. They took radical levels of responsibility & become obsessed with finding a way out of this...

I remember years later when they told me how much fear they had when they first got diagnosed; how they would talk about what would happen to us (me & my brother) if cancer got the best of them. Despite this fear, they knew that they created this in part & therefore could undo it with their efforts.

They changed their thinking first. Then, their diets & health habits. Which all resulted in them completely revolutionizing their health & cured themselves of these medical problems.

Of course, this isn't medical advice, but merely an example of how their mindset helped them go through one of the toughest times in their lives...

THE RESPONSIBILITY SCALE

> *"A hero is someone who understands the responsibility that comes with his freedom"*
>
> *- BOB DYLAN*

Are you a victim of your life or the creator of it? Are you the slave trapped & hostage to reality, hoping for good things to happen, or are you the architect of your life-shaping ught your thoughts, decisions & actions? Really? Truly?

The best way to know is to test yourself. To self-assess yourself consistently on **'The Responsibility Scale.'**

Based on a scale of 1 - 10, where 1 is a 'low level of responsibility, ownership & proactiveness' & 10 is a 'high level of responsibility, ownership & proactiveness, where do you find yourself in a given situation?

A high ranking on this index - *a high level of responsibility* - is a way of thinking that gives you greater personal power & lead to better solutions, more action & greater results.

A low ranking on this index - *a low level of responsibility* - is a mindset that doesn't support you. It keeps you in 'victim mode' in which you're *unlikely* to take action & get results.

In given situations each day, stop for a second & ask yourself where you would rank *(which may change during the day...)*

One moment you may be very proactive in your thinking, but in another situation, you might be incredibly 'victim-minded.' What you'll get by doing this is greater self-awareness, as well as a tracking measure which supports you in being your best.

EXERCISE: RESPONSIBILITY SCALE
Draw a scale 1 - 10 on a big sheet of paper (it'll only take 30 seconds to start this exercise).

On one side of the scale (1) put *'low level of responsibility'* & on the other side (10) put *'high level of responsibility.'*

Then hang this 1 - 10 scale somewhere you frequently see - in close proximity to you. It could be above your desk, on the fridge, in the living room, in the office, etc *(you can also draw up multiple charts if you want - or carry 1 with you.)*

Then, take a pin, magnet, piece of tap, blue-tac (whatever you choose) & throughout the day, pinpoint on the chart where you currently stand on this scale. You can also get another piece of paper (or a computerized version) to track these numbers over the upcoming days & weeks. You could even make some fancy charts out of it afterward if you want.

Are you being a victim right now? Go to your chart & pinpoint how much of a victim you feel like you're being.

Are you taking full responsibility, ownership & being proactive? Go to your chart & pinpoint where you would self-assess yourself on the scale.

The pin is likely to move up & down the scale many times per day as you react to different situations. In these times, move the pin to show this. Your goal (if you choose to accept of course) is to move towards a 'you' whose pin is always up at the top of the scale.

IMPORTANT: As Sigmund Freud said, **"Being entirely honest with oneself is a good exercise."** *Be as objective & completely honest with yourself as you can. This means you may want to self-assess yourself <u>after</u> the heat of the moment - you'll be more honest & accurate then.*

This is a simple exercise that takes pretty much no time at all to do, yet a very powerful one for bringing this concept back to your attention during the day & helping you become your absolute best self.

IT'S <u>ALL</u> A CHOICE!

> *"Find joy in everything you choose to do. Every job, relationship, home... it's your responsibility to love it, or change it."*
>
> - CHUCK PALAHNIUK

Often, we get caught up in thinking: *'I <u>have</u> to do this,' 'I <u>have</u> to go to work,' 'I <u>have</u> to live this way,' 'I <u>have</u> to do things I don't want to do,' 'I <u>have</u> to be this way.'*

The reality is that we don't "have" to do anything. You could just lay in bed (or on the street) your whole life, not doing anything. You probably shouldn't, but you could. *Everything beyond that is a choice!*

You could just wait until death - not eating, not taking care of yourself, not fulfilling your basic human needs. You probably shouldn't, but you could. Continuing to live & experience this beautiful, magical journey of life is a choice too. *It all is!*

Like it or not, you *choose* to go to work. It's not something you "have" to do, but something you choose to do.

"But Bogdan, I really have to. I have bills to pay. I really do have to go to work. I don't have a choice."

What you're doing is weighing up the consequences & you're going to work as a *choice* that leads to your survival.

You're choosing it. Nobody is holding a gun to your head. You could *not* go. You would probably get fired if you repeat that & have financial troubles. Which is why you go in the first place - to avoid those consequences. But, it's still a *choice*.

Even if you don't like doing it, you *choose* to do it to survive, avoid starving or being homeless. *To avoid pain.*

Within this, you *choose* how you work & at any moment you can change the work you do - people do it every single day.

Same with your relationship, your friendships, how you spend your time & pretty much anything else. We don't have to do anything, but *choose* too. Sometimes we do it to avoid negative consequences. Other times to get something we desire. But ultimately, it's a choice we make.

Knowing this gives us the power to *choose* differently (if we *choose* to, of course).

And, as to the greatest choice we have in our lives, it's...

THE CHOICE OF INTERPRETATION & MEANING

> *"You have power over your mind – not outside events. Realize this, and you will find strength"*
>
> - MARCUS AURELIUS

"I'm stressed because of him" "I'm angry because of this" "I'm sad because of that" "I broke because of this " "It not getting the results I want because of that thing outside of me."

When things we don't want come into our lives, we tend to blame external things for our stress, pain, anger or suffering.

See, while generally-unpleasant circumstances may come up, or situations you didn't wish upon yourself happen, what you always have is **a choice of interpretation** - *the freedom to choose the 'meaning' you give to that situation.*

Just imagine how incredible it would be forge an 'identity' - a way of thinking & outlook on life - which allows you to stay calm, peaceful & even filled with bliss when you would have previously gotten angry? Or to see joy & beauty when you would have previously seen pain & suffering? It's possible!

To explain this, we must go first back to this visual:

As you can see, between *'information'* (message; stimulus) & the *'interpretation'* (meaning; response) is your <u>*'identity.'*</u>

And a part of that *'identity'* is your freedom to choose your response to a given situation.

This is best, not just explained but demonstrated, in Viktor Frankl's extraordinary book, *Man's Search For Meaning*.

Viktor Frankl was a prisoner of the concentration camps during the Holocaust. However, he was also a neurologist & psychiatrist, which enabled him to approach these terrible circumstances a little differently than most.

As he wrote, the Nazi's in these concentration camps took away everything one could take away from human being. Belongings. material possessions. Clothes. Their ability to *choose* what they do, what they eat, where & when they sleep - it was all taken away. These prisoners seemed to have their every human freedom - their every human right - taken away by the Nazi's & had to do exactly what they were told to, slaving away to complete Nazi orders. They had no freedom (no ability to "choose" anything). *Or, that's how it seemed...*

Viktor Frankl found that there was 1 thing that - no matter how much they tried - they could never take away from him (unless he let them they take it away)...

In his book, he refers to this as *'the last human freedom,'* & it's our capacity to choose our *interpretation*, meaning & *response* to a piece of information, stimulus or circumstance.

He found - as shown in the above graphic - between incoming *information* (message; stimulus) & *interpretation* is <u>freedom to choose</u> (a permanent part of your *identity*.)

For example, the Nazi's could force them to work tirelessly in the freezing cold conditions, punish them & not give them food, but they couldn't (unless he let them) choose how he

POTENTIAL | 89

was going to interpret this information & therefore approach the situation. *Only we can choose this meaning we associate to given situations & circumstances.*

He realized that he could choose to think about this situation differently. He could choose to interpret this situation as 'temporary,' remaining optimistic for the future. He could choose to find little elements of joy despite these hardship conditioned by choosing to focus on different things. He could choose to close his eyes & see his family in his imagination.

He had many *choices* because he realized that he controlled the interpretation & response in his life.

And this is what the greatest individuals were, not born with, but recognized & trained themselves to do. They were able to interpret & associate meaning greater than their environment.

Nelson Mandela, for example, was a man who wrongly spent 27 years in prison. However, he didn't let this define him. He left the prison, not filled with anger or hatred (as one would expect), but with forgiveness, peace & an even greater sense of meaning than before. *Why?* Because he chooses a different to give this situation a different interpretation (a new meaning), seizing the 1 power that nobody could ever take away from him (or anybody else).

He recognized that the 'stimulus' (whether, in our lives, that's an angry co-worker, a coffee shop running out of your favorite blend of coffee or, in his case, wrongly spending 27 years in prison) didn't dictate his response, but rather he choose that.

When people come to me & say that they are *'stressed because of this,'* or *'angry because of that situation outside of them,'* I share these examples with them. Specifically, the concept of *'the last human freedom,'* Viktor Frankl wrote about.

I share that while we get conditioned into a worldview in which a *'stressful <u>situation</u>'* equals a *'stressful <u>you</u>,'* or an 'angry *situation*' that others would get angry in must equal an 'angry *you*,' it actually doesn't have to be this way.

That's a life in which you lose your free will to your environment & your emotions are being thrown around by everyone & everything around you. It's a limited life.

True bliss comes from recognizing that between information & interpretation - between stimulus & response - is *freedom to choose* (specifically, to choose the meaning we give.)

In my first book, *Skilled Success*, I shared this example:

> A great meditation teacher once shared that there shouldn't be any difference between, meditating in a cave, or meditating in the center of a city, because peace is inside us and not dependent on what's going on around us.

A peaceful person can see peace & acceptance in any situation - irrelevant of whether that's a hospital room, a stock trading floor or a battlefield. This is because that's 'who they are,' & peace comes from within.

Meanwhile, a stressed-out person will find stress, even if things seem to be ok. As Marcus Aurelius said, *"If you are distressed by anything external, the pain is not due to the thing itself, but to your estimate of it; and this you have the power to revoke at any moment."*

Or, as Epictetus said: *"Men are disturbed not by things, but by the view which they take of them"*

People will often blame external situations for their stress, 'If this didn't happen, I wouldn't be stressed,' 'Once this is over, I won't be stressed,' 'I'm stressed now, but once I complete this, I won't be stressed anymore,' or the typical line of thinking, 'I'll be happy when (this) happens.'

It's a fallacy; like running on a hamster wheel, because you'll never able to reach that supposed, dreamed-about happiness you're looking outside of you. No external circumstance can bring you long-term happiness joy, peace & bliss. *It has to come from within.* It all does - peace, happiness, sadness, anger, stress, fear, bliss, meaning & fulfillment.

'Who we are' inside shapes what we see outside.

You're not stressed, for example, because of a situation (outside yourself), but rather because of your interpretation (based on your identity) of the given information.

Meaning: you're not stressed because someone said or did something that "stressed you out" (that's mere information), but because of your interpretation of that information (based on, once again, *'who you are,'* which we know if made up of beliefs). Change what's inside you - 'who you are' - & suddenly things that used to bring you to stress, you'll find acceptance & peace (& even perhaps bliss) within.

As the African Proverb says, *"If there is no enemy within, the enemy outside can do you no harm."*

Remove the demons inside yourself & suffering disappears too (not because of the world changes, but because *'who you are'* changes so your interpretation of the world changes too.)

What this all means is that nobody, nothing, no situation in your environment or no event in time can hurt you (unless you allow them.)

Don't get me wrong though; people will still be able to cause you physical, economical & material damage (such as stealing from you, scrapping your car, physically hurting you, etc) but situations or circumstances will *not* be able to cause you emotional suffering (not unless you let them.)

Why? Because you know the stimulus doesn't control your response. *You have freedom of interpretation & choice.* As Gandhi said *"Nobody can hurt me without my permission"*

Think about it: *If someone gives you a gift, yet you reject the gift, have they really given you the gift?*

If a courier comes to your house, but you're not in - or you decline the package - is the package 'delivered'? No & no.

Only if you accept what is given to you have you received it. Whether that's a pigeon-holing label, stress or anger, it's your choice to accept it or not.

It's said that a snake bite has never killed anybody, but rather the venom that flows through your bloodstream after the snakebite that kills. In that same sense, an insult has never hurt anyone's feelings, but the acceptance & holding onto that insult - thinking about it, dwelling on it for weeks, months or years later - hurts someone. *Your interpretation & response (which you control) dictates the effects.*

One more example: If someone yelled "you're stupid!" to you but you couldn't actually hear them for whatever reason - loud crowd, conversation with someone else, headphones in your ears, whatever - did they really offend you?

Technically, they sent out the information. They even yelled it in an angry tone to really cause you pain. Except: you didn't hear it so you weren't affected by it.

In this same way, if someone insults you, but you don't allow yourself to be hurt by their words, are you really hurt?

See, someone may be able to insult you - that's outside your control. But your response to their insult is fully within your control. You can choose how you react to that. You can accept it as fact, or just as 1 person's opinion. You can accept it or discard it & move on *(but, more on this later in the book...)*

Big picture: knowing this, we have a choice to continue to believe the same things we always believed. It's a choice to remain the same person when we could equally choose to improve. And, specifically here, it's a choice to continue maintaining an *'external locus of control'* when you can equally choose to recognize your true power, tapping into an *'internal locus of control'* to live the life you truly want.

I still remember when I first learned this many, many years ago, how hard - difficult - it was to catch myself & avoid blaming, replacing it with radical responsibility, ownership & proactiveness. It sure wasn't easy...

My mind (or more specifically, lower levels of consciousness of mine & not my true, best self) keep finding reasons to blame others for things that didn't work out in my life. It took time, energy & effort to start thinking differently, but it was worth it. *I know you'll see the same thing in your own life (if you implement the lessons in this chapter.)*

CHOOSING INDIRECTLY

When I say that you can *"choose"* to change anything in your life, I mean that you can choose it indirectly. Who we are, what we believe, what we think & what we do every day - these are all choices that we make & can change at any moment. We can *choose* to be, think & do differently, but we must make these choices indirectly...

To better explain this, think of laughter. Laughter is also a choice. And it's also one you can't choose directly, but must choose indirectly. You can't 'choose' to laugh by saying 'I want to laugh now,' but you can absolutely *indirectly* "choose" to laugh at any moment of your life by *giving yourself a reason to laugh* - by "choosing" to watch a funny video, have a conversation with a hilarious friend of yours or read a list of the worst puns ever created, for example.

In other words, you can "choose" to spark laughter at any moment. It's a choice. But, one you must make, not directly, but indirectly - by choosing to _give yourself a reason_ to laugh.

And in that exact same way, we can change who we are, change our beliefs, make new decisions & create an incredible life for ourselves.

You can't choose these things directly. You can't just say *"I want to be this type of person right now"* & expect yourself to change all of a sudden. But you can *indirectly* choose to create change by choosing to give yourself reasons to changed.

Sure, you want to become this type of person, but why? Why do you want to become this type of person? What will it lead to? How would this type of person think & behave? Convince yourself that this change is a wise one that's in alignment with the future that you want to create *(more on this later!)*

Just like you can _indirectly_ "choose" laughter by choosing to watch a comedy or read a list of jokes, you can indirectly choose to become a new you, adopt new beliefs or live life differently by experiencing & implementing what you learn here & giving yourself reasons to make a change real for you...

YOU'RE THE ARCHITECT OF YOUR LIFE: DESIGN YOUR LIFE AS YOU FREELY CHOOSE TO...

> *"The strongest principle of growth lies in the human choice"*
>
> - *GEORGE ELIOT*

Even if this may not seem true right now ("You're the architect of your life"), it will be - assuming you make that choice. Any change starts with awareness (which you now have) & an *indirect* set of choices (which you can make at any moment). If you're ready, decide that blame & an 'external locus of control' are not for you anymore.

Decide that's not what the best version of 'who you are' looks like; that it's just the survival, lowest-level-of-consciousness 'you' & not the *real* 'you'. Rather, choose the path of radical responsibility, total ownership & proactiveness in your life!

Life is not happening to you, but for you. Through you. Your thoughts, efforts & actions matter!

Your results are the effects of your previous ways of being - take ownership of this. And from there, step into this new, better 'you'. Be the architect & design your life. **You can!**

Just like an architect designs a building, you're designing your life. And, I'm sure you'll agree that living the life that you consciously designed for yourself would be much better than living a life that just randomly "happened" to you.

At the end of the day, being the architect of your life is much more exciting & fulfilling than being the victim. Step into this potential & start tapping into new possibilities today.

Now, while *'radical responsibility'* starts with yourself, it can go beyond this. Highly successful people tend to think (& take responsibility) beyond themselves & think in term of their family, their communities & even the world as a whole...

THE BIG PICTURE: HOW TO CHANGE THE WORLD

> *"We are made wise not by the recollection of our past, but by the responsibility for our future"*
>
> *-   GEORGE BERNARD SHAW*

Discrimination (race, age, gender, etc), economics, global issues (war, corruption, deforestation, animal slaughter, poverty, etc) are rarely our 'fault.'

It's unlikely that you can claim direct 'fault' for many of these global issues. In fact, most of the time, nobody can. These are rarely issues that any 1 person creates, but that are created by the small, seemingly-insignificant actions of the majority. We all contribute to (or don't proactively work to fix) these issues.

And with most believing that *'if things are their fault, they don't need to do anything about it - responsibility isn't theirs'* is it any wonder these become the issues they are today?

Perhaps the answer to solving them (& making the world a better place) can arise from what Albert Einstein wisely said:

"The world will not be destroyed by those who do evil, but by those who watch them without doing anything"

As you now know, we are conditioned that if something isn't our fault, we shouldn't do anything about it. We shouldn't take responsibility for it. We shouldn't take action to affect it.

I've found - as Einstein's quote reaffirms - it's this thinking that, with time, creates the worst things in this world.

The beauty though is that whose you take responsibility in their own lives can - if they're willing to do more - take responsibility for things outside of themselves.

The world's highest achieving individuals take radical levels of responsibility, for themselves & others too...

Not only do they take total ownership for things that happen in their own lives (not blaming the media, the government, the weather, their friends & family, the job market or the economic landscape), but they also take greater ownership for the lives of those around them.

They are constantly choosing to expand their **'Circles of responsibility'**...

CIRCLES OF RESPONSIBILITY

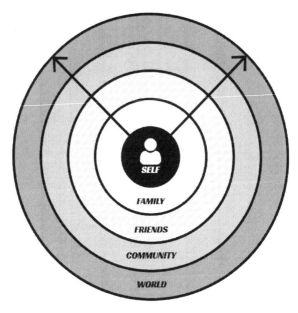

Of course, responsibility starts with *'self.'* If you're not being fully proactive, responsible & in total ownership within your own life, you can't serve others to the best of your ability.

There's a reason flight attendants tell passengers to, in case of an emergency, put on their own oxygen masks first (before helping others).

By taking responsibility in your own life, now you're able to take a greater level of responsibility for those around you, including your partner, family, friends, all the way up to your community, your company, your nation, group & even the world as a whole.

When you grow, shall you choose, there's more of you to give. But, it starts with self - a lot of people forget this.

See, when you're stepping up to taking responsibility for not just your life, but that of your family, your community or the world, seeing a piece of trash on the street, while 'not your fault,' you now view as your 'responsibility' to help with. Your company, community, organization or the world is in turmoil & you feel (& act) 'responsible' to fix it. *That's a higher level of responsibility than most ever experience.*

And while there is absolutely nothing wrong with living for yourself (as we'll talk about in further chapters), the choice to take responsibility for something bigger is always there.

It's not for everybody, but if this world is going to change for the better, it's thanks to those expanding their levels of responsibility from themselves to things bigger & bigger.

So, if you're interested in serving a cause greater than yourself, to lead others, to create true change in this world, leave a dent in the universe & leave your family, community or the world as a whole better than you found it, then *'Circles Of Responsibility'* is a great concept for you to follow & embody in your daily thoughts, decisions & actions.

Begin to expand your level of responsibility. Ask yourself:

How can you take greater responsibility for your family, for your friends, for your community, organizations you're a part of & even the world as a whole?

This is the path of greatest leadership!

And always remember - either way, whether you choose to live for yourself or expand your responsibility - take *radical responsibility* for that which you create, as it gives you great personal power to change things.

It's with this thinking that you should enter the next 2 sections of this book, which will build on the foundations covered here, giving you the research-backed understandings, proven strategies & practical steps you can take to follow the path of *self-mastery* & help you create the life you want...

2.
AMBITION:
ALIGNING INTENTIONS

"Unhappiness is not knowing what we want and killing ourselves to get it"

DON HEROLD

Without a sense of deep meaning, purpose & direction, life can quickly lose its rich vibrancy, value & magnetizing appeal. With a sense of crystallized & clarified ambition though - knowing what you truly want - life becomes an exciting adventure again!

A part of the fulfillment that comes from this journey also comes from our willingness to question & challenge 'social norms' (which can something squash our big dreams & dimish our connection to our true potential) instead opting to follow our truest aspirations. Let's intentionally, thoughtfully & with passion use this incredible gift we've received - consciousness - to plan out & go on to create the lives we truly desire...

4 | CLARITY: SET & ALIGN INTENTION

"Clarity is the counterbalance of profound thoughts."

- *LUC DE CLAPIERS*

If someone asked you...

- What do you want?
- What are the 'ambitions' you're pursuing?
- What are you good at?
- Where do you see yourself in 5 years?
- What are your plans for the next 6 - 12 months?
- What is required of you - knowledge, skills, abilities, focus, attention - to achieve what you want?
- What drives & motivates you?
- What does a great 'quality of life' look like for you?
- Who do you want to become?

...how would you answer?

Would you answer... confidently? Quickly? With certainty?

Would you hesitate or eloquently answer the questions? Would your answer clearly convey that you know what 'success' means to you? Or would you hesitate, feeling caught off guard by these questions as these are clearly not things you have spent much time considering?

This is <u>clarity</u>: knowing what you want, why you want it, what you value, who you are & who you want to become.

And it's this *clarity* (or lack of) that forms the 1st big predictor of whether you'll achieve what you want & live the life you really desire, or not (& the research proves it.)

In multiple studies, the people who can answer questions like those above more quickly, more clearly, more confidently, with more certainty & less hesitation are those who have achieved more in the past & go on to achieve more in the future (across all areas of one's life: career, health & fitness, relationships, overall happiness & emotional wellbeing, etc).

In other words, the data shows, if you have *clarity* in your ambitions - you know exactly (specifically) what you want - you're far more likely to get it.

However, it's not just about generic, vague ambitions - *'I want success,'* or *'I want to be happy,'* - but rather about true, real, personalized & crystalized clarity - that's what's required. It has to resonate - to be meaningful - to you. Do that & you've taken the 1st step to creating anything extraordinary in life.

ARE YOU GOING IN THE WRONG DIRECTION?

Have you ever started walking (or driving) somewhere only to later realize you're going in the wrong direction? I'm sure you've had this happen in your life before; I know I have. *It feels very unproductive, doesn't it?*

Yet, how often do we do this in our own lives, pursuing things that we think we want, working hard, only to later realize that the direction may have been wrong to begin with.

Don Herold put it best when he said, *"Unhappiness is not knowing what we want and killing ourselves to get it."*

We go after things we 'think' we want, killing ourselves to get them, only to realize that this wasn't really what we wanted. Or worse, we don't know what we want in the first place & so just sway with the winds of culture, tradition, social pressure

& the countless 'shiny objects' available to us, never truly stopping to realize what we deeply want, what we value, why we're doing what we're doing or where to from here...

| If You Don't Know Where You're Heading, You're Going To Get Lost!

A pilot wouldn't start flying without first checking the course, a train conductor wouldn't get the train into motion without first verifying its direction. So why would we go through our lives without contemplating where we're going, what we want or what's going to make our lives magnificent? We shouldn't. *And that's what this section, 'Ambition' is all about...*

It was Abraham Lincoln who famously said, *"Give me 5 hours to chop down a tree and I will spend the first four sharpening the ax."* Well, in our lives, 'sharpening our axe' is not just developing knowledge, skill & understanding, but also (& most importantly) gaining *clarity* about what we want.

Develop this sense of direction &, just as the research shows, your odds of tuning into the possibilities you really, deep down, desire are skewed in your favor. It becomes possible for you, but it starts with clarifying what you truly want.

Plus, as you develop this sense of clarity in your life & you feel on purpose, filled with meaning & fueled by direction, it aids your motivation & challenges becomes easier to overcome.

Research has shown that the 'reward centers' in the human brain are triggered by the potential of a reward (e.g. setting a goal, imagining the achievement of something, spotting a new opportunity, etc) in a similar way as they do when you actually achieve the goal you're after. This, of course, brings us great motivation, inspiration & drives us to take action.

Beyond all of this though, *clarity*, not just helps you achieve what you want, but has shown to bring incredible new levels of happiness, meaning & quality of life. Those who feel like they are on course in life, doing what they truly love doing, knowing what they want & acting accordingly (as we'll explore in this chapter) are happier, more joyous & more fulfilled.

It's time to start living by design (to take responsibility & create your life) instead of living by default. It's time to get some more *clarity* in your life...

CREATING CLARITY; PIECE BY PIECE

When people talk about clarity & 'knowing what you want,' they assume these are things that people 'stumble upon.' Like in a movie, in one-moment clarity just washes over them; a grand epiphany out of nowhere. Clarity just hits them over the head one day with all of life's answers. *In reality, it rarely (if ever) doesn't work like this...*

Clarity is not something that just 'happens.' A more accurate comparison is that of a jigsaw puzzle. If you sit down every day & put pieces together, with time, all the pieces fall into place & have a grand picture of what you want in life.

Each puzzle piece in this metaphor represents time spent thinking, asking yourself questions, reflecting or journaling, letting your mind wander into the future to see what's available to you, focusing on deep thoughts & questions about your existence, exploring new possibilities, testing new things & identifying what resonates (as well as what doesn't).

And just like you build a puzzle piece-by-piece, you build a strong sense of clarity in your life in that same way (though constant thinking, experimentation, testing & putting pieces together in your life.)

Except, unlike a puzzle, the seeking of greater & greater clarity never end; it's an infinite process of iteration.

Think about it... you probably want different things today than you did 10 years ago. You may want some of the same stuff, but details in your final puzzle changed. And they will continue to change as you experience more possibilities.

Clarity is an ongoing, never-ending process of experiencing life & evaluating (or re-evaluating) what you really want, value & find truly meaningful to you.

And it's created, not through one magical moment where everything in your life just comes together, but in the day-in, day-out thoughts, considerations & exploration that make this possible. Once again, the research proves this...

When following up studies were conducted to uncover why some could answer the questions we started this chapter with more quickly, more confidently, with more certainty & less hesitant than others, these individuals reported thinking, reflecting on & even talking about their ambitions more often than those who didn't have such a strong sense of clarity.

For these individuals, questions like the ones at the start of this chapter, were not just fleeting thoughts a few times a year, like for most, but a frequent, ongoing part of their lives.

Compare this to what most people do, just going 'through the motions' of life, not thinking about anything bigger, not creating their life & only stopping a few times a year to think about clarity. Birthdays, crisis's & when the calendar flips on New Year's: those are pretty much the only times most people stop to ask what they truly want out of life.

Meanwhile, those who have a strong sense of clarity (& as a result, are more likely to achieve what they want & experience the reality they desire), think about this more often & more deeply. They're in a constant process of thinking about, reflecting on, clarifying, assessing, planning & adjusting their ambitions to what they really, truly want.

EXERCISE: THINKING TIME

Beyond just the results of the follow-up studies on clarity, there are numerous cases in which top CEO's, for example, will actually schedule 10 - 30 minutes every week (or for some, every day!) just to **think**. To think about the future; their future. future of the company, future of the brand, what they want their business & brand to stand for & represent in the future. Time to think about goals, ambitions & aspirations for the companies they are leading (as well as their own personal goals outside of work).

This exercise is a chance for you to do the same - once now & if you choose, consistently in your life (recommended!)

Firstly, before you keep reading, just stop for 15 minutes & think about your life & future. Don't do anything else. For not, just sit & think.

Then, you can also schedule specific 'thinking time' into your calendar on timeframes that work for you. That's this exercise & it's profound (assuming you do it; not just skip it)

The research shows us this is what creates clarity, which is the term, helps you achieve more (which we'll cover in a moment). And this is what many successful individuals do in their own lives to give themselves an edge. And you can too with this exercise. So, pause for a moment & complete this exercise before continuing...

EXERCISE: JOURNALLING

More than just thinking about your life, writing it down has also shown to be a powerful practice, labeled *'journalling.'*

Plus, as you search through history, you'll find it's filled with extraordinary people who kept a journal, regularly taking time to pause & just write (often daily; every morning or evening). Examples include Marcus Aurelius, Benjamin Franklin, Mark Twain & George Lucas (amongst others.)

> And you too can build this habit into your rituals, allowing yourself to write down your thoughts, journal on questions you've been pondering & find great clarity amidst confusion.

And this process of thinking, mentally exploring & clarifying is, whether we realize it or not, fueled by *'curiosity.'* In fact...

| **Curiosity** Is The Path To *Clarity*

Clarity comes from the willingness to engage not just in small talk within one's one mind (thinking) but in asking the biggest, more existential questions. It comes in that deep exploration, playing with possibilities, until slowly the puzzle pieces fall into place & the next level of *clarity* is attained.

And *'curiosity'* - knowing that there is something you may not yet know & wanting to figure it out - is that path that, when you walk, gives you that *clarity*.

As Eleanor Roosevelt once said, *"I think, at a child's birth, if a mother could ask a fairy godmother to endow it with the most useful gift, that gift should be curiosity."*

Or as Walt Disney put it, *"We keep moving forward, opening new doors, and doing new things, because we're curious and curiosity keeps leading us down new paths."*

By being curious, we open ourselves to new answers; new clarity for what is real & what is worthy of us engaging in. And the foundation of curious, as you likely already know, is the act of asking questions. We must begin to question again...

To question what is around us. To ask questions about our life, our future, possibilities & what is available to us. *By staying in these questions, answers begin to appear.*

For example, if you hold the question of, *"What do I truly value & finding meaningful in my life?"* in your mind long enough, you will start to find answers. Those answers build your sense of clarity & put you on a path to amazing things.

"The important thing is not to stop questioning. Curiosity has its own reason for existing," Albert Einstein once said.

And it's also the reason children learn so fast. Think about the tremendous strides in growth, understanding & ability a newborn displays in the first 10 years of life. This is largely thanks to their insatiable curiosity. They ask questions all the time, *"What is this?" "How does it work?" "Why can't I do this?" "Who is that?" "Why should I do that instead of this?"*

And while parents may find this irritating & the education system can largely take this out of us (as Einstein also said, *"It is a miracle that curiosity survives formal education"*), this curiosity it's actually the greatest gift for clarity.

We must return to that curious state by beginning to ask questions again, to question what we know & what we've done up until now in search for something greater.

As Sylvia Earle, once said, *"The best scientists and explorers have the attributes of kids! They ask a question and have a sense of wonder. They have curiosity. 'Who, what, where, why, when, and how!' They never stop asking questions, and I never stop asking questions, just like a five-year-old."*

That's the path of *clarity*. Which, not only helps people achieve more but also gives them a greater sense of happiness, as clarity is often the difference between joy & misery (as we'll explore in this chapter).

First, though, we're going to build on previous understanding to form this connection between clarity & achievement. We're going to answer the question, *'Why exactly does clarity - knowing what you want - help you achieve it?'* Let's dive in...

EXERCISE: ASKING BETTER QUESTIONS

"Judge a man by his questions rather than his answers," was what Pierre-Marc-Gaston de Lévis once wisely said.

And since 'thinking' is nothing more than the process of asking & answering questions in your mind (& as a result, asking better questions is instrumental in the process of gaining clarity in life) it's time to start asking better questions in your life.

| Better Questions Lead To Better Answers

When you change the quality of your questions, you change the quality of your answers, changing your 'thinking' & ultimately creating different (better) results in your life!

Hence this exercise (journal on this!):

What are 20 questions, that if you could find great answers to, would completely change your life?

Here are some examples...

- What would make me truly fulfilled in my life?
- How can someone achieve more in the next 6 months than they did in the last 5 years?
- What do I think is impossible right now that is in fact very realistic for me (& how do I achieve it)?
- What does an extraordinary life look like for me?
- How do I become the best possible husband / wife / partner / parent / friend / family member?

Take 10 mins (minimum!) to create your own questions. It's valuable to word them as you would - personalized to you.)

Then, put these questions in various places (on your phone, hang on your fridge, etc) where you'll constantly be able to ask them to yourself, reflecting on the possibilities...

WHAT YOU SEEK IS WHAT YOU'LL FIND: WHY CLARITY LEADS TO ACHIEVEMENT

> *"My favorite words are possibilities, opportunities, and curiosity. I think if you are curious, you create opportunities, and then if you open the doors, you create possibilities."*
>
> - MARIO TESTINO

First & foremost, our ambitions are a part of 'who we are.' And as you know from chapter #2, we filter possibilities, opportunities & situations (information) differently based on 'who we are,' or more specifically, what we've been primed & conditioned to focus on.

So, by clarifying your ambitions & reminding yourself of what you truly want, you're conditioning yourself to pay attention to things differently in your life. To spot new possibilities you may not have seen before you set this goal. To seize opportunities differently. To response & react in a new way.

To best explain, let me ask you this: *have you ever looked through catalogs or searched online to find the exact version of something you really wanted - a specific model of a car, a certain watch, a certain type of jacket, etc - & as soon as you found this, you suddenly started to see that car, watch, jacket or 'thing' (whatever it was) everywhere?*

You never realized that car, watch, jacket, gadget, app or anything else you just picked out for yourself was so popular, but now you seem to see it everywhere. People are driving, wearing or using that same thing you wanted all the time.

Another example: you learn a new word & suddenly start hearing it everywhere around you *(which is strange as before you don't remember hearing anyone use this word.)*

Or, you're in a crowd of people & you're able to tune out what they are saying (not focus on it), however, when they say your name (or something that sounds a little like your name), you recognize it immediately & listen.

This group may have been talking for a half hour, saying a total of about 3000 words, yet your mind didn't pay attention to 2999 of them & only focused when it heard that 1 word that sounded like your name (or was, in fact, your name).

These are all examples of your mind reacting appropriately to what you've primed & conditioned it to spot around you.

It's not that the car, watch or gadget wasn't around you, or that new word you learned wasn't being used. It was. It's just that before you weren't primed to spot it. These things were around you all along, but your mind didn't pick them up. Just like when you go watch a movie again, except this time you spot something new that you didn't spot last time. It was there before, you just didn't see it last time.

This is also one of the most common explanations for 'manifestation' or 'the law of attraction.' When you go to 'manifest' something, you condition your mind to look out for certain things that you often end up finding. In reality, they may have been there all along, you just didn't realize them before. Now you do because you're primed yourself to do so.

Knowing all this, we can condition ourselves to spot new information, new possibilities & new opportunities around us by implanting what we want to focus on into our mind.

For example, if I told you to count everything around you what was of a certain color - e.g. brown - your mind would instantly hyper-focus on that which is brown, counting it all.

Previously, you may not have been focused on any of these things - the brown button on friend's jacket, the brown text on that box in the corner of the room, the brown spots on the lion painting hanging in the room - but now you notice it all. *Why?* Because your mind is filtering the information around you differently, based on what you've (or in this case, what I have) conditioned it to focus on.

See, there are literally thousands of different things you could be focusing on in just your immediate environment.

At any moment, your mind could choose to focus on any of these things, or not. The things, objects, people, etc, around you. However, you don't.

There's no way your mind can pay attention to everything at the same time, so your mind makes choices - it pays attention to that which is important, useful, valuable, necessary, as well as aligned with 'who you are,' above everything else.

However, once again, these aren't just pretty metaphors & examples, this is how your brain works & why we do what we do - biologically & psychologically. *It's a part of 'who you are.'*

In fact, dissect your brain & you'll find what is called the 'Reticular Activating System' (or for short, 'RAS'). This bundle of nerves at your brainstem are the part of your brain in charge of exactly what we talked about here; filtering incoming information & bringing to your conscious attention only that which is important, useful, valuable, necessarily & aligned with 'who you are,' above all else.

See, our brains are incredibly complex (as is the world around us). Billions of bits of information are created & processed by us all day long. Over & over. It never ends. And somehow, our brains don't explode. *Why is this?*

Because we don't consciously process everything around us, but merely a small part of it that our mind considers 'important' to us *(thanks to the 'Reticular Activating System')*

And this is the first (& arguably) greatest explanation for why gaining *clarity*, knowing what you want & setting ambitions for your life actually helps you achieve it.

It's because as soon as you know what you want (& especially, when you think about & imagine it often, as in the case of people in the follow-study mentioned before) your condition your mind to filter information differently so you can see that which you may not have seen before.

New possibilities & opportunities seem to appear out of nowhere, but in reality, they were there all along.

Except, before they were being filtered out (discarded as 'not important' or 'useless' information), but now that they align with 'who you are,' (specifically, your ambitions) they are being filtered as 'important' & *'useful.'* Therefore they are now being brought to your conscious attention.

I remember years ago when I first heard the phrase, *"seek and you shall find"* & got a little confused by it. Back then, I didn't understand this. However, I researched it & learned how the brain operates. And, as it turns out, that phrase is spot on:

Seek long enough, with a specific, clear image or goal in your mind & (just like the color 'brown') you will find something that matches that because your brain has been conditioned to look out for that.

Hence, by constantly seeking clarity about important things in your life, focusing on what you want, outlining your ambitions & pursuing them, what you're doing is conditioning your mind into new possibilities, new opportunities & a new life.

That's why in this chapter, we're going to explore various frameworks for gaining *clarity* in your life, starting with the most important aspect of this...

MOTIVE: 'WHY' MORE IMPORTANT THAN 'WHAT'

"Millions saw the apple fall, but Newton was the one who asked why."

- BERNARD BARUCH

We often get obsessed with the 'what,' & assume it's the first place to start with *clarity - <u>what</u> you're going after, <u>what</u> ambitions you're pursuing, <u>what</u> actions are you taking, <u>what</u> things are on you to-do list every day* - but research shows us the motive (the 'why') behind your ambitions & actions actually matters much more in terms of happiness, motivation, inspiration, creativity & fulfillment.

Or simply put: *"Why" we do what we do matters more than "what" we do or "how" we do it for the things we value most.*

This isn't just some inspirational jibber-jabber but based on over half a century of research looking at human motivation.

See, our understanding of what motivates us (human beings) has evolved a lot over time...

And, it's the author of many books on the topics of business, economics & behavioral science, *Daniel Pink*, who conveys this information best by comparing our understanding of the 'motives' behind our actions to that of software development.

In his hit book, *Drive: The Surprising Truth About What Motivates Us*, he describes these upgrades in understanding as *Motivation 1.0, Motivation 2.0 & Motivation 3.0.*

Motivation 1.0 refers to our first understanding of what motivates us, which is our *biological urges: our basic human needs*. If there's a lion running towards you, you're going to be 'motivated' to do something, whether you like it or not. You don't need to sit down & journal or visualize your goals turning into reality. Motivation is automatic. Fight or flight.

Your body even reacts biochemically, raising your cortisol levels (cortisol; the stress hormone) to make you take action.

This first level of motivation - *motivation 1.0* - served us (human beings) well in the past when the world was more dangerous, we were in constant threat from predators & our main goal in life was mere 'survival.' With time, more was required though...

Now, don't get me wrong: this 1st level of motivation (1.0) is still applicable today & helps us every single day. Abraham Maslow best theorized this in his 1943 paper, *"A Theory of Human Motivation,"* in which he first introduced us to the now-household, *Maslow's hierarchy of needs*.

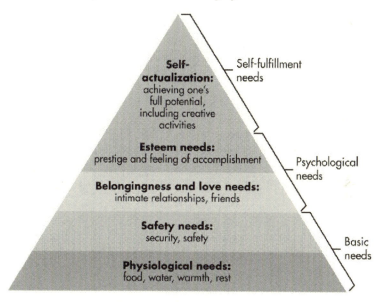

He shared that at the base of everything are our *basic human needs*. These include the needs of food, water, shelter & sleep. If we are in a state of deprivation in these areas, we aren't able to see anything greater - until these needs are met.

For example, you're likely to be concerned about your legacy, spiritual practices or work in your community if your basic needs are not met & you're roaming the streets as a homeless person, starving, thirsty, cold & with no place to stay.

The first step is to meet our *basic needs* - which *Motivation 1.0* (our biological urges) help us with this with.

When you're hungry, thirsty or sleepy, your brain & body signal this to you & you're automatically 'motivated' to act accordingly. Beyond this though, our biological urges don't motivate us to do anything more than merely 'survive.'

Hence, if you want to, not just survive, but thrive - to live a great life & experience a magnificent experience - *Motivation 1.0 isn't* going to help you here. That's why society evolved, with the introduction & practice of *Motivation 2.0*.

This 2nd upgrade to our understanding of why we do what we do now included extrinsic, external 'motives' for action.

The idea that to motivate ourselves (or others) we must incentivize or reward the behavior we want more of & punish the behavior we want less of. Or, as it's commonly referred to, 'the carrot & stick approach.' That's *motivation 2.0*.

The idea was that to motivate human beings, like a donkey, you dangle a carrot (money, social status, a reward or sorts) while using a stick to beat out unwanted behaviors (a punishment, getting grounded as a child, getting a fine, etc).

Reward & punishment. Positive & negative reinforcement. Just like you would train a dog or a dolphin. This was our understanding of why we did what we did; beyond biological urges (motivation 1.0), *we did what we were rewarded for & didn't do what we would be punished for* (motivation 2.0).

And this became our main method of motivating ourselves & others to do anything. Businesses dangled carrots (incentives) to employees to make them harder or punished unwanted behavior. Pay someone more (financial incentive) & they work harder. Punish someone & they don't repeat that behavior. Parents rewarded or punished children with gold stars, allowances, praise, etc & punished them by grounding them or taking away their tablets or game consoles.

Much of what we experience today & why people do what they do is based on this understanding of motivation (v2.0) The idea is that we only do things for extrinsic, external reasons.

That's until 1949, when psychology professor, Harry Harlowe, discovered something new about our motivation.

In an experiment, he gave 8 monkeys a mechanical puzzle. However, since the primates wouldn't receive any reward (such as food or praise), nor where they punished for not completing the punished (no extrinsic motivation), he was convinced the monkeys would not concern themselves with it.

To his surprise, the monkeys gave the puzzle a go, recognized how it worked, & without any extrinsic incentives, solved it with great enjoyment. They repeated playing with the puzzle until they were able to solve it fairly quickly.

This brought into question our understanding of why we do what we do. The monkeys were not motivated by biological urges (motivation 1.0), nor any extrinsic rewards (motivation 2.0; reward or punishment), so they shouldn't have been motivated to do anything with the puzzle. *But, they were!*

Similar experiments were performed with more intelligent, more aware, smarter monkeys - a.k.a. human beings - which confused the researchers & challenges what we know about motivation. *Perhaps there was another level at play here?*

It wasn't until 2 decades later though that the idea that there was more to motivation than just biological urges & extrinsic rewards was taken seriously. It really got attention when 2 researchers, Edward Deci & Richard Ryan, performed various experiments building on what Harry Harlowe had found. They shared this in their 1975 book, *'Intrinsic Motivation.'*

In the following years, continued research kept resulting in similar conclusions: that when a task is enjoyable within itself, external stimulus is not required. And it's this work that moved us to a new understanding of motivation - upgrading us to *Motivation 3.0* (as Daniel Pink called it).

This new understanding (3.0) now included, not just extrinsic motivation, but also factored in the great power of *intrinsic motivation*; the idea that when a task is fulfilling - we find it interesting & is worthwhile within itself - no external reward is required to 'motivate' us to do it.

And that brings us to one of the cores (& most useful) categorizations we have of motivation today. Outside of motivation 1.0 (our basic human needs), motivation can be divided into *'intrinsic vs extrinsic motivation.'*

Intrinsic Motivation: *motivation to do something for its own sake; for an internal, innate benefit you get from an activity.*

Extrinsic Motivation: *motivation to do something for external reasons (e.g. earn a reward, financial incentive, avoid punishment).*

INTRINSIC MOTIVATION	EXTRINSIC MOTIVATION
- Learning a topic or skill because you find it interesting or enjoyable.	- Learning a topic or skill to get a good grade or avoid punishment from teachers.
- Participating in a sport because you love it - for its own sake.	- Participating in a sport to win a trophy & make your parents proud.
- Playing an instrument because you love it & find it meaningful.	- Playing an instrument to impress other people or make more money.
- Building a business because you want to freely share what you have with the world around you.	- Building a business & make money to be popular, 'keep up with the joneses' or make your friends jealous.

While we're mostly aware of this first basic categorization of motivation - *intrinsic vs extrinsic motivation* - what you may not know is just how this affects our happiness & joy when it comes to the ambitions we set in our lives...

EFFECTS OF LIVING FOR EXTERNAL MOTIVES

In the 1980s, scientist Tim Kasser & his team of researchers set out to test how living life for external (or 'extrinsic') motives (money, social status & popularity, approval from others, material possessions, etc) impacted ones happiness, joy & overall wellbeing in life, compared to doing things for internal (or 'intrinsic') reasons.

What the researchers found at first shocked them. The results showed that people who achieved goals for external motives (such as money, social status or material things) over time, showed no increase in day-to-day happiness. *Absolutely none.*

Sure, they were 'happy' at the moment, but that happiness didn't last. It dissipated quickly. In the same way that nobody walks around happy about a financial target they hit last year, or a new watch or car they bought 2 years ago. Short spike of happiness (like when you get a hit of energy after drinking a coffee or energy drink), but it quickly fades away & you need to have another to get be happy again.

What this means that while your new watch, new iPhone, hitting a million followers or big commission check may give you a short jolt of 'happiness,' it's unlikely to affect your day-to-day, ongoing, lasting happiness (just like that coffee you drank last week doesn't give you increased energy today.)

The researchers also discovered that people who live their lives dominated by external (extrinsic) values had a worse time in almost every respect. They felt physically worse, were angrier, experiences less joy in life, had worse relationships & even felt more insecure.

On the flip side, those who pursue goals that motivated them intrinsically - like being a better parent, dancing for the sheer joy of it or helping others, become significantly happier, less depressed & less anxious in their lives.

Meaning: their happiness actually lasted. This time, a better metaphorical comparison is not that of a coffee or energy drink, but that of hitting the gym as a method of increased energy - it lasts. You go to the gym to workout & now, on a day-to-day basis you feel increased energy & strength; that's how intrinsic motivation affects your happiness.

In another study, graduates of the University of Rochester were asked about their main ambitions & aims in life. While some shared about extrinsic goals (e.g. profit targets they wanted to hit, ambitions to become rich & famous, etc), others specified more meaningful, intrinsic goals: to develop themselves personally or to help others (for example by working for international aid organizations.)

Some years later, the researchers interviewed the participants to find out how things had turned out for them. The students with profit goals (extrinsic motivation) were no more content with their lives than before, despite many having achieved positions as managers in large firms, earning large paychecks.

In fact, those in 'extrinsically-motivated' group suffered from depression & anxiety more frequently than the other group. While, those in the 'intrinsically-motivated' group reported greater happiness in life & only very rarely suffered from depression or anxiety.

22 different studies since then have all found that the more materialistic & externally motivated you are, the more depressed and anxious you will be.

As Joseph Campbell once said, *"We're so engaged in doing things to achieve purposes of outer value that we forget the inner value, the rapture that is associated with being alive, is what it is all about."*

Or as Democritus once put it, *"Happiness resides not in possessions, and not in gold, happiness dwells in the soul."*

However, it doesn't stop there. Studies also showed that when people are *intrinsically-motivated* they are more creative, more inspired, often perform better (productivity) & report both greater work & life satisfaction.

See, the difference between intrinsic & extrinsic motivation for happiness is like the difference between fool's gold & actual, real gold. On the surface, they look mostly the same - it's why 'gold' must be inspected by an expert. But, under the surface, they are very different. And real gold is many, many times more valuable (despite the on-the-surface similarities).

In this same way, doing something for intrinsic or extrinsic reasons may look exactly the same on the surface. At the end of the day, the actions are exactly the same: building a business, playing the piano, learning a topic or skill, etc.

However, the _motive_ (the 'why') behind your actions is the real factor that best determines whether that activity will really bring you lasting happiness, creativity, inspiration, joy & emotional wellbeing.

IS EXTRINSIC MOTIVATION BAD?

It's a very human thing (based on our past conditioning) to assume that if something shows more promising results that sometime else, or certain studies go against the positive effects of something to assume that it is 'bad,' or 'ineffective.'

A more realistic view of much of the things in life is that nothing is 'good' or 'bad' all (or none) of the time (it's why I don't like to this absolute term, as they are often flawed).

Extrinsic motivation is not bad. Far from it. Let me explain...

As I've shared many times already, there are no right or wrongs & everything has its pros & cons. It's our job to learn to use these different tools & methods at the right times.

Is a screwdriver good for hitting in a nail? *Not ideal, right?* A hammer would be a much more effective choice. However, for screwing in a screw, the screwdriver is a more effective choice.

Self-mastery *is learning about these various philosophies, concepts & 'tools,' as well as knowing when to use them to create (& live) the life you freely choose for yourself.*

And the same applies to intrinsic & extrinsic motivation...

For example, for less creative & more mechanical tasks (like working on a manufacturing line, filing papers, driving, etc) which don't require creative thinking, but mere compliance, repetition & efficiency, research continues to show *extrinsic motivation* is the best tool for the job.

Also, as many jobs today still fill into this category of largely mechanical work (although, they are fading away in the modern world because of outsourcing, automation, machinery & advancements in robotics & AI), the world would fall into chaos if extrinsic motivation wasn't used. *It's a valuable tool (it just needs to be used correctly)*.

Plus, for other tasks for which we don't have any real intrinsic motivation (things we don't particularly want to do but know we should) extrinsic motivation is a still great choice too - like kids doing chores or parents filing taxes.

Lastly, *extrinsic* motivation has always been shown as a great gateway to exploring new things that can lead to *intrinsic motivation* down the line.

For example, you may not be *intrinsically motivated* to play tennis right now simply because you haven't done it before.

However, you use *extrinsic* motivation just to get yourself (or someone uses to encourage you) to go to your tennis practice. This new exposure to this new sport can lead to you enjoying it & becoming *intrinsically motivated* to play tennis with your buddies every weekend.

THE JOURNEY VS THE DESTINATION

In the book, *The Happiness Hypothesis*, social psychologist Jonathan Haidt wrote...

> *Richard Davidson, the psychologist who brought us affective style and the approach circuits of the front left cortex, writes about two types of positive effect.*

The first he calls "pre-goal attainment positive effect," which is the pleasurable feeling you get as you make progress toward a goal.

The second is called "post-goal attainment positive effect," which Davidson says arises once you have achieved something you want. You experience this latter feeling as contentment, as a short-lived feeling of release when the left prefrontal cortex reduces its activity after a goal has been achieved.

In other words, when it comes to goal pursuit, it really is the journey that counts, not the destination. Set for yourself any goal you want. Most of the pleasure will be had along the way, with every step that takes you closer.

The final moment of success is often no more thrilling than the relief of taking off a heavy backpack at the end of a long hike. If you went on the hike only to feel that pleasure, you are a fool.

People sometimes do just this. They work hard at a task and expect some special euphoria at the end. But when they achieve success and find only moderate and short-lived pleasure, they ask (as the singer Peggy Lee once did): Is that all there is?

They devalue their accomplishments as a striving after wind. We can call this "the progress principle": Pleasure comes more from making progress toward goals than from achieving them. Shakespeare captured it perfectly: "Things won are done; joy's soul lies in the doing"

Extrinsic motivation is about the *destination*. It assumes that the journey (the task at hand) is <u>not</u> enjoyable & so you get rewarded for getting through it & reaching the destination.

If there is something you know you should do, but you don't want to do it, *extrinsic motivation* is a great tool for you for you to use in these moments - it'll help you endure painful, non-interesting tasks because of the reward at the end.

Intrinsic motivation is about the *journey*. It assumes that the journey (what you're actively doing) is the greatest part. The joy of learning. The fulfillment of discovering something new.

The happiness of doing something for the reason of just doing it; because you love it - like dancing, playing tennis, writing, singing, having a meaningful conversation with someone, etc.

No reward (extrinsic motivation) is needed here. If one does show up, that's great & you accept it, but that's not the motive. That's just a bonus; a side benefit. *The intent is the journey.*

So when a successful athlete talks about loving (or being motivated) by '*the game*' itself, an inspirational speaker talks about 'loving & enjoying *the process*,' or a guru in a movie talks about '*loving the journey*,' what they are referring to is <u>intrinsic motivation</u> & it's incredible benefits.

Extrinsic motivation may be a powerful tool you can use (as you know), but for big picture, joy-driven, fulfillment-fueled ambition-setting that'll give you great motivation, creativity & meaning, *intrinsic motivation* is the best tool for the job.

To better understand why we explore some of the greatest frameworks we have for human consciousness today *(as well as question 'the meaning of life' itself)*...

HIGHEST DEGREES OF CONSCIOUSNESS

The higher up you go on '*Maslow's hierarchy of needs*' & the higher levels of consciousness you want to tap into, the more you're going to need to rely on *intrinsic motivation*.

This is because the very things we value most (happiness, joy, connection, freedom, love, peace & fulfillment) come from within, not from outside - just like intrinsic motivation.

Plus, these are intangible things - you can't hold them or sell them. They are more brain chemistry (emotion; internal) then they are about the material or physical - a situation in which doing something for an intrinsic reason is often your best bet.

See, motivation #1 - your biology - takes care of the base level for survival - your basic human needs.

Beyond that, while *extrinsic motivation can do a great job motivating you to a certain point, it can't get you to the levels of true self-actualization of self-transcendence.*

Self-transcendence (or just, 'transcendence') is the highest level in *Maslow's hierarchy of needs*, although it doesn't appear in initial research, conception, nor in most of the graphics & explanations that exist today. Before his death in 1970, he started to introduce & expand on this idea that there was another level beyond *'Self-Actualization.'*

'Self-actualization' refers to the idea that one must fulfill their potential & for 2 decades it was the top of Maslow's hierarchy of needs; the highest human need. Maslow himself said this about it, *"What a man can be, he must be. This need we call self-actualization."*

And while *self-actualization* is a great lofty, ambitious & worthy ambition to pursue, Maslow added *'transcendence'* as the next level of growth later on...

As Maslow described it: *"Transcendence refers to the very highest and most inclusive or holistic levels of human consciousness, behaving and relating, as ends rather than means, to oneself, to significant others, to human beings in general, to other species, to nature, and to the cosmos"*

According to Maslow, *self-transcendence* brings someone what he described as 'peak experiences.' Experiences in which people transcend their own personal concerns to see life from a higher perspective, bringing strong positive emotions like joy, peace, and a well-developed sense of awareness.

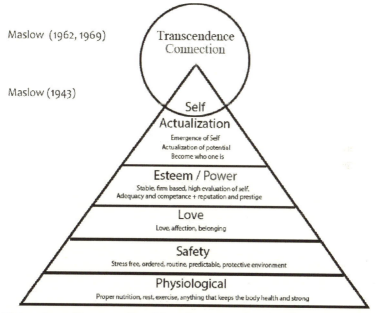

This also aligns well with what David Hawkins discovered about the various levels of consciousness we can operate at.

In this famous, *Map of Consciousness*, the highest level, isn't happiness, love, joy or bliss, but *peace & enlightenment*. At this level, one's view of life (including the situations within it) isn't that life is 'good,' 'bad,' or 'perfect,' but that life just *'is.'*

One's existence is all-encompassing & transcends both time & space. The process is described as *pure consciousness*.

Lastly, this is also what we talked about in chapter #2 - the most inner level of 'who we are' (before even our 'beliefs') is *energy*. We are nothing more than energies & frequencies experiencing life. *Pure consciousness. True transcendence.*

Meaning: it's not just what the greatest physicists have told is who we truly are, but it's also what the greatest, most respected theories of human motivation & consciousness point us to as well. *The idea that there is greater meaning to life (more than what may be visible to us right now) & that we must transcendence our past, our environment, our body & our circumstances to fulfill it. That we are here to just experience life. Fully. Truly. In its full possibility.*

As to how we do this, the specific meaning we associate to our lives (& the direction we choose to take it), is for us to decide.

'Self-Actualization' & 'Transcendence,' are the highest needs in Maslow's hierarchy, but how we express these can vary...

For one person, fulfilling their full potential & transcending to a higher level of consciousness is about maximizing happiness & joy, stepping into unconditional love, or feeling true bliss.

For some, it's about freedom & choice more than anything else. For others, it's more about giving, while for some it's about acceptance of what was, what is & deep introspection.

At the end of the day, we choose how we're going to express this in our lives & the meaning we associate to our lives in the 1st place - that's the ultimate 'why' we must uncover...

BIG PICTURE: WHAT'S THE MEANING OF LIFE?

> *"There are two great days in a person's life - the day we are born and the day we discover why."*
>
> - WILLIAM BARCLAY

"What is the purpose of existence?" "Why are we here & what are we here for?" "What is the purpose of one's life?" "What are we living for?" Or simply, "What is the meaning of life?"

You may have asked yourself these question before & may even have gotten some answers (*clarity*).

Whether you, me or anyone is ever able to truly answer it, I don't know. However, 1 thing is certain: mere consideration of life's meaning - elevating so far beyond typical small talk or small-minded thinking - can help us gain massive clarity. It can help us tune into what truly matters to us & give us great direction (a 'why') we can use to make better decisions & live extraordinary lives.

And to further probe at this clarity, here are some popular views (answers) to 'life's meaning' for us to consider...

- **Happiness:** to maximize happiness & minimize suffering; to experience life to its fullest (e.g. to experience new things, meet new people, do what you find joy in, enjoy life, have fun). *To be happy.*

- **Freedom:** to live life on one's own terms; to seize choice & choose your life freely, as you want (e.g. to do what you want, when you want, how you want, with who you want & if you want). *Total freedom & choice.*

- **Potential:** to realize one's truest potential; to see what is possible & do what one can (e.g. to find & chase dreams, to learn, to get as good as one can get at the topics, skills or areas that they choose to focus on). To strive for excellence & become better every day; mentally, physically, emotionally, spiritually, etc.

- **Love:** to tune into, express & radiate love. To connect with people. To be kind, caring & treat others in the absolute best possible, most loving way. *To love fully & unconditionally.*

- **Contribution**: To live beyond one's own desires, contributing & giving to others; to aid the happiness, success, ability & life experience of others. To leave the world (or, at least, one person's world) a better place than you found it (e.g. to add value, reduce suffering, share & contribute, to bring peace). *To give.*

- **Peace / Enlightenment:** To accept what simply 'is' & view life without judgment of what is wrong or right. To connect with something beyond oneself & accept all of life unconditionally. To transcendence the physical & engage in the spiritual, energetic & all-encompassing - see life from a higher perspective. *To embody peace & transcendence.*

These are popular views about the meaning of life, but not to be taken as the only views. You could resonate with one, many, a combination, none or something completely different than what's shared above.

Also, while these options are similar, they are also wildly different & capable of producing a very different experience of life. Like a highway with many exits - you may be driving on the same highway, in the same direction, but each exit can ultimately take you in a completely different direction.

What I've found important is *personalization* here; it's about what resonates & is meaningful to *you*.

Just as nobody can do pushups for you, or go to the bathroom on your behalf, nobody can decide what the meaning of your life is, except '*you.*' **You're in charge here.**

And I've found this is perhaps the biggest reason for a lot of the sadness, sense of loss, helplessness, depression & even suicide in this world: people attempt to live someone else's life, based on someone else's views, opinions & meaning.

From an early age, we are pushed into a view of the world from those around us instead of given the choice to pick what we really want: including the very meaning we choose to give to life itself.

It's as if we're given the greatest gift one could ever receive - life itself - yet told we can't only play with this gift in a certain way, at certain times & assuming we follow all the 'rules' (or, 'social norms') that others follow (as we'll talk about later.)

And if we play with this gift any different, we get punished by parents, teachers & society in general (*motivation 2.0, remember?*) so we become 'normal,' - just like everybody else.

And we grow up, with a whole list of things we 'should' do (because it's what others do), even though these things may not align with what we want in this adventure of life.

And then we can sometimes fall into feeling bad for being different; for being unique. Guilty for not liking, loving or accepting the things that others around us do. And we continue to repeat & reinforce these beliefs our entire life, forgetting about what we truly value, what we truly want & the possibilities that are available to us.

Continuing to live out this pattern - living your life only based on the values, opinions, views & beliefs of others - is a surefire way to an experience of life you may end up regretting.

See, if you attempt to live your life based purely on the views, opinions & meanings of others, you may end up hating this incredible gift of *life* you were given. *Live life as you choose (& play with this gift of life as you truly want) & now you can create a life you are absolutely overjoyed with!*

As Joseph Campbell wrote, *"The meaning of life is whatever you ascribe it to be."*

Ultimately, you get to choose what you value, what you want & what aligns with this. *It's up to you.*

So, perhaps the best question is not, *'What is the meaning of life?'* but *'What is the meaning of life for you?'* as your view of life may be different from that of your friend, neighbor, parents, teachers or anyone else you connect with in this life.

Also, even if asking these big existential questions doesn't bring up immediate answers - as we talked about, *clarity* is a lifelong, never-ending process of questioning & exploring - just the sheer act of staying in this thinking can help you gain great insights into what you value & what truly matters to you.

> **EXERCISE: JOURNAL ON LIFE'S MEANING...**
> Take 10 minutes & journal (write as much as possible) on this question: **What is the meaning of life *for you*?**
>
> It doesn't matter what you write; just write. You'll find that one thing will lead to another & another, so just begin, be open, be curious & write whatever comes to mind.

Knowing this (our true values & meaning of life) - even in part - can help us better reflect on our 'motives' for doing things in our lives & better decide what is right for us...

ASSESSING YOUR 'MOTIVES'

As you now know, the next time you set an ambition, form a plan in your mind or put a task on your to-do list, don't just assess whether 'what' you're pursuing is correct, or whether your 'how' (method) is optimal, but assess your '<u>why.</u>'

All 3 are important (*'what,' 'how,' 'why'*) but for a magnificent existence, <u>it must start with the *'why.'*</u>

Assess the 'motive' behind your goals, plans & actions <u>first</u>, then check the other stuff. This is a critical part of the *clarity* required to create what you want. Get used to asking yourself:

Am I setting this ambition for an extrinsic or intrinsic reason? What's my 'motive?' Why am I <u>really</u> doing this?

Is this ambition (as well as these actions) being motivated by the prospects of some financial reward, popularity or social status (extrinsic motivation) or is it driven by an intrinsic drive for some more, something greater, a new version of myself, my highest values & love of the process?

Am I going to find fulfillment in the process of doing this? Is it meaningful & aligned with what I truly want in life?

For example: do you really want that Ferrari because you're a true car fanatic & enjoy the 'journey' & 'process' of driving new cars (intrinsic) or do you want that supercar on your vision board because deep down you think it'll make you more popular, 'cooler,' make your friends jealous or the destination of owning the car will make you happy (as in 'when I have this car & this house, then I'll finally be happy' thinking.) Which is your true motive?

Do you actually want to be a part of the community or social circles you're involved in, eat the food you're eating, marry the person you're planning on marrying, etc?

<u>Why</u> are you dating that supermodel or driving that supercar? Is he or she really someone you love who also just happens to be smoking hot or are you really just in love with the idea of dating a supermodel & how your friends will look at you? Why do you want what you want & do what you do?

Are the things you want really things <u>you</u> truly want or merely things you '<u>think</u>' you want because of the doctrine & programming of society? (more on this in the next chapter!)

Are your ambitions truly aligned with the life you truly, deep down, want to live? Are you doing these things for the journey (intrinsic) or for the destination (extrinsic), thinking that they will make you popular or happy down the line?

You see, most of the time people say 'I want that,' it's not really 'that' which they want. We want 'that' because we think it'll bring us what we truly want - such as happiness, joy or freedom. It's a means to an end.

"I'll be happy when I have this" we tell ourselves. And we chase things accordingly. We chase things outside of ourselves thinking they will make us happy - like money or fame - but they will not. Not in a lasting way.

If anything, money & fame (amongst other external motives) will just amplify what's within. If you're happy within & you're doing things for a deeper purpose & you add money on top, you'll enjoy that. But, if these external motives are your core source of your supposed future happiness - *'I'll be happy when...'* - you may end up a little shocked by what you find.

The more aware we become of this (what we truly, deep down value, want & find meaning in), the more likely we become to, not just achieve our ambitions, but to tap into great happiness & fulfillment in the process. See, while you can achieve a goal without a strong motive, you're unlikely to find happiness.

'What' we do & 'how' we do it gives us results, but it's the 'why' that, like fuel in a car, powers it all, as well as gives us a deep sense of meaning in life. *It's why we start with 'why.'*

Then, once you have clarity of 'why,' the 'how,' the 'what,' & everything else comes next. And the goal here is total alignment. That's how you build clarity; piece by piece.

TOTAL ALIGNMENT: FIND THE 'HOW,' THE 'WHAT' & TAP INTO THE POWER OF INTENTION

> *"Happiness is when what you think, what you say, and what you do are in harmony."*
>
> - *MAHATMA GANDHI*

The key to achieving your ambitions (& living a great life) is nothing more than *total alignment*.

Specifically, <u>total alignment</u> between your ambitions, beliefs, thoughts, feelings, decisions & your actions.

Plus, when what you believe, think, say, decide & do is all moving in the same direction - with time, attainment of your ambitions is almost guaranteed. *You will find a way. Or, if you can't, you'll make a way!*

The challenge is we tend to struggle with *alignment*. It's not easy to live in a place of true congruence as we are not taught this growing up. However, this doesn't change the goal; to live in total alignment with what we value, want & find true meaning in. Where the 'how's' & 'what's' align with the 'why.'

That's the path of lasting life meaning & the place from which you create a magnificent existence.

Nw, let look at where we are right now (current reality) so we know the gaps we may need to bridge...

For example: we say we want to be healthy, fit & look good naked, yet we stuff our faces with sugar-filled, modified, unnatural foods that we know very well will harm our health. We don't exercise regularly (like we know we should).

It's not that we don't know that the things we put in our mouths are bad for us (we do) or that we're not sure whether exercise is truly beneficial (we know it is).

It's just we don't do what we say - a lack of alignment between knowledge & implementation. Or, otherwise put, what we say we want & what we do is *misaligned*. It creates poor health.

Or, wee say we want a loving relationship, great friendships, great interactions with other incredible people, as well as amazing connection with members of our family, yet we don't devote quality time to this, we're not present in our interactions & we do things that create conflicts.

Or, we say we want to attain financial freedom, build a big business & to change the world in some way, yet we spend our time on high unproductive, meaningless things we know 'waste our time,' we shy away from taking risks or fail to persevere in the face of challenges.

We say we want happiness, joy & peace, yet we don't take time to be grateful, to forgive or be present, living in the moment.

And these actions are driven out of misaligned thoughts & feelings, as well as, at the core, *misaligned beliefs* - limiting beliefs rubbing up against empowering beliefs, pulling you in different directions & creating conflicts within you.

Success, failure, happiness or sadness simply came back to *alignment* (or the lack of it.)

Just think about it... Think about the areas of your life in which you get the best results & most satisfaction. Then look at the areas of your life that you get the worst results, matched with the most frustration, sadness, guilt, pain or plain suffering. Ask yourself: *What's the difference between the successes & failures in your life? Between the areas of your life you're thriving in & those you may be struggling in/*

I may not know you personally, but I can say with confidence that the difference comes down to *alignment*.

In the areas you're more successful & fulfilled in, you're in higher *alignment*. What you want & what you do is on the same track. Same lane. Going in the same direction. *Aligned*.

While, in the areas of your life in which you're not getting the results you want, odds are, you're in much lower levels of *alignment*. What you truly want is far from what you're doing right now. You say you want one thing & you're doing things that are completely unrelated to this.

For example, you say you want to quit smoking & tell people, *'you should never smoke - a very bad habit,'* while you hold a cigarette for the 4th time today - a lack of alignment. Or another word for it, 'hypocrisy,' - the act of being a hypocrite.

Or knowing that you should invest (or at least, save your money) instead of splurging it, yet find yourself on shopping sprees with not just, no money, but lots of credit card debt.

It's this *lack of alignment* that causes the conflicts in our lives, sabotages our achievement, keeping us going in circles & blocks us from tapping into greater meaning in life.

Plus: just as in an interaction with someone, saying one thing & doing another creates distrust, in our own lives, it creates a distrust (& lack of belief) in ourselves. We begin to doubt ourselves because we feel so off track.

Our goal here is to move towards *total alignment* - do this & you've taken the most pivotal step to the life you want.

IT'S ABOUT 'ALIGNED ACTIONS.'

We think that we feel good or bad because of the 'right' or 'wrong' actions that we take, but really it's the *alignment* between our actions & ambitions that makes that difference.

For example, if you value Mother Earth (the environment), yet find yourself in situations where you know you're harming the environment through your actions, you'll likely to feel guilt, sadness or disappointment.

Although, you're not actually feeling bad because of the actions you're taking (e.g. not recycling, driving with high fuel consumption, using plastic, etc) themselves. Those are just actions (the 'what.') It's not the actions that make you feel bad as someone else could take the same actions & feel completely normal. *Why?* Because they may not value the environment like you do.

Simply put: *it's not the standalone actions that make us feel good or bad, but their alignment to our what we value.*

If you are driven by freedom as a core value of yours, yet you spend your time primarily slaving away at a job you hate, where you have absolutely zero say or choice, you'll likely to be unhappy. *Why?* Because there's a lack of alignment between what you value & the reality you live in.

On the flip side, if you value safety or security more than you value freedom, you'll be less likely to feel trapped in this job you're in, but rather feel 'safe' in it. It's protection. It keeps you alive. You view that same job very differently because of its alignment to your values.

See, at the end of the day, success & fulfillment do not come from taking the supposed *'right'* or *'wrong'* actions, as there really are no *'right'* & *'wrong'* actions for everybody.

That's a very one-size-fits-all view of the world - assuming there are 'right' things that everybody in the world should do.

In actuality, people value, want & desire different things. You may want different things from life than your neighbor, your friend, me or best buddy. And they may want different things from life than those in their family. *Different people want different things.* And different people find success, a feeling of accomplishment & true joy from different things.

And if we want different things in life, it's only logical that our thoughts, feelings, decisions & actions should differ too. Our actions should be the ones that 'align' with what value.

| It's Not About 'Right' Or 'Wrong' Actions; It's About 'Aligned Actions.'

And when do what aligns with what truly value & want in life - when we live in total *alignment* - we feel a great charge, energy & vibrancy about life. We feel on purpose. We feel 'true to ourselves,' fully 'who we are,' & filled with inner meaning that guides us to continue living in this state of being.

As to how we begin to tap into this *alignment* in life, it all starts with the simple, yet profound…

POWER OF <u>INTENTION</u>

When a great painting is painted by a great artist, it is not accidental. Brushstrokes are not just 'random,' acts, with the hope of coming together. No. They are intentional. Each & every brushstroke is completed with intention - with complete alignment to the end goal of creating a masterpiece.

The same applies to the masterful sculptor or the Chessmaster - each move is done with clear intention; in total alignment with the desired result.

The businesses that thrive operate in the same way, as do the communities, movements, organizations, & individuals.

Yet, how often do we leave our own life to <u>randomness</u>; it's a surefire way for <u>not</u> getting what you want.

We just go through life doing whatever comes up. We wake up in the morning, check our emails & proceed to spend all day - our entire attention - reacting to the world around us. Going from one *unaligned* activity to another, not stopping to ask whether what we are doing is actually *aligned* with what we value, believe & want from life.

Doing things just to pass the time or merely to survive, wandering through life without clarity & intention isn't going to get you the results you want. You must know what you want, what you value & then map your actions to this through the power of intention.

We must be intentional. Not to leave our life to default or to randomness, but to get behind the steering wheel of our time, our attention, our results, our emotional reality & life in general, to shape it as we truly want - *one decision at a time.*

So, as you wake up each morning, or before starting anything in your day, ask yourself if this is aligned with what you want.

And it's out of this thinking that all the best decisions in our lives (that allow us to tune into new possibilities) come from...

MAKING THE BEST DECISIONS IN LIFE

In my work, a lot of people I've taught & coached asked me questions along the lines of, *'What should I do?'* or *'What decision should I make?'* across various areas of their lives.

The challenge: these are not questions you can fully answer without first asking yourself, *'Well - what do you want?'*

This is because, as you now know, it's the *alignment* which makes a decision an effective (or ineffective) one.

One person could make a decision & it could be the worst possible decision for them, yet another person can make that same decision, yet it turns to the best decision they've ever made in their life. It's very subjective. It's why...

| The Best Decisions Are The Ones <u>Most Aligned</u> With Your Values & Ambitions

As you now know, the things that are most aligned with what you value are the best use of your time, energy & attention.

And *the power of intention* is your ability to stick to this in your life. To look at the countless things that you 'could' be doing each & every day & be selective - intentional - in the things you choose to do (or don't do).

And to fully harness the power of intention (& make the best possible decisions) do this as you look through your schedule, list of opportunities or potential to-do's for the day. Just ask yourself, 'Is this all in alignment with what I want?'

In fact, in my life, the #1 question that keeps me on track, helps me plan & enables me to make my best decisions is this:

| Are My Thought, Decisions & Actions Aligned With My Ambitions Right Now?

It's a question I ask myself many times a day sometimes. When I'm doing things that I know I shouldn't, it quickly pulls me out of this by reminding me I'll find more joy elsewhere. 'Alignment is over there,' it shows me. And when I am on track, it reinforces that & helps me build momentum.

This question acts like a GPS (a navigation device) guiding me (you, or anybody) to the destination you want to get to.

So I implore you to ask yourself this question as you go through the hours in your day, the days in your week & weeks in month & year, as it'll serve you to truly align your decisions & actions with your values & ambitions.

And when you have important decisions to make, step back to what you want, before proceeding with what best aligns.
Lastly, here's a great tool (framework) to help you further...

A TOOL FOR TOTAL ALIGNMENT

The '*5 W's & 1 H*' is a foundational journalism & story tool designed to help create a more complete, full, congruent, coherent & aligned story, which omits fewer details & better covers the full spectrum of what actually happened.

And it's a framework that I've adapted into this environment to help us assess our actions & move towards *total alignment*.

TOTAL ALIGNMENT

See, at any given moment - no matter what you're doing - all 6 of these parts in a play & build upon one another: *why, how, what, who, where & when.*

Firstly, the *'why.'* Everything you do has a *motive* behind it. Even if that motive is just *'I'm bored & have nothing better to do, so why not?'* We *do things for a reason.* Plus, it's that reason behind our actions that, more than anything, impacts, not just your results, but the joy & happiness you get from what you do.

Secondly, the **'how.'** This is your *method* of doing something. You can do the same task, yet do it differently & get very different results. How you do what you do differentiates you from others; it's your uniqueness. It's the expression of your 'why.' And it's about finding the best, most aligned methods & strategies for doing what you do.

Thirdly, the **'what.'** This is the specific actions you take in an hour, day, week, month & year. Different people do different things. And again, what you do in life is an expression of *'who you are.'* People should not be like robots, machines or slaves, all doing the exact same thing that they were told to do, but rather *should* do different things in life - *the things that are 'aligned' with what they truly want.*

Next; the **'who?'** This is about people & responsibility. *Who is doing the task at hand? Is it you or something doing it for you - or with you? Are you going after this goal alone or are you part of a team working together? And who is in that team?* It's another important area we must bring into alignment; the idea of surrounding yourself with like-minded people & spending time with those who value what you value falls into this category of *'who.'* For example, in various studies, employees who work alongside people who they actually like, report greater job satisfaction. The job is exactly the same, yet the people who are in the job alongside them actually make them enjoy the job as a whole more *(which also applied to all areas of your life.)*

After that: the **'where?'** *Location & physical environment* is another important thing that impacts your level of success & happiness in life. Put yourself in environments that align with your values & you'll feel greater meaning, connection, joy & fulfillment from what you do.

Lastly, the **'when?'** This is about *timing. When are you doing certain things? Is your 'timing' in alignment with what you want?* For some, they find it much better, more effective & enjoyable to do certain things at a certain period of time, while others prefer other timings. Once again, it's about aligning this with what *you* want & value.

And don't worry, just like we've gone in depth with the 'why' so far, we'll go deep into the other things in this book as well.

Now, let's put this all together. Let's look at an example for *great alignment vs poor alignment* (& how it's likely to affect performance, results & happiness.)

Imagine... you're working on a project that's meaningful to you & you're doing it because you love the cause you're working on supporting (a well-aligned 'why'). You're very passionate about the thing you're doing & likely you would do it in spare time as a hobby or something - even if you weren't getting paid for it.

You're also taking very specific actions that others haven't taken before that allow you do better serve this cause than others have done in the past. You're clear on what gives you the edge & have total clarity regarding the things you'll do

AMBITION | 145

today, tomorrow, next week & next month to bring this project to success ('how' & 'what'). *Confidence is on your side.*

You're also working on this project with a team of like-minded people who are equally passionate about this cause. They're *not* working for the money primarily, but out of passion. In fact, many of them turned away higher-paying jobs to work here in a lower-paying one because they love what this organization & project stands for.

They are proactive - finding solutions, not dwelling on issues. They are passionate, hard-working & make stuff happen.

And mixed into that, you just connect with them so well. You have so much to talk about, so much in common & similar values to those you work with on this project. They are like friends - not just co-workers (sharing similar values & interests). The team is great & you love working them ('who').

Additionally, you're working in a very specific office space fully aligned with the cause. For example, if the cause is about the environment, this is an environmentally-friendly, natural office you absolutely adore. If it's a different cause, it's an office space that aligns perfectly with that. You have all the 'resources' you need to carry out the project & everything you may need later on is in close physical proximity to you. Like a great, small, cozy cafe in the perfect location, you're in the perfect place to make things happen ('where').

Lastly, you have schedules & timelines you're very happy with. They are ambitious but allow you to work on your own terms & make great things happen. You have autonomy & can work when you work best (as can the others.) And you do. You work when you want & create great work ('when').

That's an example of *alignment* based on this framework. Each of the 6 areas is in alignment & working together. And I hope you can clearly see how each of them builds to create greater success, as well as happiness & fulfillment.

In fact, for a contrasting view, feel free to read this example again, but this time, taking alignment out of certain parts.

Imagine everything else is there, but now the project you're working on is one you find meaningful & useless... ('why')

Or, the project is meaningful, but the way you're doing things doesn't align with you or the cause... ('how' & 'what'),

Or, everything else is great, but you're working with people you don't like working with - who constantly complain, find fault, do the least amount possible, don't contribute & don't share similar values with you or the project.

See, how any of these things can take away value from the whole? How one piece out of place can take away from the whole - like a stain on an otherwise fresh, clean shirt?

When we tune into higher & higher levels of *alignment*, we do more, achieve more & in the process, love what we do & find great meaning & value in it.

We should strive for great congruence & harmony in all that we do - all 6 areas in total alignment.

EXERCISE: 6 AREAS OF TOTAL ALIGNMENT
This is an opportunity for you to personalize & put into practice the power of this tool.

Take 10 minutes (minimum), pick an area on your life you want to start with (more on this coming up) & journal. Write down how these 6 areas look now, how you would like them to look & what you can do to make this happen...

While this instruction is rather general & open, that's the point. You can get creative here when assessing & planning areas of your life. But, use it. Don't just read & forget, but put into practice that what you're learning here.

AMBITION CIRCLES: 3 CATEGORIES OF AMBITION

"You can do what you want to do. You can be what you want to be."

- *DAVE THOMAS*

The next framework for understanding human ambition & planning your amazing future is titled, **'Ambition Circles.'**

In this framework, all ambitions, aspiration & goals fall into 1 of 3 categories. And, by understanding these 3 categories you can gain even greater clarity into why you do what you do, what you value & what to do going forward. *Let's explore...*

AMBITION CIRCLES: 3 CATEGORIES OF HUMAN AMBITION

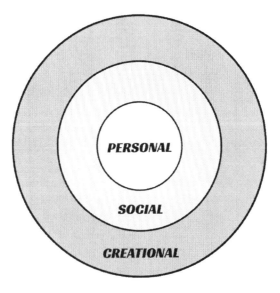

The first of these 3 categories is **'Personal.'** This is about *'who you are,'* your identity, your mind, body, thinking & feeling. It's about introspection & taking care of your mind & body through focus, time, learning, growth & care.

Goals related to being a certain type of person, thinking a certain way, learning certain topics or developing certain skills, as well as looking a certain way, having good health, having energy & meaning in life, all fall into this first category of ambition. These are *'personal'* ambitions - they come from within & nobody else is required for you to achieve them. You could be the only person alive & still become a certain type of person. It's within your control & therefore come with the greatest choices in life.

Beyond this, goals about meeting certain people, building certain friendships & relationships, having certain social experiences, friendships, relationships, romantic connection & love, all fall into this second category of **'Social'** ambitions.

While *'personal'* ambitions are about you & who you want to become (what you want to know, experience, be able to do) *'social'* goals are about how you want to relate with others.

How do you want to relate to & share the experience of living with people close to you? What type of shared experiences & emotions do you want to have? How much connection, trust, love & fun do you want to experience together (& with who?)

Lastly, goals related to creating anything beyond yourself fall into the third category of **'Creational'** ambitions. This includes everything from wanting to build a business, start an organization or create a movement around a certain cause, to aspirations such as to publish a book, write a screenplay, release an album, paint a painting or build your dream house.

Anything you're creating beyond yourself - including wealth, impact, a legacy or a difference - falls into this 3rd category.

And the reason this 3rd category is titled **'creational'** is, firstly, these things don't just happen, rather you create them.

Create: *bring (something) into existence*

You turn something that didn't previously exist (except in your thoughts, feelings & imagination) into something others can see, observe, interact with & get value from. That's the first reason - you're *'creating'* these things (even if you don't think you are).

And secondly, because it comes from *you* - you are creating it.

Just like a child takes on traits & influence from the parents (which we'll explore in the 'Psychology' section), *creational accomplishments* (such as books, movies, songs, paintings, companies & movements) take on the traits of their creators.

Apple is known for its design because the company took on that personality & influence from its a founder - it's creator - Steve Jobs. Tesla & SpaceX are brands that fundamentally embody the personality of Elon Musk. How Elon thinks is similar to how these companies think.

And the same applies to any 'creation' that ones from the imagination, intent & effort of an individual - whether that's a book, a movie, a painting, a song or an organization.

To see this in action, the next time to read, listen to or watch someone's 'creation,' study the person behind it...

Watching Lord Of The Rings, Star Wars or Matrix movies next week? Get online & read about J. R. R. Tolkien, George Lucas or The Wachowski siblings. You'll quickly realize how their identities - *'who they were'* - shaped their 'creations.'

And the same will happen for anything you 'create' because 'you' are the one creating it based on your outlook on life.

Like women birth children, authors birth books, screenwriters birth screen players, musicians birth music & business owners birth products & services. You create ('bring into existence') that which did not previously exist.

While this comparison may seem strange between children & albums or screenplays, it's a rather accurate one. Although I'll never know this from personal experience, I've talked with enough mothers (who are also 'creators') to see this strange comparison. In fact, as *Ruby Wax* wrote at the start of her book, *How to Be Human*:

> *After writing my last book I said to myself, never again. It's like having a baby: you're in such pain during the birth, all you want to do is chew your arm off; it's the same with writing a book, except you're dilated for more than a year. But, when it finally comes out and it thrives (hits number 1 on that bestseller list), oh my god, all you want to do is get fertile and do it again.*

And I've found it's those who look at what they do in this way that get the most meaning from what they create. Their work, career, hobbies & passions aren't just things ways to pass the time, but something more - almost like a form of parenting.

Giving birth to new things ('creation') & then caring to ensure those things navigate through life, helping others & contributing to the world in some way. Everything that comes out of you is your 'creation.' Therefore, every goal to create something beyond yourself falls into this 3rd category.

Now, knowing these 3 categories of human ambition enables us to gain more clarity about our lives. It allows us to assess whether we're really stopped to think about these 3 categories & what we want in each of them...

- *Who do you want to become? What type of person? If you were to describe 'who you are' what would you like that description to look like? What knowledge, experiences & skills do you want to develop? What do you want to get good at? What would make you feel like you are being your 'best self?'* **(Personal)**

- *Who do you want to surround yourself with? Who do you want to spend time with, care for & support? What do you want in your intimate relationship, friendships & family connections? How do you want to relate to others? What shared adventures, trips, experiences & memories do you want to have (& who do you want to have them with?) What would make those social experiences amazing?* **(Social)**

- *What do you want to 'create' beyond yourself? How do you want to express your unique abilities & ideas into the world? What do you choose to contribute beyond yourself? What would make you feel truly alive in your work, career, hobbies & passions? What do you want to 'bring into existence' that may not otherwise get created?* **(Creational)**

Also, you can ask yourself: *which of the 3 categories are you most drawn to? Perhaps you're more drawn to one of them?*

I say this because depending on your 'meaning of life' (what you value most) you may be more drawn to a certain category:

HOW IT COMES TOGETHER: MEANING OF LIFE

For example, if your meaning of life is (& core values are) about *peace, acceptance & spirituality*, you may more highly prioritize the 1st of the 3 categories: ***'Personal.'***

You're more likely to enjoy time alone with yourself as that quality personal time is important time for you to find peace within yourself - to enjoy the present moment & little things filled with beauty in this world.

You may be less likely to put things out into the world or to get heavily involved in the lives of others, as you're on your own journey of introspection, self-discovery, acceptance & spirituality (which is of greatest significance to you).

In another example, if your meaning of life is connection & love, then you may be more likely to look outwards into your *social circles* as this matters a lot to you: **'Social.'**

You're less likely to enjoy time alone, but prefer spending time with others. Where you are matters less to you than who you are with. You care about giving, about loving & helping others. And you're likely to set more goals that reflect this, asking yourself *'What can I do for others?'* or *'How can I be a better friend, partner, lover, family member?'*

Lastly, if your meaning of life is to express yourself, to create, to innovate & bring new things into this world - driven by the values of freedom, expression, power & impact - then you're likely to prioritize the 3rd category: **'Creational.'**

Tapping into creativity & inspiration is important to you. Putting your ideas, inspirations, opportunities & creations out into the world matters to you. Creating something - whether that's poetry, new invention or a massive organization - is important to you. Helping not just an individual, but changing the world as a whole in some way drives you.

Once again - & I can't stress this enough - there are no 'right' or 'wrong' answers here. In reality, we are most fulfilled when we tune into what we truly want.

And this is just another framework to help you reflect on what really matters to you. All 3 of these categories impact you, but some may matter more to you than others.

And this too can change throughout your life. *It all can* - as change is life's only constant. What's important is that we constantly put ourselves in situations where we can zoom out of our daily life & think about the big picture, asking ourselves these big existential questions (like the ones here). That's how *clarity* is built & new opportunities for success open up...

EXERCISE: SET YOUR TRUE AMBITIONS

This chapter has the potential to change your life in more ways than you even imagine right now. However, only if you take the time to put everything in this chapter into practice.

Reading (consuming new information) is not enough if you don't act on these new insights. And that's why this exercise is here; to challenge you to block out at least 30 minutes, go back through all the profound concepts & understandings in this chapter & begin putting them into practice.

During those 30 minutes, explore yourself, your past & present actions & results. And see just how everything in this chapter affects your life. Ask yourself...

First, big picture: *What do you truly value in life? What gives your life meaning? What is the meaning of life for you? Why do you do what you do & what would truly make your life a magnificent experience?*

Just as you would plan a holiday, it's time to plan your life for maximum joy, freedom, peace, fulfillment & meaning.

In the past, were the goals you were pursuing based on intrinsic desire or extrinsic motives? And what do you want your future ambitions to be based on? And how?

What life ambitions would you love to spend your lifetime pursuing, achieving & on the journey towards? What makes you feel truly alive in life?

What ambitions do you have for your life, based on the 'Ambition Circles' concept, in which all ambitions fall into the 3 categories of *'Personal,' 'Social,'* & *'Creational?'* What goals do you have in each of those categories?

Who do you want to 'become?' How do you want to 'relate' to others in your life? What do you want to 'create' in life?

Look out 2, 5, 10 or 20 years into the future - what does your ideal life (& lifestyle) look life? What does your ideal day, week, month & year look like?

Now, let's zoom in a bit: *What ambitions would be truly meaningful for you to pursue over the next 6 - 12 months?* What goals do you have for this week, this month or this quarter that can inspire you & excite you to pursue?

Each & every single one of these questions can be pondered on for hours (in fact, do that & clarity is almost guaranteed). So, take time to think about each question deeply; to think about your life deeply & fully. *Then act in alignment!*

EXERCISE: DIARY ENTRY FROM THE FUTURE
Imagine you had just lived a great day in your life 1 year from now & before going to bed, you stopped to think about, reflect on & write about this great day you just had...

Take 5 minutes right now & journal on this day as if the day 1 year in the future had already happened.

Design your perfect day & write about it as if it had already happened, including the details, feelings & what made this day so incredible in your eyes. As you write, ask yourself...

What time did you wake up? What was the first thing you did in the morning? What did you think about as you started your day? How did you feel? What things did you do during this day & why did you find great joy in these?

Include descriptions of all 6 of the areas of total alignment, including who you were with, what you did & how you did it.

This is a simple exercise, yet it's profound because it not only helps you gain *clarity* as to what your perfect day looks like but also gets you to feel it as it's already happened (coming from a much higher level of emotion & belief).

Then, you can choose to repeat this exercise regularly to remind yourself (& your *Reticular Activating System*) what really matters to you, what you want to look out for & create.

CONSTANT CLARITY CRYSTALLIZATION: **TEST, TASTE, EXPERIMENT & EXPERIENCE MORE.**

Before we wrap up this chapter on clarity, I want to share with you 1 more critical thing that'll help you crystallize what you want & tap into greater levels of clarity (& success) in life.

What you read so far is profound content which has been curated & crafted to make you think, reflect & plan - to help you really step back & think about the big picture. To support you in looking inwards & finding answers to life's questions.

However, it's just the beginning as clarity (like *self-mastery* as a whole) is an *ever-lasting, ever-expanding process*.

Your life is a constant journey of recognizing, refining & crystalizing what you truly want (or don't want) & adjusting accordingly to live in total alignment & create a great life.

And this leads me to this 1 strategy - outside of reflection - for continuing your journey of *clarity*. This strategy is simply to *immerse yourself in possibilities*. To test, taste & experience more. It's basic, but it's really the secret to true *clarity*.

The reality is that, unless you first see, hear or experience something (gain awareness that it even exists or 'could exist') it won't be inside your scope of what you think you can create.

If people don't know an island exists (it's never been seen before), people don't know that it's possible to travel here.

However, as soon as the island is discovered, experienced & charted on the map for the first time, now that possibility opens up. And just like humans have outlined the countries on the planet, putting them on a map, you too must go outside of the known to find new things & put them on the map of your life. For clarity & greater possibility, you must...

| Test. Taste. Experiment. Experience. <u>More.</u>

Each time you do this, you expand your awareness & better understand what you want (or don't want). This allows you to better plan your future, condition your mind to achieve it, make better decisions & live a more fulfilled life.

One of the reasons (of many) that families in poor countries sewing clothes for $2 per day, never go beyond this is that they simply don't know what else is out there.

Imagine being born in a small village somewhere in the middle of nowhere with no connection to modern society. Of course, your thinking would be limited & your ambitions wouldn't do anything beyond, *'get a good $2 per day job & survive,'* as nothing else is within your awareness. You don't know about a lot of the possibilities that most people in the modern world are aware of. The key is to...

| Immerse Yourself In Possibilities

This is why, fueled by curiosity, we must continue to do things outside of the familiar to expand our awareness. To immerse ourselves in new possibilities & opportunities.

We must *test, taste, experiment & experience* new things. And then reflect on those things as it's this powerful combination of *constant experimentation* & *thoughtful reflection* which gives us new answers & awakes new possibilities for us to tune into (that you may not have known ever existed in the past).

So, if you're lacking *clarity* as to which career path you should follow, what you want your perfect partner to be like, what type of lifestyle you want (or anything else) you now know what you need to do...

It's simple, but it's the answer that's going to get you the results you want. That answer is to **test, taste, experience & experiment more** (constantly reflecting in the process - as you've done in this chapter) to gain *clarity*.

For example, you may not have known a certain instrument even existed until you went to the music store & saw one on display. You then searched it online & saw someone play that instrument. You thought it was very cool, so you bought one, taught yourself to play it & it became your amazing career.

Before, you didn't know this instrument even existed. You had never heard of it. So, if someone asked you what you wanted to do for your career in the future, you wouldn't have been able to give them a proper, clarified answer as the thing you ended up doing (& loving) was something you didn't even know was a 'thing.'

The more you experience, the more things are now in your scope for what you want to do, be or achieve!

To find the things that will truly light you up, you must do a lot of things, knowing that each thing leads you to something truly amazing down the line.

Personally, I'm incredibly grateful that my parents introduced this outlook on clarity & finding what you want into my life early on. Growing up, me & my brother did everything. We played many sports. Multiple instruments. Travelled a lot, seeing different places, cultures & people. Learned dozens of topics. Pursued many interest & hobbies. And this allowed us to develop clarity very quickly & set us up for a great life. *It's one of the main reason why I was able to discover my career path (& life purpose) when I was about 14 years of age.*

Test. Taste. Experiment. Experience. Do more & you'll have more to reflect on. Reflect on more & you'll get more answers. It's simple, yet most will overlook this incredibly powerful strategy for clarity - don't do that. Use this!

As Paulo Coelho's once said...

"Be present. Make love. Make tea. Avoid small talk. Embrace conversation. Buy a plant, water it. Make your bed. Make someone else's bed. Have a smart mouth and quick wit. Run. Make art. Create. Swim in the ocean. Swim in the rain. Take chances. Ask questions. Make mistakes. Learn. Know your worth. Love fiercely. Forgive quickly. Let go of what doesn't make you happy. Grow."

That's how you build clarity: *piece-by-piece.* With each question. With each new experience. With each new test. With each moment spent pondering life's infinite possibilities & countless opportunities.

By knowing that *clarity* is a <u>*lifelong process*</u> of exploring reality, life, possibility, what you value & what you want. And then living out this process. Tapping into clarity, gaining awareness & tuning into new possibilities.

5 | HEIGHT: PLAYING A BIGGER GAME

"Big results require big ambitions."

- HERACLITUS

Am I dreaming big enough? Am I playing up to my fullest potential? Am I creating & contributing fully for myself, those around me & the world? Is there more available to me? Is there another level for me? That's what we must ask next...

Why we do feel like we should set small goals that are considered 'realistic,' instead of daring for something greater that would stretch us, make us grow & lead us to big things?

And how can we (if we choose) raise our height of ambition, & feel confident in shooting for big ambitions in our lives?

Once we have *'clarity'* regarding the direction we want to take our life in - what we value, what drives us, what fulfills us, what we're passionate about & what matters to us - it's time to see how big a game we want to play (the 2nd key: *'height.'*)

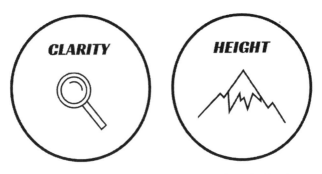

'*Clarity*' is the 1st key to ambition, while *'height'* is the 2nd.

160 | SELF MASTERY

And it's these 2 keys that work together to help you aim your truest potential & get on to path to an extraordinary life...

THE PROBLEMS WITH DREAMING SMALL

> *"Many people simply settle for finding some level of contentment with their 'lot in life.' They've long ago given up on their dreams. And most people never consider the possibility that life is something they can control. But it is."*
>
> - NEALE DONALD WALSCII

The challenges of dreaming & playing small are 2-fold:

1. Small Goals Don't Mobilize Committed Effort

Uninspiring. Unlikely to fully motivate & mobilize. Less likely to fill us with a greater sense of meaning. Simply put...

Small goals are unlikely to mobilize the inspired, motivated & committed effort needed to achieve something great.

They end up becoming a *'self-fulfilling prophecy.'* You dream small because you may feel anything bigger is out of reach. These smalls goals then lead to less motivation, inspiration & committed action, resulting in you only achieving small things (instead of bigger things) & reinforcing it to yourself.

'If I had aimed any higher, I wouldn't have achieved it,' you may think. Except: you're failing to account that it was your small goal which only mobilized the little effort you needed to achieve this small goal. And, had you set a bigger one you would have been more inspired, motivated & committed to thinking greater, doing more, being more resourceful & willing to do whatever it takes to achieve that greater goal.

As Italian sculptor, painter, architect, poet & icon of the Renaissance Age, *Michelangelo* put it:

"The greater danger for most of us lies not in setting our aim too high and falling short, but in setting our aim too low, and achieving our mark."

The reality is you *can do more. You really can.* We all can. *Much* more, in fact. However, you won't know this until you set ambitions that truly mobilize your full dedication & effort.

As the American Psychological Association found, people who set goals which are both *specific (clarity)* & challenging (*height*), were 90% more likely to achieve what they set out to achieve. And, according to the data, in almost all examples, those who set goals that stretched them performed better than those who set easy goals, 'do your best' goals or no goals.

| Small Goals Mobilize Small Actions. Big, Challenging & Engaging Goals That Stretch Us, Compel Us To Do (& Become) More.

For example, *'I just want to make a little more money each month,' 'I just want to stress a little less,'* or worse of all, *'I just want to make it through the week...'* are not only lacking *specificity* (clarity) but are not the type of ambitions which lead to motivation, inspiration & full emotional buy-in.

So, you may want to replace *'I want to stress a little less,'* or *'get through the week,'* with, *'I want to create a magnificent existence in which I wake up overjoyed most - if not all - of the time, create great happiness & fulfillment from what I do & become an incredibly joyous person, living a great life!'*

That's the type of 'height' of ambition that, when you read, is likely to naturally put a smile on your face & inspire you to put in the work bettering yourself (& your life) to achieve it.

You can then set *'stepping stone'* goals, which are specific & measurable, to get there, but you start with the end in mind.

You start with something that's going to mobilize you to grow, improve & better yourself. And that's a job only big, inspiring, challenging yet exciting, goals can do.

Or as Daniel Burnham poetically put it...

"Make no little plans; they have no magic to stir men's blood and probably themselves will not be realized. Make big plans; aim high in hope and work, remembering that a noble, logical diagram once recorded will never die, but long after we are gone be a living thing, asserting itself with ever-growing insistency."

Small goals lead to small thinking & uninspired action. However, change the ambition & you better mobilize yourself (& those around you) to create something magnificent.

2. Small Ambitions Can Lead To <u>Regret</u>

Ask people who are approaching the end of their lives to talk about their experience of life & you'll quickly see the pattern. Their sentences will start with, *'I wish...' 'I wish I did this...' 'I wish I did that...'* or *'I wish I had the courage to pursue this...'*

They don't often regret the things they failed at (those feelings don't stick around as strongly), but the things they knew they could have done, but never did.

That's what we - human beings - <u>regret</u> the most. Not the possibilities we pursued yet failed at, but the ones that we were too scared to even pursue in the first place.

These people coming to the end of life, experiencing regret, talk about the possibilities & opportunities they never seized; the places they wanted to visit but never did, the things they didn't do, the courageous actions they didn't take, the relationships they never fully committed to, the people they didn't treat better, how they didn't do what they could with their health & fitness, how they didn't dream bigger & do more of the things on their 'bucket lists.' You get the idea...

They don't dream that they did less, but that they did more in life! That they dreamed bigger, did more & lived fully *(instead of being scared, putting off what's important for later.)*

You may have heard the phrase, *'you regret the things you don't do more than the things you do.'*

It's a saying attributed to Mark Twain. Full quote: *"Twenty years from now you will be more disappointed by the things that you didn't do than by the ones you did do. So throw off the bowlines. Sail away from the safe harbor. Catch the trade winds in your sails. Explore. Dream. Discover."*

If this is true & we regret the things we don't do more than the things we do, then dreaming big (& playing big) are not things we *'could'* do or *'should'* consider, but things we <u>must</u> do if we want to live an extraordinary & magnificent life.

As, in the long term, dreaming small, setting goals below your means, denying possibilities & settling for what's comfortable instead of tapping into courage to live fully, can lead to you looking back at your life filled with *regret. And that regret may just haunt us with the things we shied away from...*

As Les Brown said, *"The graveyard is the richest place on earth, because it is here that you will find all the hopes and dreams that were never fulfilled, the books that were never written, the songs that were never sung, the inventions that were never shared, the cures that were never discovered, all because someone was too afraid to take that first step, keep with the problem, or determined to carry out their dream."*

So, not only do small goals not mobilize the efforts required to create great things & become 'self-fulfilling prophecies,' but also lead us to look back at a life filled with regret. *'So why do we dream small then?'* you may think...

5 BIG REASONS WE DREAM SMALL

In my research & personal experience, as well as based on the teachings of great men & women before me, I have identified **5 big reasons** - *biological, psychological & environmental reasons* - that stop us from dreaming, aiming & playing big.

And I've seen the detrimental effects each of these 5 reasons has on our level of personal power & ambition. They often leave us feeling caged. Limited. Restricted. Trapped.

The reality is for a lot of people, their <u>height</u> of ambition is too low for the life they truly want in life!

Deep down they want more, but they don't let themselves go for anything higher. They suppress this desire to dream bigger & do more. Why? Usually because of 1 (or more) of these 5 reasons you're about to discover...

I must warn you though as these 5 reasons often operate unconsciously. Like background programs on a computer, they are running your life (affecting the ambitions you set for yourself) without you even being aware of it.

Meaning: we often follow these reasons without consciously thinking about it. Like background programs, they affect us, our dreams, our targets & our goals, yet we don't even realize it. They are so deeply ingrained into us (as you'll learn) that it takes great awareness to even recognize their effects.

As Albert Einstein said, *"Of what is significant in one's own existence one is hardly aware, and it certainly should not bother the other fellow. What does a fish know about the water in which he swims all his life?"*

Or as the figurative translation of the African Proverb goes...

"A fish is the last to acknowledge the existence of water"

Just as fish would find it hard to acknowledge the existence of water, we - humans - are swimming in *beliefs & programs* to the point it can be hard to even acknowledge their existence.

That's when we must train ourselves to be as *objective as we can*; to see incoming information with reason & perspective.

Plus, as you read about these 5 reasons, your instincts may start to protest, claiming they don't apply to you. I assure you, they do. All 5 of them. More or less, but they apply.

Why? Because you're human (I assume) & these are part of the human condition. These are often deeply biological & psychological reasons that are wired into us in one way or another. They can also be sneaky, disguising themselves behind things like "safety" or "comfort," so that we don't recognize their influence on us *(as you'll see!)*

That's the warning I attempt to give whenever I lead people through this work. It's because I want them, as I implore you to so right now as well, to be open to something new. So you can create something greater in your life. And clinging to the known isn't going to do that. *Be bold. Be open. Be willing.*

5 REASONS WE DREAM SMALL

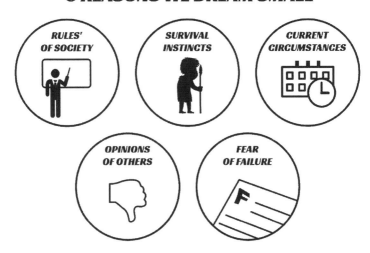

I implore you to read through this part of the book carefully, intentionally & consciously. It's important! *Now, let's begin...*

1. **'Rules' Of Society:** Big Ambitions Aren't What We Are Taught To Pursue Growing Up.

The typical *'rules'* for living a 'good life' (that usually come from school, society, media, parents & the world) go like this:

- Go to school & get good grades.
- Go to college & graduate with a piece of paper that'll show the world you're good at what you do.
- Get a good, stable & well-paying job (& work hard).
- Find a partner, get married & start a family.
- Buy a house, car & nice 'stuff' (upgrade this regularly).
- Spend time with friends, travel & seek entertainment.
- Retire (& enjoy life now that you no longer work).
- Die.

Those are the 'rules' - social norms; default path - for living.

Unlike laws, they are not written anywhere. Yet, they exist...

Ask people (especially those who haven't engaged in this type of work before) what a 'good life' looks like, or 'what we are taught to do in life growing up' & the answers will come back mostly the same. While they may vary slightly between cultures, they are similar for most of the modern world.

These 'rules' exist - but only in our minds. Despite this, they strongly influence the *ambitions* we set for ourselves in life.

The average person in the modern world will be told to plan & do these things countless times growing up & through *repetition* we are taught that 'this is how the world works.'

Often, we are not even asked if we agree with these things, or whether we're logically considered them, but these things are just assumed for us...

We are not asked, *"Are you going to have a job growing up?"* but *"What job do you want to have when you grow up?"*

Not, *"Are you going to get married & start a family?"* but *"What does your dream wedding look like? How many kids are you going to have?"*

Not, *"Are you going to buy a house, a car & save for retirement?"* but *"Have you started saving for that house, car or retirement yet? Let's build your credit score so you can get a big loan for that house you'll want later on..."*

The world around us hooks our attention & then - through repetition - passes these social norms *('rules')* to us: what we should believe about ourselves & others, how the world works, what is right & what is wrong, what's acceptable & what's not.

At school, you listened to the teacher teaching you. At home, your parents & family. You read, listened to & watched information on TV, videos on the internet & words in books or magazines. You were taught the 'rules' you needed to comply with in order to 'fit in' with society & be like everybody else.

The challenge is this path - these 'rules' laid out for us - don't encourage ambitions above or beyond this socially-accepted scope. Nor are they *personalized* to us, what we value & want.

For example: I went to school (to supposedly, learn how to live a 'good life') for around 9 years - age 5 to age 13, before dropping out - but don't remember once hearing a teacher encourage me to question or break out of the rules,, to explore the world, to create a great lifestyle for myself, to pursue a 'calling' or a 'mission,' instead of living paycheck to paycheck for somebody else, to ponder the meaning of life, to volunteer, to start a foundation, to write a book, to gain & share wisdom, leave a dent in the universe, attempt to change the world in any meaningful way or to leave a legacy.

Despite the fact these things have shown some of the greatest things we can focus on for our own happiness, fulfillment & sense of meaning in life, as well as things that serve humanity at the highest level, they simply are not in the 'rulebook' we are given growing up.

It's why most never dream big - anything beyond these 'rules' isn't taught to us. *Or, simply put: we've only ever been taught & encouraged to dream & fly so high (& no higher!)*

Secondly, **personalization**. When your high school teacher stood in front of your class & said, *"one day, if you study hard, you'll get a good, high-paying job & you'll be happy,"* they weren't talking to you specifically. That guidance wasn't *personalized* to you.

That teacher didn't know what you value, what interests you, what a 'great life' would look like for you, or if you ever wanted a job or not - these factors were never considered.

And so the teacher (because she got herself a job for herself is merely passing that along to you). The teacher passes along the 'rule' to you, just as it was passed along to him or her.

Don't get me wrong though: not all rules are bad. Some are great & you would gladly accept them - even if you weren't taught into them. For example, getting married, starting a family, having kids - personally, I find these great rules to follow. However, others, I've found limiting & have worked to break out of. It all comes down to *personalization*. Not *'is this what people want?'* but *'Is this what you want in your life?'*

Some 'rules' may be very different from what you truly want & you're only following them in your life today because you feel socially-pressured into doing so.

Like getting a job, buying a big house or nice car, or saving for retirement - these may not be aligned with what you want.

Maybe you don't truly accept these 'rules' & you want something different? Or bigger?

Richard Branson owns an island, not a house. Enzo Ferrari founded the company of Ferrari, not just owned a car. Many successful individuals don't have 'jobs' they hate, but 'careers,' 'missions' & 'callings' that they wake up Monday morning ecstatic to work on. Not waiting until the weekend to finally enjoy life, but spend their whole week doing what they love.

Saving for retirement? Many of these individuals never plan on retiring - ever! Personally, I never do. *I love what I do.*

Why would you want to retire when your work is something so joyous & so fulfilling that you can't stand the idea of <u>not</u> working for the rest of your life?

Others are financially free & don't work (or work very little).

These are all possibilities, yet as you may realize, are not what your teachers in school probably told you to aim for.

These are not part of the 'rules' of society, but often higher, greater, more fulfilling ambitions to pursue.

As Steve Job's famously said: *"When you grow up, you tend to get told that the world is the way it is and your life is just to live your life inside the world. Try not to bash into the walls too much. Try to have a nice family life, have fun, save money. That's a very limited life. Life can be much broader once you discover one simple fact. This is – everything around you that you call life was made up by people no smarter than you. And you can change it. You can influence it... Once you learn that, you'll never be the same again."*

This all begs the question: *Why do we even have rules in the first place?* (by understanding this, it might help you tap into the greater potential that is available to you).

WHY WE HAVE 'RULES'...

The main reason is to provide order & structure; to prevent confusion or chaos. Like herding sheep, *'rules'* are created to move everybody down a similar path, at a similar speed.

They <u>weren't</u> created with success in mind, but mere survival. Designed to just help you *'get through life,'* rather than *'thrive in this magnificent adventure called life.'*

Plus, they are designed for the lowest common denominator within society. Like the curriculum in the education system, as well as a method of delivery (which hasn't changed very much for many decades), they are build for *everybody*.

Meaning: anything that everyone (or at least, most people) wouldn't be willing to (or interested in) doing wasn't included within these 'rules' & therefore isn't necessarily encouraged. They are built to make people *average* - like everybody else.

That said, rules are not necessarily bad. They work well to provide order, structure, mediocre achievement & average life satisfaction for 7+ billion people. They do a good job getting a large number of people to live an average life; to *'survive.'*

If you're ok with that, then there's nothing for you to do here. If you're *not* though & you want something greater *(not an average life, but a magnificent existence)* you must learn to think & dream <u>beyond</u> the 'rules' that society shares.

In this instance, the *'rules'* were not made for you. They were not personalized to what you want & so following them will not give you the life you desire. *So, you have to do things differently than most to get different results you really want.*

Why should we follow the conventional 'rules' of society, that 1) were designed for mass-scale mediocrity & 2) may not be personalized to what drives, inspires & brings joy to <u>you</u>?

As Steve Jobs - as well as countless other highly successful & fulfilled people - said, *we shouldn't*. At least not *all* of them.

We should be more <u>deliberate</u>. More <u>intentional</u>.

Remind yourself: While you may not have chosen these 'rules' that were conveyed to you, now that you're aware of this information, you can *choose* to think differently. To re-evaluate how small or how big you really want to play.

Just as you were taught to only aim so high & you did (in the past), only achieving so high as a result, you can teach yourself to play bigger (& achieve bigger!)

HOW 'RULES' ARE CREATED...

Take an idea &, if deemed valid, it can form a 'belief,' within an individual. It doesn't matter if this 'belief' was accurate or not, as long as we believe it, it shapes our thoughts, feelings, decisions & actions.

Now, take that idea (now a 'belief') & repeat it enough times to those around you, with enough examples, convincingly enough & it may spread. With time, it can become part of the *'culture.'* Or in other words, a *'rule'* that people now follow.

Not necessarily because it's right or wrong, accurate or not, backed by fact or not, but simply because it's accepted by the majority of people *(remember: reality is subjective)*.

Examples of ideas that became part of the 'culture' include:

- *You need to get good grades in school.*
- *You need to get a college degree.*
- *You need to get a good, stable job.*
- *You need to eat meat to get protein.*
- *You need to drink milk to have strong bones.*
- *You need coffee to feel awake.*
- *You must drink alcohol in social situations.*

- *You must wear makeup & dress a certain way.*
- *You must get & stay married.*
- *You should buy & own a nice house & car.*
- *You need to save for retirement & then retire.*

These are all 'rules.' They've been socially accepted & now, the majority of society follows them (at least for now.)

What's important to remember is each & every one of these started with a single idea from a single person. *All rules did!*

A single idea somebody believed & shared with enough examples, convincingly enough, frequently enough that it spread & now the majority of people agree with it.

Now, both the beautiful & harm of an idea is that if you repeat it enough times, with enough examples & evidence, you can get people to believe it to be the truth.

And this works whether the idea is what people would naturally consider a 'good' one or a 'bad' one. Whether the idea is based on fact or fluff, helpful or sabotaging, small or big, if it's packaged beautifully enough, people will believe it & it might spread into *'culture.'*

In fact, it was Adolf Hitler who once said: *"If you tell a big enough lie and tell it frequently enough, it will be believed."*

I know this book may get some hate now because it referenced Hitler. I'm aware of that. And if you're offended by this, imagine how offended I should be - I'm Polish. I was born in Gdansk, Poland & my grandparents & great-grandparents were actually involved in (& affected by) the war...

I share this quote because it's a good example of how he managed to convince the good people of Germany to do things they never would have considered before.

I bet it had run a survey asking the people who later become the staff running the concentration camps if they would ever see themselves doing the things they ended up doing, they would have all told you *'No way, I would never do that. That's evil. That's not me - I'm a good person'*

Hitler understood though that if you tell a big enough lie frequently enough, it'll be believed.

So, he decided to spread his own ideas (based on *his* views of the world). Ideas such as:

- *Races fall into a hierarchy where some are superior & others are inferior (Racism)*
- *Jews are part of an inferior race (Anti-semitism).*
- *Germans are a superior race (German nationalism).*
- *Disabled people, homosexuals & other minorities don't deserve to be part of the superior German race.*

And he knew that if you share a *belief* (based on an idea), with enough conviction & frequency, people will buy it *(especially when it appeals to their best interest to do so).*

He also knew that if you get enough people to accept these beliefs, it becomes part of the *culture;* 'rules' (social norms) that people blindly accept & live by. And it did become part of Germany's 'culture' during the second world war.

But, there's one more layer to this & that layer is *'tradition.'* If you pass a 'belief' down through generations, it becomes not just part of the *'culture'* but also a *'tradition.'*

And 'tradition' is simply an amplified degree of 'culture,' in which people reason their actions with not just *'because everybody is doing it,'* but with *'this is how it's always been done.'* It basically becomes an even more deeply ingrained *belief* about how the world works...

HOW 'RULES' ARE CREATED

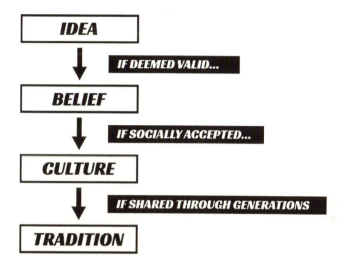

See how it works? An idea (good or bad, useful for you or not) is accepted by somebody & becomes their 'belief,' about how the world works. If this individual's *belief* is shared & socially accepted, it becomes part of the *'culture.'*

And the more socially-accepted a belief becomes (*culture*) & the longer it's been passed around (*tradition*) the less likely we are to challenge the validity of a *belief* in the first place; we become more & more likely to just follow it blindly.

That said, it doesn't have to be that way. And, as you know, the path of **self-mastery** is about putting your own *beliefs* under the microscope, asking whether they actually support us in creating the life we want & then adapting accordingly...

THE UNCONSCIOUS 'PROGRAMS' WE RUN

A young woman is preparing a pot roast while her friend watches her. She cuts off both ends of the roast, prepares it & puts it in the pan. Watching this, her friend asks, *"Why do you cut off the ends?"*

"I don't know. That's how my mother always did it & I learned how to cook from her" she replies.

Curious, during the next visit home, she asked her mother, *"How do you cook a pot roast?"*

Her mother proceeded to explain, *"You cut off both ends, prepare it, put it in the pot & then in the oven."*

"Why do you cut off the ends?" the daughter asked.

Equally confused, the mother replied, *"That's how my mother always did it & I learned to cook from her."* This made her equally curious to learn why she cooked it this way, so the next time she went to visit her mother (grandma) in the nursing home, she asked, *"How do you cook a pot roast?"*

The grandma slowly answered, *"Well, you prepare it with spices, cut off both ends & put it in the pot."*

"Why do you cut off the ends though?" she then asked.

The grandmother's eyes sparkled as she remembered, *"The roasts were always bigger than the pot we had back then, so I had to cut off the ends to fit it into the pot I owned."*

The story is simple, but the message is profound.

How often do we make decisions & take actions based on out-of-date 'rules' that we've been programmed to act upon - that don't best serve us based on the new information, access & capacities we have in today's world?

How often do we do things simply because that is 'how they have <u>always</u> been done' when in actuality, there is a better, more effective way that could yield much greater results, happiness, joy, as well as a more magnificent existence?

You may think that the daughter & mother were silly for cutting off the ends when they didn't have to anymore - as there pots were now big enough not to require this - but this is an example that transcends just cooking into life in general.

In this example, the daughter just wasted lots of pot roast over the years, but what happens when you substitute 'wasted pot roast,' for wasted time, money, potential, love, happiness, joy, freedom or possibility?

Or what if you substitute 'pot roast,' for that big thing you've always, deep down, wanted (e.g. to start your own business, to be a music instructor, to be a content creator, to write a book, to write a screenplay or start a movement), but never pursued it because you were programmed to spend your life following the typical 'rules' of society instead?

The challenge, of course, is that we don't know what we don't know; which flawed, unconscious programs we still run. And it's why it's so important for us to question that which we don't normally question, with curiosity & reason.

In fact, the difference between people who go & break free of many of these beliefs & as a result, tend to live happier, more free, more aware, more joyous, lives, is that they're willing to question the things they do & why they do it.

'Why am I doing what I am going?' is a powerful question that digs under the surface to uncover the cause of our actions, as is *'what belief is driving this action & where did this 'belief' about myself or how the world works come from?'*

CHANGING THE 'PROGRAMS': BECOME AWARE OF WHAT YOU MAY NOT YET KNOW ABOUT...

These 'beliefs,' we have that make-up *'who we are'* & form the lens through which we see reality can be divided up into those that *we know about* & those that *we don't (yet) know about...*

BELIEFS: THOSE YOU KNOW ABOUT & THOSE YOU <u>DON'T</u>

Firstly, we all have 'beliefs' which we're aware of & know that they influence our thoughts, feelings, decisions & actions.

Then, there are *'beliefs'* you have which you <u>don't</u> even know you have, yet they still influence you. Like it or not, we all have these unconscious programs we run simply because it's what we've been conditioned to do, that lead us to waste the very things we find most valuable in life.

Our goal, of course, is to constantly expand that inner circle within that diagram by gaining awareness of what we believe, how we first acquired those beliefs & how they influence us. *As we do this, we're able to better understand ourselves as well as become the best versions of ourselves.*

Plus, as I've found in my work, the more we learn about ourselves & what drives our behavior, the more we want to dig deeper & learn more. It becomes a positive cycle of constant exploration, greater consciousness, growth & *self-mastery*.

And keep in mind: those 'beliefs' you have, but <u>don't</u> know you have only remain in the darkness, unknown to you, silently controlling your behavior, until you shine a spotlight (your conscious focus & attention) onto them.

So, the next time you do something that you look back on thinking you shouldn't have done - like lash out at someone, get frustrated at a situation, do something that moves you away from what you want or any other form of self-sabotage - don't just discard it (or get mad at yourself further) but rather look to find the *cause* of that action.

What 'beliefs' drove you to act in that way? Are you aware of them or are there 'beliefs' that drove your actions at that moment that you're not yet aware of? What are they?

As you explore in this way, you're able to then re-examine these beliefs & act differently (in a way that's more aligned with what you truly want) the next time a similar situation occurs. *This is how you change your unconscious programs (or 'beliefs') that run your life.*

And, as we talked about before, these 'rules' (or 'programs') can be further categorized into those at the 'culture' level & those deeper at the 'tradition' level. *Let's explore both...*

'CULTURE' SAYS: 'BUT, <u>EVERYBODY</u> ELSE IS DOING IT LIKE THIS...'

'If they told you to jump off a cliff, would you do it?' a mother might say to her son or daughter in response to those 5 words we often use to justify our actions: *'everybody else is doing it.'*

Turns out mum or dad may have been spot on when pointing out how ludicrous it is to do something just because it seems *'everybody else is doing it.'*

'Everybody' may be wrong. Or more likely, what it seems like 'everybody' wants may not be what <u>you</u> want in <u>your</u> life.

You must think for yourself & live the life that will make you joyous, not what you think will please others & make you 'fit in.' And nothing demonstrates how ineffective doing things *'because everybody is doing them'* better than history...

Did you know that during the 1950s, half of Americans smoked? This is because smoking wasn't considered bad. If anything, it was considered 'healthy' back then.

In their advertising, cigarette companies would even advertise that doctors smoked - & they did. It was not only common for doctors to completely dismiss any risks of smoking, but occasionally they would actually appear in cigarette ads saying things such as, *"cigarettes provide temporary relief of paroxysms of asthma."* Cigarettes are great & *"20,679 physicians agree"* an ad would say. One ad even said that cigarettes are no worse for you than a glass of water.

Now, you might think the doctors were lying. *'Deception!'* your mind might yell. Perhaps. Although, the more likely conclusion is the doctor's too didn't know any better as they too smoked. They too stopped questioning this *belief* & just bought into cultures view that *'if everybody is doing it, it must be ok.'*

That's until research, study & science caught up, finding that smoking was causing lung cancer, heart disease, as well as many other health issues.

Finally, some researchers decided to think for themselves & fact-check what culture believed about cigarettes.

Today, with few exceptions, everybody in the modern world knows that smoking is harmful to your health. It's actually a law for smoking companies to write that *'Smoking Kills'* on their product packaging.

A single product idea turned into a cultural norm which, through people's blind acceptance of it, lead to the death of countless people over the decades. *If only more people stopped to question this cultural norm sooner?*

People smoked back then because there was no reason not to. Plus, *'everybody was doing it.'* It was part of the *'culture.'* Yet, *was it right?* No. *Effective?* Definitely not.

Once again: just because everybody is doing it, doesn't mean it's what we should be doing, in the same way that just because 'everybody' is going to college, getting a job, drinking soda, eating meat, drinking milk, complaining about the world, sleeping in, watching TV, spending hours per week on social media or spending money on fancy cars to impress others doesn't necessarily make it the right thing to do.

You must decide consciously <u>what's right for you</u>, instead of burying your head into the sand & rationalizing your actions with 'everybody is doing it.' We must all step up in this way!

Another example is that of how even morality has changed. This example is that of slavery. For hundreds of years, slavery was the norm in many countries in the world. It was 'no big deal' & 'everybody doing well financially had a slave.'

'Everybody was doing it.' It as part of the culture. So, it must be morally ok then, right?

I'm sure you would agree that it's definitely not right, making it another good example the 'rules' we are taught aren't necessarily the best things for you (or anyone) to follow.

What if it turns out the things that are part of 'culture' today - such as that list shared above - turn out, years later, to be wildly ineffective ways for living a great life as well, yet you continued following them as 'everybody else was doing so?'

Plus: at the end of the day, if you believe the same 'beliefs' as everybody else, you'll think, feel, make decisions & take actions just like everybody else, in turn, getting the same results as everybody else. You'll be just like everybody else. You'll be average. Mediocre. *Same input, same output.*

To achieve something different, you must believe different things, driving different thinking, feeling, new decisions, new actions & in turn, - yes, you guessed it - new results.

To achieve bigger things, for example, you must 'belief' different things about your future & set higher ambitions for yourself. You must pursue your true ambitions *(not just what 'everybody else' does, believes & aims for.)*

As Mark Twain said: *"Whenever you find yourself on the side of the majority, it's time to pause & reflect."* Otherwise put:

| If You Want To Achieve What Only 1% Of People Achieve, You Have To Do Things Differently Than 99% Of People

If you aim small, setting ambitions below your true capacity, thinking about your future just as the 'majority' of people do, you'll get the same results as others.

If you find yourself in this situation, yet you want something more, as Mark Twain said, pause & reflect on what 'rules' you're buying into. Decide whether they truly serve you & how you should think differently to get the results you truly want.

'TRADITION' SAYS: 'LOOK - THIS IS HOW IT'S <u>ALWAYS</u> BEEN DONE...'

Have you ever stopped to wonder why, despite all the possible options, the lives of most people in the modern world look mostly the same, in terms of what they've done in the past to get to where they are today, how they spend their time & the behaviors they display?

The similarities are uncanny when you bare in mind that each of us is born as a blank slate with absolutely no understanding of what a 'job' is, what 'school' is, how the world works, what food should be eaten or not, what behaviors are considered appropriate, how to mate or how to live.

We are born without any of this information, yet end up living in very similar ways - similar education & skills, a 9-5 job, taking time off on the weekends, eating similar foods, watching similar shows, spending time in a similar way, etc.

It's either a massive coincidence or there's something that works to guide most people in the modern world in a similar direction? Upon further research (as you're doing here) you'll find it's 'culture' & 'tradition,' guiding us down the same path.

However, while 'culture' tends to influence you more while later on in life (when you're already a kid, teenager or adult), the influences of *'tradition'* are there from the beginning. *They start from the very moment you are born...*

Meaning: during the first few years of your life - before we even developed consciousness *(more on this in the next section)* - we're already getting conditioned by ideas & beliefs about the world held at the 'tradition' level. Just ask yourself...

Did you decide what religion you were going to be raised in? Did you choose the food you were going to eat growing up?

Did you consciously choose whether or not you wanted to go to kindergarten or school, or was this decision made for you? Did you decide you wanted to go to college / university or was this something that was just assumed for you? Perhaps your family already set these plans into motion for you?

What about your career? Did you choose it or were you nudged down a certain career path from the moment you were born (like becoming a doctor or a lawyer)? Perhaps, you were subtly conditioned into the same career path as your mother or father?

Like it or not, we didn't consciously 'choose' many of these things, but rather are just conditioned into them. Long term, this can lead to a lot of *internal conflicts* as you realize what you were conditioned into may not be what you really want...

For example, you may be raised with 1 religion, but your whole life, deep down, felt resistance to fully devoting yourself to that religion. Some of the practices & beliefs of that religion just didn't fully resonate with you & your views of the world.

Yet, because of your environment (the 'rules' you were given), you never expressed these doubts. You feared what would happen if you rebelled & instead redirected that doubt inwards. *Perhaps you felt like a bad person, felt guilty or even felt resentment toward yourself. You wondered why you couldn't just be 'normal' like everybody else. "Everybody else just accepts this, why can't I too?" you may ask yourself.*

Perhaps, we should explore why we even subscribed to this religion in the first place? Did we choose this or was it chosen for us? Is it really what you want? Is it fully aligned with how we want to think, feel & experience life?

What about food? The 'rules' condition us that we must eat meat for protein & drink milk for strong bones, but if we explore this, we'll find these beliefs really don't hold up.

Lots of compelling research has come out showing how destructive these foods can be for our health.

Is how you eat, as well as think about your health right now something you choose or something that was decided for you from an early age (through tradition)?

Schooling? College? Good stable job? *Are these things you choose for yourself, or did someone choose them for you?*

We now know that just because something is the 'rule' doesn't mean it's necessarily the right thing for us.

We should be open & curious to fact-check our own beliefs...

Personally, I dropped out of high school when I was 14 years of age & it was the best decision of my life!

What about your career? *Did you choose it? Are you doing it because you truly love it (intrinsically) or because you felt pressured to get involved in the career you're in right now?*

Parental pressure is common today, which leads parents to push children into certain careers that make the most money or hold the greatest prestige (like that of a doctor or lawyer)...

However, what if you don't enjoy these things? What if your current career doesn't interest or fulfill you?

What if the only reason you're in it is to please your family & the only reason your parents are in this field is because of the pressure that was put on them by their parents growing up (just like with the pot roast example)?

Are you going to stay in a career you hate your whole life because of the conditioning of 'tradition' or change into a career you love?

Many of the things that you believe, subscribe to & follow in your life right now, 1) you often haven't chosen yourself & 2) have come from a single idea from a single person that may or may not be the best, most effective approach for you.

What all this means is that we shouldn't follow the 'rules' of society just because *'everyone else is'* or that *'this is how it's <u>always</u> been done.'* Fortunately though...

RULES ARE BREAKABLE (& YOU'RE REMEMBERED FOR THE RULES YOU CHOOSE TO BREAK)

See, while 'rules' operate best as a fallback, we get conditioned to treat them as *fixed, unbreakable & 'must-be-followed.'* In reality, this is not the case...

You can break out of certain 'rules' that limit you as the only person locking you into the prison of them is yourself. *Let yourself out to create the life you freely want for yourself!*

It's possible. People do it every single day. To leave the old behind, create change & set new ambitions for their lives.

Plus, as Douglas MacArthur once said, *"You are remembered for the rules you break."*

At the end of the day, hundreds of years from now, when we're all going to be dead, you'll be remembered for the *'rules'* that you choose to break. Your great-grandkids may think of you are the granddad or grandma who challenged *'tradition,'* went against the grain & led the family in a new direction...

Perhaps... 'the grandad who changed how future generations eat for the better so everybody in the family is healthier & lives longer,' or 'the grandma who <u>didn't</u> become a sad, but compliant doctor because of the conditioning she received growing up, but a happy, joyous & fulfilled artist, author, musician or business owner that showed future generations that choice is in their hands.'

In history, it is those who question the *'rules'* ('social norms') that become known for it...

For example, what is Rosa Parks remembered for? What is Gandhi known for? What about Martin Luther King Jr?

They are remembered because they broke specific *'rules'* - challenged specific social norms - that others did not.

Others may have thought that those same rules were unfair or unjust, but didn't break them *(they didn't have the courage).*

Rosa Parks rejected the social norm of racial discrimination. As did Martin Luther King Jr. While he was not the initiate of the civil rights movement, he was the figurehead of it; the most empowering leader who was a living embodiment of the racial discrimination 'rule' he broke. Gandhi is remembered for his stand on non-violence even when violence was the norm. The status quo; what 'everybody else would do.' He broke that rule & propelled people in the direction of peace.

These greatest men & women were those who didn't just walk through life on autopilot, accepting the 'rules' as they were given to them, but those who were willing to challenge them, to question & consciously decide the best path. They were able to think & dream *above & beyond* the 'rules.' And you can too.

Ultimately, as Harley Davidson said, *"When writing the story of your life, don't let anyone else hold the pen."*

Not society. Not tradition. Not me. Not your friends or family. Nobody, but yourself. *You choose the story you write...*

2. **Survival Instincts:** Our 'Reptilian Brain' Is <u>Not</u> Built For Success, But Mere Survival.

There are 3 parts of the brain that control what we think, feel & do *(especially at first, when things are not yet habitual).*

This model for understanding the human brain (these 3 parts) was first developed by Paul MacLean in the 1960s. And while this model remains a very simplified version of how our brain actually works, knowing it can serve us well here.

Plus, greater details of the brain's structure & function go beyond the scope of this book. They would add a few hundred extra pages to its length while adding little value for someone just looking to better their lives without learning the in's & out's of the brain & names of all it's fancy-sounding parts.

By understanding these 3 core parts of the brain, you'll be able to better recognize (& interpret) the mixed information that your brain may often send you.

For example, that feeling of wanting something but knowing you shouldn't pursue it (emotion vs logic), or knowing that something would be beneficial & wanting it (like a big goal), but fearing it at the same time. *Let's begin - the 3 parts are:*

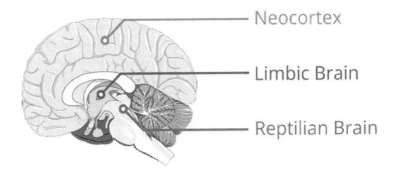

1. **Reptilian Brain:** Survival Instincts

The reptilian brain is found in all animals, including, of course, human beings. It's the oldest of the 3 parts of the brain & controls vital body functions (e.g. breathing, body temperature & balance.)

Its role is to make sure you <u>survive</u>. To keep you alive; which is why it's the brain's center for aggression, impulse & mating. It makes sure that you fulfill your basic human needs & starts to act out if you don't, to ensure that you comply.

Have you ever felt very unmotivated to work, disengaged in your conversations or more easily-annoyed while you were hungry, tired or wanting to go the bathroom? Well, now you know why. Your *'survival instincts'* took over, making it hard to focus on anything but the survival needs at hand. As the

Snickers chocolate bar ads have said for years, *"You're not you when you're hungry."*

The reptilian brain controls your 'survival instincts' - those automatic instincts, reflexes & reactions we demonstrate.

It's the reason we flinch when someone goes to punch, hit or kick us (even if it's a joke from a friend just goofing around which we *logically* know isn't going to hurt us). Or when an animal gets closer at the zoo & we feel a threat - even though we're completely safe on the other side of the protective glass.

In those moments, your 'fight or flight response' is activated, motivating you to act to protect yourself. Ambition is switched off. You're not thinking about tomorrow, next week, or what you have to get done later in the day. You're not pondering the meaning of life. You're just focused on *'surviving.'*

Put this all together & you have a great tool for *survival* in your reptilian brain. The downside though is that these same *'survival instincts'* that keep you alive can also keep you playing small, achieving very little & being very unhappy with life *(as we'll talk about in just a moment, after covering the basic details of the other 2 core parts of the brain)*...

2. Limbic Brain: Emotions & Feelings

The limbic brain is the part of the brain that controls feelings & emotions. It's the brain's emotion factory, turning sensory information & thoughts into feelings & emotions.

So, while the heart may be energy center for love - as mind & body are connected; which we'll explore later - it's actually the limbic brain that's generating that emotion of love. As it does with all emotions, including hate, jealousy, excitement, joy, enthusiasm, peace & tranquility. *After all, the 'limbic brain' is also known as 'the feeling brain.'*

Although, it's also the part of your brain responsible for memory formation; helping you form short term & long term memories from experiences that you've had.

3. Neocortex: Logic & Language

Lastly, you have the newest, most evolved, largest part of the brain, the *Neocortex*, which controls logic, reasoning, forward-thinking, planning & overall consciousness. If the limbic brain is the *'feeling'* brain, the neocortex is the *'thinking'* brain.

The neocortex is present in all primates, but most developed in humans, making up over 80% of the brain's volume. It's a big difference maker between humans & other species.

The neocortex is also flexible, with almost infinite learning abilities. Plus, mostly operates on the conscious level of mind.

And now that you have a basic idea of these 3 mains parts of your brain, there are 2 big understandings that can truly serve us in playing a bigger game & living a great life…

GREAT FOR SURVIVING, NOT FOR THRIVING

The 1st key understanding is that while your reptilian brain - your 'survival instincts' - are an incredible tool for survival, they also form the 2nd big reason why we dream & play small.

Fear, resistant, doubt, alway seeing the worse-case-scenario & seeing things as 'threats' to our survival, are the tools of the reptilian brain. And while they served us well when the world was a dangerous place in which, you could get attacked by a tiger, in today's world, they are rather counterproductive instincts. They have their time & place, but listening to these instincts all the time is a sure way of living an unfulfilling life.

We fear to set a big goal because we might fail, or get hurt, or rejected, or judged in some way. We fear to talk to a stranger because our 'survival instincts' see this stranger as a 'threat' instead of a 'friend.' We fear striking up a conversation with a member of the opposite sex. We fear to speak our truth or speak in public. We fear the unknown as our 'survival instincts' again, see this as a 'threat' & not an 'opportunity.'

Our neocortex (controlling logic) knows these fears are often irrational & unjustified, yet we still fear them because of our reptilian brain. And we buy into this fear, which stops us from doing that which will help create an extraordinary existence.

For example, while the *neocortex* understands that the odds of a plane crashing are 1 in 40 million (& daily things such as driving, public transport or even riding your bike are, statistically, more dangerous), your reptilian brain may still be terrified when you're on the runway, about to take-off.

'But, what if I'm the one in 40 million?' your reptilian brain asks. We know we can't live our lives this way, yet we listen to this & get scared when doing new things. It's the reason why some people never travel - fear. Or in the case of this chapter, when wanting to pursue bigger & higher ambitions in life.

Studies have now shown more than 90% of things we fear & bad things we imagine happening, don't actually end up happening. Although, I'm sure you know this intuitively as well, based on your own life experience...

Remember when you pictured getting rejected by someone, playing out in your head how embarrassing it could become, only to end up striking up a pleasant conversation? Or, when you went skydiving & feared your parachute not opening, yet it did & you had an incredible experience? Or you spent all week scared because your boss wanted to have a meeting with you & you thought you were going to get fired, but you didn't?

These things - these 'worst-case-scenarios' we picture - almost never happen (90+% of the time). And even when they do, they are almost never life-threatening. Yet, we fear them &

worry. Largely, for no good reason. Or more accurately, our reptilian brain fears them.

Because of this, we live scared & terrified of testing new things & playing big in our lives; doing what we're truly capable of.

It's in these moments - especially when setting ambitions & making commitments - that we must remind ourselves that our fear & doubt is not our own. It is coming from the survival instincts of our reptilian brain & is largely unjustified. We must lower its influence when setting ambitions & thinking about our future by disassociating from it, telling ourselves *'This is not me being scared - it just my survival instincts, worrying about something that I know won't happen.'*

The reptilian brain is not wired for success or happiness, but for mere survival. Hence, while the reptilian brain serves us well in dangerous situations - when our lives are at risk - in other situations, it only hinders our progress & limits our potential, making it this 2nd big reason here.

And, just like with the others, you can train yourself to counteract these instincts. You can condition yourself to override your fear. To, not be fearless (fear will always be there), but to *fear less & less* in your life. And, when fear is there, not to let that fear stop you from playing big!

ALIGNMENT OF THINKING & FEELING

The effects of your brain can be compared to that of 2 people working together. If you have 2 people that are working together *effectively*, 1 plus 1 could equal 7 in terms of their combined output & results. They make each other better. Support each other. And combined, there's little they can't do!

If 2 people are working together *ineffectively* though, 1 plus 1 could equal 1.2 (or even, 0) in terms of their combined output & results. They could distract each. Waste time arguing. Or worse, sabotage each other's work.

The same happens within each of us; from our different parts of the brains (specifically, the *neocortex* guiding our thoughts & the *limbic brain* guiding our feelings).

If they are working together - in *total alignment* - you can create & achieve extraordinary things. You can do & become anything; growing, getting better & tapping into possibilities!

If, on the flip side, these 2 brains are in constant conflict with each other, sending completely mixed messages all the time - pulling you in different directions - like 2 people working together ineffectively, it can be very counterproductive. Plus, it can lead you to doubt yourself, get confused, overwhelmed, to spin in circles or even self-sabotage yourself completely.

Here's an example: You've made a conscious & logical choice to avoid chocolate because you're on a diet (*neocortex*). When you get home though & saw chocolate on the kitchen counter, your brain (the *limbic brain* this time) sent you a different signal to that of your initial choice.

"Chocolate! I love chocolate! Feed me. I want it - it's going to taste so good!" it says to you. At first, you stopped yourself (*neocortex*), reminding yourself that you're strong & you can do this. However, you may have ended up eating the chocolate later on because the desire grew too strong (*limbic brain*).

See the mixed signals that different parts of your brain can send you at different times? And see how this can, not only stop you from creating the changes you want to create, but also cause doubt, confusion & conflict within you?

Or, in an example of setting ambitions for your future, your *neocortex* understanding the content in this book & wants to finally go after that big thing you've always wanted. Logically, you get it, but emotionally, you're still reluctant to implement.

Or, reversed this time: you start feeling great (*your limbic brain*), but then you attempt to rationalize your joy & fall into a downward spiral of overthinking & overanalysis. Your *limbic brain* just wanted to be happy, but now your *neocortex* started overthinking & before long your 'feeling great' goes away. *2 parts of your brain pulling in different directions.*

See, both the limbic brain (emotion) & the neocortex (logic) are powerful in their own way, but it's when they are truly working together - in <u>total alignment</u> - that you tap into your highest levels of thinking, feeling, motivation, personal power, inspiration, creativity, meaning & success.

WHICH INFLUENCE WINS?

The influences of your survival instincts (reptilian brain) & your greater self (limbic brain & neocortex) on your behavior are like 2 wolves in a battle. As to which influence wins & ultimately guides the direction of your life is, as the Native American tale concludes, *"the wolf that you feed."*

If you feed your survival instincts (your fear, your resistance, your small-mindedness, your goal of *mere survival* in life), with your focus, attention & energy, buying into it's irrational & unjustified fears, it'll win & guide the direction of your life.

It'll also become stronger & stronger, making it harder to counteract next time, becoming all-consuming; controlling every part of your life experience. It'll hold you under a barrel, with the idea of mere survival as the goal for life & nothing more. It'll trap you from a great life. Which, if that's what you want, is ok. But, if that's *not* what you want, it's like being held hostage against your will by your own mind.

See, not only does dreaming big - *height of ambition* - often go about the 'rules' of society, but it often goes against this part of your own biology. Often, the things we truly want are the things our 'survival instincts' are more averse to pursuing. And it will remain that way if you feed *that* wolf.

On the flip side, if you feed the other wolf - the one of greater consciousness, possibility, beauty, love & freedom (the *limbic brain* & the *neocortex working together*), your higher levels of thinking & feeling will ultimately shape your future.

These 2 parts of the brain equip us with everything we need to live an extraordinary life. However, just like with a tool or new gadget, we must learn to use them (something the education system forgot to teach us!) *You must learn it. Train it. Do it.*

Just as you can train yourself to be physically stronger, you can train yourself to be *mentally* stronger; for your reptilian brain to influence you *less* & your higher consciousness to be the real driver of your life. *So ensure you: feed that wolf.*

EXERCISE: STEP INTO YOUR FEARS

One of the best ways to lessen the negative influence of your reptilian brain, fear & self-doubt, instead replacing it with confidence & greater proactiveness is to constantly face (& step into) your fears - reducing their power over you.

As Eleanor Roosevelt said, *"You gain strength, courage, and confidence by every experience in which you really stop to look fear in the face."* And she also said, *"Do one thing every day that scares you."*

And this exercise is based on exactly this; it's a challenge (or, mission) of sorts for you (should you choose to accept!)

Simply put: firstly, take time right now & make a list of things that would scare you to do (things that are currently outside your comfort zone) & then do them - *at least 1 per day for the next 30 days.*

Here are some examples of things you *could* do:

- Strike up a conversation with (or hug) a stranger
- Live karaoke or sing in public

- Ask for a discount at a store
- Take a dance class
- Take a cold shower (or jump into a cold pool)
- Hold a snake or a spider
- Make a video, or live stream (or public speaking)
- Start doing pushups in public (e.g. in a store)
- Ask a stranger if you can take a selfie with them
- Go paragliding or skydiving

The point is to make these easy things you can do (usually short 5 min daily challenges you can complete) although you may want to add in a few bigger, more time-consuming challenges into the mix as well. *It's up to you how you do it!*

If you choose to do this challenge over the next 30 days, you're likely to find that much of what you fear is much scarier <u>before</u> you do it than <u>after</u> you complete it.

Your comfort zone (what you feel comfortable doing) will stretch & you'll gain more confidence!

You may also want to journal your experience after each day's challenge for even greater benefit.

Remember: it's not about removing fear altogether *(fear is helpful at times)*, but to learn to fear less & act in spite of it.

Courageous people are not fearless - they still feel fear - but those who know fear is an illusion & act in spite of it.

Take the 30-day challenge now!

EXERCISE: MEDITATION & MINDFULNESS
Another great way to 'feed the wolf' of higher consciousness, profound thought & feeling is by dedicating more of your time to your mindfulness & meditation practices *(although, 5 or 10 mins per day, if done consistently, is a great start!)*

Why? Well, over 1000 scientific studies now document the profound benefits of consistent meditation & mindfulness. These documented benefits include lower stress, less aggression, better sleep, better focus, elevated mood during the day & even increased productivity.

Hence, if there's was 1 new thing you could start (in just 5 or 10 mins a day) that would have the most profound impact on your life, daily meditation would be it...

Remember: it's the metaphorical wolf which you feed that shapes your life (either the wolf of fear & your reptilian brain) or the wolf of profound thinking & feeling. *You choose!*

3. **Current Circumstances:** We Base Our Ambitions On Our Current & Past Circumstances.

Back in chapter #1, we talked about how believing that the past equals the future can turn into a *'self-fulfilling prophecy'* in which you continue to get the same results as before.

In that same way, basing the *height* (or intensity) of your future ambitions on your current or past circumstances can have the same effect.

And this forms the 3rd big reason why we often dream small - another one that when we break free from, we can achieve much greater things...

BORN LIMITLESS. RAISED INTO LIMITS.

Imagine if this is what you thought to yourself when you were a child, as you were learning to walk. You had the desire to walk, but you doubted yourself & didn't take action to learn, rationalizing it with, *'But, I've never walked <u>in the past</u> & I can't walk <u>right now</u> so why would I be able to in the future?'*

This example shows us just how irrational basing our future ambitions on our past (or on *current circumstances*) really is.

A child will just get up & give it a go - never stopping for a minute to even consider this feat as impossible just because it's not something they are *currently* able to do (or did in the past). Even after falling a few times, the child isn't going to give up, quit & think, *'Maybe, I'm just not a walker..,'*

Not a chance! The child is going to keep going, pushing, learning & pursuing that ambition until it's achieved. That's what I do. That's what you did. And that's every person who knows able to walk did growing up.

It's natural. It's how we are born: *limitless*. We're are born naked, bare & incapable of anything, yet filled with potential.

And we're still filled with potential today - infinite possibilities that co-exist for us in the future - but this understanding has been clouded by 'beliefs' that don't serve us about how the world works (*'beliefs' we can change!*)

We get taught to rationalize things in a certain way. We attempt to lose weight, build muscle or to succeed in business, but when we fail, we form 'beliefs' about what we think is possible in the future. With time, we stop dreaming & only settle for that which is the same (or maybe a tiny, little bit better) than what we've had in the past or have in the present.

When, in actuality, it doesn't matter where you were (past) or where you are (present), as your life can change at any time. You can choose to change it & tune into new possibilities at any moment in your life.

Hence, an ambition should never be diminished or discarded just because it's 'new' & not something you've successfully done before. Of course, you haven't. Just as you hadn't walked, before you did. It's new & that's ok. So, dream big *(beyond your current circumstances)* & be relentless in the pursuit of that ambition *(just like when you were a child!)*

The past doesn't equal the future; nor do your current circumstances. The future is what you make it (through your thoughts, feelings, decisions & actions - or your 'trajectory')

WHAT IS REALLY 'IMPOSSIBLE?'

Look around you. Look at all the 'impossible' things around you right now as you read this book.

You may think, *'Bogdan, what 'impossible' things? There's nothing like that around me...'*

What about the electricity that's powering the light, heating & everything else in your house right now?

Imagine going back in time & telling someone a few hundred years ago about 'electricity,' explaining how it works & how it powers your house. They'll tell you that you're crazy. That this explanation sounds too good to be true. *"That's 'impossible!"* they may say. And it was 'impossible' - until it wasn't.

What about the bookshelf in your living room? Hundreds & thousands of years of compiled wisdom & story. Someone could have written a book based on the last 5, 10 or 20 years of life lessons & in just a few hours you read that & learn those same lessons. You can buy biographies of some of the greatest people who have ever lived & read them in an afternoon.

And, if you want, you can even take all those hundreds or thousands of books, put them on your tablet or e-reader & take them with you wherever you want. Something that, in the past, would have been called 'impossible.' *Until it wasn't.*

And don't even get me started on 'the internet,' which is nothing short of a miracle. Like a 2nd world - a virtual one - where people share, learn & connect. The internet has created more job opportunities & more access to information than any individual company or government could ever wish to...

I mean, just imagine the chaos that'd erupt if the internet suddenly disappeared, never to return. It's incredible. Totally 'impossible.' *Until it wasn't.* And today, we take it for granted.

As the author of the book, *Abundance: The Future Is Better Than You Think*, Peter Diamandis, wrote on CNN:

"Right now, a Masai warrior on a mobile phone in the middle of Kenya has better mobile communications than the president did 25 years ago. If he's on a smartphone using Google, he has access to more information than the U.S. president did just 15 years ago."

Pretty incredible, don't you think? Now, imagine attempting to explain the internet to your ancestors, 20, 30, 50 or 60 years ago. Imagine explaining to them that in the 21st century someone in the middle of Kenya will have access to more information than the president of the U.S.

"Are you ok? You sound delusional. Crazy. Perhaps you should get tested..." they may think or say. They'll think you're going mad. But, you haven't. They just can't see what you can see, so they pawn it off as 'impossible.'

This is all because we often set expectations for the future based on the past & a linear trajectory through time. We assume if something wasn't possible in the past & isn't possible now, it's unlikely to be possible in the future.

This thinking is obviously flawed though - as you know. That's just not how innovation, improvement, change & the world as a whole, works. It works very differently from that.

In reality, we don't know what we don't know. We're quick to write something off as *'never going to happen,' 'crazy,' 'too ambitious,'* or *'impossible,'* without considering that there is something beyond our awareness that can open up to us as soon as we realize something as 'possible' & set that ambition.

Plus: ambitions & opportunities are like the chicken & egg. You're unlikely to see opportunities to achieve what you truly want unless you first set that big ambition for yourself & believe that it could happen for you.

This is where many of the world's greatest - game-changers & world leaders - thought about their ambitions very differently. They didn't set ambitions based on what was possible right now (current circumstances), but on what they wanted (even if it seemed 'impossible') & then worked to make it possible, probable & eventually accomplished. *You can do the same!*

A GOOD RULE OF THUMB FOR POSSIBILITY

As to what's possible in your life, the first good rule of thumb is simply this...

| *'If Anyone Else Has Ever Done It, It Means That You Can Too.'*

It's a good baseline for what's possible for you in your life & a great place to start with your thinking...

See, I don't care where you are right now. I don't care how beautifully blissfully, or how terribly awful your life might be *right now* (current circumstances), as with time, your results can do a complete 180 based on your ambitions & trajectory.

You could weigh 300 pounds right now, yet the ambition of 'weighing only 150 pounds' is still not considered 'impossible.'

To reason this, ask yourself (based on this first rule of thumb): *has anyone else ever lost this much weight?* Yes - no doubt. Research it. Look it up. *And if they could do it, that means you can do it too!*

In this same way, how much money you have in your bank account *at this moment* (current circumstances) shouldn't be a deciding factor when setting ambitions for how much wealth you would like to have accumulated in the future.

Statistically, very few people are born into wealth, while most of the wealthiest people in the world started from the bottom. There was probably a time in the past in which Jeff Bezos, Bill Gates, Warren Buffett, Mark Zuckerberg or Carlos Slim also had little or no money to their name. A close-to-empty bank balance or even being in debt. *However, they didn't base their future ambitions on this. And you shouldn't either!*

If anyone else has ever done it, it means you can too.

Although, in reality, there's even more than this. This is just the first rule of thumb & doesn't always apply. Possibility stretches much further, so even if someone else <u>hasn't</u> yet done something, you can do that too (*I mean, someone has to be first anyway, so why not you?*)

And even if something appears 'impossible' I've found it much more effective to consider it as *'may be possible,'* than to rule it out completely. This is because our stamp 'impossible!' is a very a powerful symbol for our mind, which totally depletes all motivation & becomes a *'self-fulfilling prophecy.'*

The great sports coach, Vince Lombardi, put it best when he said: *"We would accomplish many more things if we did not think of them as impossible."*

Or, as Paulo Coelho said, *"Go for the impossible. I always tried to find my own limits. So far I did not find them, so my universe is in constant expansion."*

Knowing all of this, base your ambitions on what you want & the infinite possibilities available to you *(not on the past or current circumstances)* as with this comes great power!

4. Opinions Of Others: People Make Assumptions Based On Their Own Subjective Life Experience.

Walt Disney was fired by a newspaper editor because *"he lacked imagination and had no good ideas."*

"You ain't goin' nowhere, son. You ought to go back to drivin' a truck," is what Jimmy Denny, manager of the Grand Ole Opry, told Elvis Presley after firing him.

Robin Williams was voted *'Least Likely To Succeed,'* & Beethoven's teacher said he was, *"hopeless as a composer."*

The 4th big reason why we sometimes stop dreaming big & settle for playing small is because of the *opinions, reactions, words & comments of others.*

They tell us we're dreaming too big, we're crazy, we lack the ability or that this just 'isn't our thing.' Sometimes we hear this & we start to doubt ourselves. *'Maybe they're right?'* we ask ourselves, o *'Who am I to dream this big anyway?'*

Their opinions influence us. They make us doubt our big dreams. They make us shrink into the majority. When you share your dream & you're met with such resistance & 'dream suppression,' it can fill you with doubt.

And it can lead you to continually lower your ambition until you're dreaming no bigger than *'I just want to get through the week.'* Other people's opinions can make your dreams shrink.

With this said, this doesn't have to be this way. And that's exactly what we're exploring here...

Personally, while I've been incredibly fortunate to have parents, friends & people who have always supported my ambitions, told me to pursue my dreams & encouraged me to think big, but that doesn't mean I haven't gone through my share of 'ambition suppression.' I have.

People telling me to *'be realistic,' 'to settle,'* to *'get my head out of the clouds,' 'to be a normal teenager,'* or *'to quit.'*

Friends. Family. Teachers. Haters on the internet. Peers. Strangers. People I worked alongside. You get the idea.

I'm sure you've been through something like this. Pretty much everybody has. Including, all of the world's highest achieving people. *So, how should you deal with it?* Or, specifically...

If we've <u>all</u> gone through things like this at one moment or another, what makes the difference?

Walt Disney, Beethoven & Elvis Presley had people who indicated to them that they were dreaming unreasonably & should settle for something smaller, yet that didn't stop them from achieving truly great things? How come? What made the difference between them & others?

The key: **interpretation & response**.

In those moments when your ambitions are met with the disapproval, discouragement & even hate from others, we most more consciously interpret this information. *We must think differently about the opinions of others.*

When Walt Disney was told he lacked imagination & didn't have any good ideas, was this a sign that he should stop pursuing any creative endeavors in his life? Or perhaps that his boss was wrong about him... he just didn't know it yet. A sign that he should keep going, get better & do exactly what he did in creating the Disney brand?

Should Elvis Presley have lowered his ambition when the manager told him he wasn't going to make it in the music industry? Should he have let someone else's opinion diminish his lofty ambitions? Or should he have done what he did & kept dreaming big anyway - & gone on to achieve them?

In these moments, we have a choice:

1) We welcome the discouragement, treat it as the truth, dwell on it & let it lower our ambitions, our goals & our self-esteem...

2) We can see it as merely *'opinion,'* learn what we can from it, use it as fuel to move us forward potentially, discard it & chasing the big things that we truly want to achieve in our lives anyway.

*It's our **interpretation** that makes all the difference.*

And to support you in forming the most beneficial & effective interpretations when these things come up, we're going to explore some of the psychology, reasoning & motives behind why people sometimes advise you to dream smaller...

This will make it easier for you to optimally react to anything that comes your way, as well as avoid dwelling on other people's opinions & letting them stop you.

'DREAM SMALL': WHY PEOPLE ADVISE YOU DO SO?

What do you think will happen when you put some crabs in an open bucket? Will they get out? Escape?

Let me give you a hint: any crab can easily climb up the side of the bucket & escape.

Based on this - that the crabs have *the ability* to easily climb out of the bucket - our first thought might be that the group of crabs would escape. They would climb up the side & get out.

Personally, I picture them hiking up the side of the bucket like heroes, yelling *'FREEDOM!'* while the soundtracks from the movie 'BraveHeart' plays in the background. Perhaps, working together to regain freedom together. That's where my imagination would take me. And, based on the fact they have the *ability* to get out, logic would conclude the same. *But, the reality is very different...*

Yes, when you put 1 crab into an open bucket, indeed, the crab climbs out & escapes. *Piece of cake. No problem. Easy peasy*!

However, when you put a group of crabs together into a single bucket, any 1 crab's efforts to get out will be undermined by the others, creating demise for the entire group.

A crab would start climbing up the side of the bucket, but the others in the group would drag it back down. And this would repeat over & over again.

The result: the crabs never escape the bucket that they so easily could. They remain stuck.

This experiment has been repeated many, many times, & the term, *"crab mentality"* has been coined amongst researchers to explain this sad phenomenal.

A similar phenomenon is, *'Tall poppy syndrome.'* A term that describes aspects of a culture where people of high status are resented, attacked, cut down, strung up or criticized because they have been classified as superior to their peers.

So when, Margaret Thatcher - prior to becoming British Prime Minister - said *"let your poppies grow tall,"* what she meant was, like the crabs, people shouldn't let their emotions lead to hate towards those striving for something greater.

The *'crab mentality'* doesn't just apply to crabs, but to us - human beings - as well.

We've all had a time in our lives when we felt a little jealous, envious or hateful - these emotions are *our 'crab mentality.'*

For some, these sides show themselves all the time, for others very rarely (if at all anymore). It's because as you change *'who you are'* & embrace kindness, human goodness & greater connectedness, you're less likely to need these emotions.

What's important to understand though is that it's these emotions that cause many of the opinions, much of the hate & a lot of the 'dream suppression' you'll get from others. It's in these darkest emotions that people hurt others. It's because, as the saying goes...

| Hurt People, Hurt People

Those who feel hurt (inside) are those who do things to hurt others. They throw comments at you designed to disappoint, dishearten or hurt you because they feel hurt within. And frankly, it's easier to reflect this onto others than to generate the courage to face it ourselves.

The negative opinions, hate & 'dream suppression' you may get when stepping up & playing bigger has nothing to do with you, but to do with them, so don't take it personally. In fact...

| Don't Take Others Opinions <u>Personally</u>

Why? Because they are not personal. They are not about you, but merely a projection of the hurt people are feeling within themselves - as well as their subjective outlook on life.

So when someone lashes out at you with a comment designed to hurt you, it's not about *you*, but merely because of the emotions <u>they</u> are experiencing in their own life right now.

I mean, odds are, we've all seen someone lash out at someone for no other reason than simply because they were in a bad mood at that time. And so, we can sometimes become the targets of his hate or cynicism just because we are in close proximity at the time - we're close by & an easy target.

Your teacher may just be having a bad day when she lashed out at you calling you *'stupid,'* & telling you *'you're useless at this & should just quit.'*

She may have had a bad morning, or a bad weekend at home with the family? She may still be emotionally recovering from something? She's talking to you, but not really. She's actually talking to herself, or her son, or her husband or someone else completely, just talking *through* you.

'Why can't you ever do anything right?' a parent may say to a child in anger, although in reality, they are saying this to themselves as a form of processing their own emotions. *Hurt people hurt people.*

The child though, not possessing this understanding you now possess may take this personally, form a *belief* around how useless or stupid they are & live our their whole life struggling & failing *(just because of 1 opinion picked up in childhood, which wasn't even really directed at them)*.

Someone says to you *"you're so ugly," "you're so stupid," "you're such a failure," "your voice sounds horrible"* or *"you'll never be able to achieve them"* but really they are just sharing through their own limited perspective of life *(their 'opinion')*.

They have a certain views - certain 'beliefs' - about beauty, intellect, vocality or success they are attempting to project to you. It's not personal. It's just their point of view. Yet, many accept this as the definitive truth...

If they call themselves 'beautiful,' they doubt that & treat it as a just their own opinion, yet when someone else calls them ugly, dumb or idiotic, they assume it's fact (it's a little ironic).

In reality, it's the other way around. In this subjective world, how you view yourself is much more real than what others think or say about you, as their words are based on *their* 'beliefs' & *their* outlook on life *(often guided by the 'rules'.)*

Equally, when people tell you *"you're amazing"* or *"you are wonderful,"* don't take that too personally either. They too are not saying that because of you but based on their view of life.

You should just do what you do & see opinions from others that come from it as clouds - mere feedback for you to observe based on other people's views of the world.

And if something does hurt you & feel personal, know that this is on you too. Their words were only able to hurt you because you had a bruise within you they got to. Had you not been bruised inside with your own insecurities, their opinions would have washed away, instead of you dwelling on them.

As Don Miguel Ruiz once wrote, *"Don't Take Anything Personally. Nothing others do is because of you. What others say and do is a projection of their own reality, their own dream. When you are immune to the opinions and actions of others, you won't be the victim of needless suffering."*

This is the path of *self-mastery*. And something we are all in a constant process of training - *so don't be too hard on yourself.*

We must learn to recognize that the opinions of others are not personal & not really redirected at us, but based on other people's views of the world (& their current moods.) When you train yourself to think about it in *this* way, you become largely immune to the opinion's, judgments & potential hate of others, freeing yourself to dream as big as you want *(not caring what others will think about it).*

And, to make this practical & start developing the muscle of *'not taking things personally'* whenever someone says or does something you feel is designed to hurt you or tear you down in some way, ask yourself, *'Are they really talking about me here, or is this their own 'stuff' they're going through & I'm just a close-by target easy to hit right now?' Is it my goals they are doubting & suppressing, or are they doing this because of their beliefs & interpretations of the world?'*

Train yourself in thinking about the world in this way as when you do (& you take nothing personally) nobody will be able to stop your fire from blazing anymore; that's how you create the life that you freely choose for yourself.

And the 2nd reason people can say things to undermine the ambitions you set for yourself is for personal self-interest.

See, if you follow through & achieve something greater, it unconsciously challenges those around you *(family, friends, co-workers, etc)* to do the same.

If you get into better shape, for example, your friend feels compelled to do the same (hey, we're a social species). They think, *'She did it; I should get into better shape myself.'*

If you're surrounded by people who always want to grow & get better, this is great. However, if you're surrounded by people who don't want to change, your new goal is, subconsciously, seen as a threat to their current way of living.

At which point, they can either change with you, or they may unconsciously undermine your ambitions, secretly hoping you fail, don't change & stay the same, so they can rationalize to themselves, *'He's in bad shape too, so I don't have to change.'*

Like the crabs, it's much easier for pull others down - by causing doubt, criticism & cynicism - than it is for people to step up & change with you (even if they are your best friends or even family). *It's not their fault though; it's just certain 'beliefs' they are buying into (as you or I perhaps once did.)*

And therefore a lot of the opinions you hear may be secretly guided by this inner-conflict. They want the best for you but don't want you to fly too high as then if they don't do the same, they'll look bad. You may even get very mixed messages from some of the people who care about you the most because of this. One moment, they'll encourage you to dream big. The next, to give up in the face of challenges. Their opinions are silently tainted by this... *(even if they - or you - don't see it.)*

Once again, by knowing this, you can better interpret the *opinions of others* & become immune to the criticism, hate or 'dream suppression' you may encounter on your journey.

Lastly, the 3rd reason people can sometimes advise you to play smaller than you're capable of, is because...

| People Base Their View Of Possibility On Their Own Life Experience

A millionaire won't ever tell you that becoming a millionaire is 'impossible,' yet someone who has struggled financially their entire life will likely do so.

Why? It's because people base their view of what's possible on their own subjective experience of life.

Because 'in their experience of reality,' making (& keeping) money is hard - they assume this is the truth. It is not. It is merely *their* opinion, based on *their* 'beliefs' about the world.

As Arthur Schopenhauer once said, *"Every person takes the limits of their own field of vision for the limits of the world."*

So when people tell you to aim lower, to play smaller, be realistic or to get your head out of the clouds, it's not that what you're aiming for is too lofty, but that, in their personal experience of life (the limits of their 'beliefs' about the world), it's seems as unreasonable. They can't see themselves playing that big a game so they project this onto you. It's not impossible - it just is to them (hence the opinion they share.)

Without knowing this, may accept this *opinion* & lower your financial targets (or any other ambitions you have) as a result. *Don't!* See the opinion as what it is: *1 person's opinion* (which is subjectively based on their view of reality, not on what's true or possible for you).

Let's go back to the foundation visual for a moment...

Not only do we filter *information* & form *interpretations* based on *'who we are,'* but so do those around you. *We all do.*

What this means is when people say anything to you, what you're getting is less likely to be the actual source of the information, but rather their subjective interpretation of it.

So, if you tell someone, *"I'm going to get into great shape this year - that's my goal,"* & they reply with, *"Don't bother. You'll just fall back into unhealthy habits. Trust me, I know this..."* what they are saying is that *they* don't feel like *they* could achieve this goal *(based on their interpretations & 'beliefs')* & not that you can't do it.

They are filtering the information they are receiving through their own prism of personal experience - *'who they are.'*

Again, people assume their limits for the limits of others, when in actuality, they are not. They are merely sharing their interpretation of a given ambition or situation - *that's what an opinion is.* It doesn't mean it's true or false - it just *'is.'*

As you read this chapter, you may have thought to yourself that people are evil, secretly against you or conspiring for you to fail. This is also a harmful & unsupportive interpretation.

In fact, the people who are going to tell you to aim lower, player smaller & play safe the most will usually be those closest to you; those who care about you the most - your significant other, parents, family, friends, co-workers, etc.

They are the ones most likely to tell you to 'be realistic,' or to 'get your head out of the clouds.' And, this is not because they don't care about you, but because they do. As counterintuitive as it initially seems, these are actually signs of love.

Ask them why they do it & they'll tell you they're attempting to 'help you.' To keep you safe. To stop you from getting hurt. That's why they do it & they believe that so it's real to them.

The problem, once again, is they're giving you advice, *'don't dream too big,' 'be realistic,'* or *'lower your expectations,'* based on their own views (& beliefs) about the world.

Remember: like anyone else on this planet, they're merely acting on their conscious & unconscious programming of how the world works. Which means unless they've achieved that goal you set for yourself themselves (or know someone who has), they may consider it 'impossible' (or 'very improbable') & are therefore going to advise you to think the same way.

If they don't have 6-pack abs, they may view this goal as 'impossible,' or the journey getting there as 'not worthwhile,' hence advising you to aim smaller, to spend less time in the gym & just be comfortable with what you have.

So when you hear your grandad, for example, telling you to be realistic and settle for a 'good, stable job' instead of to pursue your dream of starting your own business, don't get mad at him. *Rather, understand. Empathize even.* It's not his fault; he doesn't know he's merely projecting his limits onto you. He just thinks he's saving you from potential pain & hardship.

Understand that & thank him for his opinion, however, interpret the information wisely. It's just his opinion (based on his limits). It equally has nothing to do with you. It's not personal. *You go do your thing; creating the life you want!*

5. **Fear Of Failure:** 'Failure' Is Viewed As A Negative Thing That Should Be Avoided, Not Embraced.

'Don't get into a relationship as you could get hurt...' 'Don't start a business as it might fail...' 'Don't aim for anything higher as you may struggle.' 'You could get hurt, lose or fail.'

You may have heard one (or many) of these as you're walked through this journey we call life; either as thoughts inside your own head or the *opinions of others.*

It's this thinking that forms the 5th big reason why we tend to dream (& play) small in life; the well-known *'fear of failure.'*

People settle for dreaming small & pursuing small ambitions over bigger ones because they fear that doing something big in their lives may lead to failure.

Sometimes they stop setting goals or dreaming all together because of this fear - which makes the attainment of anything great very, very unlikely.

If you lower your ambitions because of a *fear of failure*, you're likely to be heading down a path to mediocrity, unfulfilled potential, untapped possibility & ultimately, regret.

And this is another 'belief' society conditions us into: *to avoid failure at all costs*. And this programming starts young...

'Don't go there,' 'Don't touch that,' 'Don't do that, you might get hurt,' 'That's dangerous,' 'You could get hurt - stop that.'

Those are just some of the phrases a parent, or teacher, may use frequently to tell a child to *not* do something. Some are justified, others not. Yet, through repetition, it's conditioned into us that it's safer to be scared. To not do things. To not test anything unknown. To fear the unfamiliar. Think about it...

'Don't talk to strangers.' 'Don't tell people how you really feel about them or they may reject you.' 'Don't speak out.' 'Don't aim too high or people will despise you.' 'Don't stand out.'

And yes, fears of rejection, abandonment, change & being judged all link to a *fear of failure* in some way.

Is it any wonder we fear ever doing anything uncomfortable (raising our ambitions) when we are not just biologically primed to move away from change (homeostasis), but this is then amplified by a lifetime of programming that we should avoid failure at all costs & just play safe in life?

However, while society conditions us to avoid failure, highly successful people view failure very differently. They see value in it & interpret it very differently.

Or in other words, they've developed very different 'beliefs,' about failure, as part of their identity, which enable them to get very different results. **Best part:** *you can do the same!*

Imagine it: *If you stopped fearing failure, how much higher you would aim, how many more opportunities would you seize, how much more action would you take & how much fuller a life you would live? What would be possible for you?*

AN OPTIMAL VIEW ON 'FAILURE'

In the famous Nike commercial, 'Failure,' basketball legend, Michael Jordan, said the following words:

> *"I missed more than 9000 shots in my career, I've lost almost 300 games, 26 times I've been trusted to take the game-winning shot, and missed. I've failed over and over again in my life, and that is why I succeed"*

Michael did not say that he succeeded *despite* his failures, but *because* of them. He didn't say that he became, arguably, the best basketball player of all time because he didn't fail as much as those around him, but because he failed *much more*.

He failed & persisted when others didn't. His failures didn't weaken him, but rather, gave him strength. In his words, they were the very reason he became the best.

He didn't fear failure. He didn't hate it or dispose of it. He didn't attempt to avoid it, looking for ways to fail less. Rather, he recognized failure was what made his success; his day-in, day-out willingness to test, to take risks, to fail, learn, change, tweak & improve brought him greatness. He understood...

| Failures Are Stepping Stones To Success

Thomas Edison didn't create the filament for the light bulb that gave the world the first, lasting source of light on his 1st, 5th or 12th attempt. No - he failed a reported 10,000 times.

10,000 times he must have thought *'this one was going to be the one; it'll work this time,'* but it didn't. Yet, once again, he viewed failure differently than most.

If a person asked him whether he was discouraged because so many attempts proved unsuccessful, he would reportedly say, *"No, I am not discouraged, because every wrong attempt discarded is another step forward."* Or as he once famously put it, *"I have not failed. I've just found 10,000 ways that won't work."*

He viewed failure optimally, seeing each failed attempt as one that was bringing him closer to what he ultimately wanted. Because of this, his failures didn't embarrass him, create doubt in his mind or make him want to quit, but rather assured him that he was getting closer.

Just as many marketing & sales trainers would say: *'every NO brings you closer to a YES,'* in his case, every failed attempt moved him towards a successful invention. *And that's exactly how he viewed his so-called 'failures.'*

What many people don't know is that Thomas Edison also went through a lot of failures as a kid. Growing up, he struggled with learning. So much so that his teachers said he was *"too stupid to learn anything."* Then, he was fired from his first 2 jobs for being *'unproductive.'*

And my favorite example which illustrates Thomas Edison's incredible ability to react to failure optimally comes from later in his life, when he seemed to lose everything, only to recover stronger & better than ever before...

It was 1914 & 10 buildings in Thomas Edison's plant - more than half of the entire site - were engulfed in flames, quickly burning down. The fire was too powerful to be put out.

Edison lost an estimated $919,788 (or, more than $23 million in today's dollars) in that single afternoon. The flames had consumed years of priceless records & prototypes, while his insurance covered only about a third of the total damage.

In a 1961 Reader's Digest article by Edison's son, Charles, Thomas Edison calmly walked over to him as he watched the fire destroy his dad's work. Edison told his son, *"Go get your mother and all her friends. They'll never see a fire like this again."* When Charles objected, Thomas Edison replied, *"It's all right. We've just got rid of a lot of rubbish."*

Later, at the scene of the blaze, Edison was quoted in The New York Times saying, *"Although I am over 67 years old, I'll start all over again tomorrow."* He stuck to his word & immediately began rebuilding the next morning without firing any of his existing employees.

After just 3 weeks, with a loan from his friend Henry Ford, Thomas Edison got part of the plant back up & running again. Edison and his team went on to make almost $10 million in revenue the following year.

How easy would it have been for Thomas Edison to just quit, or at least lower his ambitions? He had already accomplished a lot. He was already 67 years of age. *Yet, he didn't do that...*

If anything, this failure just made him stronger. As did his teacher telling him he was *"too stupid to learn anything,"* & each one of the 10,000 failed attempts at the light bulb.

And this was not because he was lucky, but because of *'who he was.'* Specifically, it was his *'beliefs'* about failure *(as part of his identity)* which allowed him to achieve extraordinary things when others would have quit. He saw things differently because of *'who he was.'*

And had he given up during any one of those failures - his teacher's comments, getting fired twice, the factory burning down, 10,000 unsuccessful attempts - he wouldn't have had the positive legacy he holds in the world today. He wouldn't have helped move humanity forward. People wouldn't have remembered him for the legacy he left. They wouldn't still be talking to him today. And he wouldn't have been written about as an example of reacting to failure optimally here.

And these aren't just one-off examples of successful people reacting to failure in weirdly-optimistic & determined ways.

Sigmund Freud, for example, was actually booed from the podium when he first presented his ideas to the scientific community of Europe. He returned to his office & kept working. Not quitting. Not lowering his ambitions. Today, he's referred to as the 'father of psychoanalysis,' (because he primarily invented it) & his work forms a lot of what we know about psychology & the unconscious mind.

Albert Einstein didn't learn to speak until he was 4. He didn't read until he was 7. Growing up, one of his teachers described him as *"mentally slow, unsociable, & adrift forever in foolish dreams."* He was expelled from school & was later refused admittance to the Zurich Polytechnic School. His childhood was packed with failure - especially, learning difficulties. He pushed through it though. And went on to question & change how we view the universe we live in.

Winston Churchill had to repeat a grade during elementary school. And, when he entered Harrow, was placed in the lowest division of the lowest class. Later, he twice failed the entrance exam to the Royal Military Academy at Sandhurst. He was defeated in his first effort to serve in Parliament. Failure after failure, but he didn't give up. He became Prime Minister at the age of 62 & led Britain through World War 2.

He later said: *"Never give in. Never give in. Never, never, never, never — in nothing, great or small, large or petty — never give in, except to convictions of honor and good sense."*

Or as Confucius once said, *"Our greatest glory is not in never falling but in rising every time we fall."*

These incredible individuals - whether that's Michael Jordan, Thomas Edison, Sigmund Freud, Albert Einstein, Winston Churchill, or others - viewed failure differently. Or more accurately, they *filtered* incoming *information* differently than others to form different *interpretations* about failure.

When these events, situations & circumstances showed up in the lives of these people - 'failures' - because of *'who they were'* they interpreted it differently & acted accordingly.

They interpreted their failures, not as signs they should give up, quit or aim lower (as many people do) but as signs that they're on the right path & should keep at it.

Michael Jordan saw each failure as learning & training that made him a better basketball player. Thomas Edison, based on this *'beliefs'* interpreted each failed attempt at the light bulb, not as a sign to give up, but as a failed experiment that'll make the next one better - with time leading him to a breakthrough invention (which it did). Sigmund Freud didn't interpret the audience's rejection as a sign that he's a failure & should give up on his research, but as a sign to keep going.

At the end of the day, failure is neither good or bad, but our interpretation makes it so...

You can use failure to get stronger, to become better, to dream bigger & become the best you can possibly become. Or you could use it as an excuse to give up & quit. *The choice of interpretation, once again, is yours...*

And, in the examples of the great people in this chapter, it was their interpretations of failures *(based on 'who they were')* that lead to new thinking & feeling, different actions & better results. They interpreted their failures differently than most & created different results. *Can you see how it comes together?*

Just imagine if Thomas Edison quit after 100, or 1000, or 5000 failed attempt at successfully completing the light bulb? What if Sigmund Freud quit when he got booed off stage when first presenting his ideas? What if Albert Einstein gave up when the teacher told him he was "mentally slow?"

Or - thinking bigger - what if everybody (now or throughout history) just quit whenever they failed the first time at anything? How different would the world be today?

How many amazing things <u>wouldn't</u> have been invented, created or achieved? How much less accomplished would humanity be?

If there's anything to fear, it's not failure, but a reality in which people quit whenever they fail at anything.

We mustn't let failure (or the fear of failure in the future) derail us from the pursuit of what's important & meaningful to us, as failure is less often a sign to quit & more often a sign to keep going.

Or, as *Sacha Baron Cohen's*, comedic character, *Ali G*, put it:

"If video games have taught me anything, it's that if you encounter enemies then you're going the right way."

When you encounter hardship or failure ('enemies,' of sorts - either internally or externally) remember that these are rarely signs telling you to quit, but more often signs telling you to stay at it as you're on the right path. That you're breaking out of your comfort zone, striving, growing, stretching yourself, testing new things & becoming a better version of yourself. *Or opportunities to reflect, learn & get better moving forward...*

As Henry Ford (who went broke a reported 5 times before succeeding financially & changing the way we travel) once said: *"Failure is simply the opportunity to begin again, this time more intelligently."*

This is important to keep in mind as failure won't just appear once or twice in the pursuit of a big dream, but many times....

For example, the classic, *The Wonderful Wizard of Oz* was rejected by publishers so many times that the author, L. Frank Baum, actually kept a journal called, *'A Record of Failure.'* In it, he stored all the rejection letters he received.

Today, of course, *The Wonderful Wizard of Oz* isn't just a best-selling book, but one of the best-known American stories of all time, translated into multiple languages, and turn into films & musicals worldwide.

Stephen King's novel, *'Carrie'* (which was a huge turning point in his career) was rejected 30 times by publishers before finally getting published. Today, Stephen King's books have sold upwards of 350 million copies worldwide.

The worldwide phenomenon, *Chicken Soup for the Soul*, was rejected by 144 publishers before finally getting published. Today, that book has turned into a series of books, which have been translated into 43 languages, published in over 100 countries & have sold 500+ million copies worldwide.

Life of Pi. Moby Dick. Dune. Harry Potter and the Sorcerer's Stone Twilight. Just are just a few more examples of famous books that were rejected by publishers many, many times before finally getting published.

Meanwhile, in the movie business, hit movies such as *Back To The Future, Star Wars, Dumb & Dumber, Pulp Fiction & E.T*, where rejected by studios & considered 'failed screenplays,' for a variety of reasons before studios finally made them.

Imagine if these authors, screenwriters & creators gave up on their ideas when confronted with rejection & failure?

The first key realization - as demonstrated here - is that:

| Failure Is Unavoidable

If you want to achieve success (of any kind) *failure* is an ingredient that's baked right in; part of the process. So you might as well dream big anyway & find value in your failures.

Every successful people has failed countless times & the only people who don't fail are those who never do anything. Author & billionaire businesswoman, *J.K. Rowling* put it best:

"It is impossible to live without failing at something unless you live so cautiously that you might as well not have lived at all – in which case, you fail by default."

Everybody fails. The sooner we realize this & individually, socially & ideally culturally eliminate any shame, doubt or embarrassment associated with failing - failing in school, in a relationship, financially, in your health, on a big project you're working on, anywhere - the more we can create & achieve.

So often we attempt to hide our failures from the world. We don't want anyone to see our hardships. The challenge is that in doing so, we cut off support, advice & guidance. We become less open to receiving support as we fill with shame inside.

Plus, when we move away from transparency & get immersed in hiding or covering up our failures, we get stuck. Our energy becomes so drained in hiding the past that we have no energy left to create a better future *(as we touched on in chapter #1).*

This is the reason why the 1st step in the well-known 12 steps to overcoming alcoholism that millions have used to get sober, is *acceptance*. Accepting that you have a problem. Admitting your failure; that you 'failed,' in the past & are now open to change. Often, openly sharing it. Seeing the problem as it is - not ignoring it or seeing it worse than it is - is that critical first step. That's when you become ready to change & can start making progress instead of spinning your wheels.

Failure is a part of life & the only people that don't fail are people who live life so timidly, fearing failure, that they end up failing in the big picture of life (filled with regret later on.)

And, once we understand it's part of the process of success, we might as well learn how to use failure to our advantage...

| Each Failure Is An Opportunity To Reflect, Learn & Get Better

A great example of this is shared by Matthew Syed in this book, *Bounce: The Myth of Talent & The Power of Practice.*

In the book, he shares a study conducted back in the 1990s in the sport of figure skating.

They found that the biggest difference between elite skaters & their less skilled counterparts was simply how frequently they fell over (failed) in training. They found: *elite skaters fell over far more often during their training sessions than the others.*

Once again: we are taught those who succeed are those who fail less. That you're either a failure or a success. Yet, this thinking doesn't hold up. Far from it.

Just like Michael Jordan, elite figure-skaters in this study or many of the most persistent authors, screenwriters & business individuals, it's those who *out-fail* others who *out-achieve* others. Or, in other words…

| People Succeed Not Because They Fail *Less*, But Because They Fail *More*

Failure should not just be accepted, but actually encouraged. We shouldn't stop our friends, our family, co-workers, children, students & those around us from failing, but actually encourage them to test, experiment, aim high & yes, fail, as much as they can, as doing will so leads to learning & growth.

To help you really get this, think about any time you've ever learned anything. It can be when you learned the alphabet, spelling or mathematics growing up. Or how to ride a bike, play an instrument, speak a new language or anything else.

Now, think back to how you actually learned that. Chances are, first, you acquired new information. You were told, read or heard something new. You gained awareness of something you didn't previously know.

Then, to memorize this information or develop this skill, you probably did it over & over again. Sometimes you did it well &

sometimes you made mistakes (you failed), self-corrected & with time, made those mistakes less & less, until you got good at it. That's how we learn; through information, repetition, failure, self-correction & an ongoing desire to improve.

Knowing this, we can also recognize that in our lives, we've already failure hundreds, thousands & maybe even hundreds of hundreds of times so far...

We said the alphabet wrong many, many times before learning to say it correctly. We spelled words wrong hundreds of times in our lives before learning to spell them well. We fell from our bikes or lost control while on skateboards, skis or snowboards. We felt like we were drowning many times while learning to swim. The list goes on & on. Over & over again, we failed in our lives & then used it to learn & improve. *Realize this & you find great strength for future failures you'll face...*

Plus, when we realize all this & live it in our lives - that each & failure is nothing more than an opportunity to learn, get better & keep going - not only do we achieve more, but we actually enjoy the journey much more as well.

This is because I've found much of the misery we, human beings, experience comes from our interpretations of failed attempts in our lives. We think failure is bad & should be met with disappointment, shame or embarrassment. Interpret this information differently (based on the principles here), find meaning in each failure & you'll begin to love the process too.

Also, built on these understandings, we shouldn't be looking to mask failure - which in my experience, is what a lot of society now does (especially with parenting & education)...

Schools & parents give students work that's easy instead of challenging, just so they 'don't fail.' And when children do fail, it's masked with a 9th place participation trophy, for example.

So, instead of diving into this pain & using it to build strength & resilience, the child gets nothing. No learning. No growth.

Plus, that's not how the world works. It's an unrealistic environment that doesn't prepare children for the real world, as in reality, there are no 9th place participation trophies. *If you underperform, you get fired, not rewarded.*

Even though the children may cry & get disappointed, this is an important part of growth. In fact, it's in those moments of emotion & pain that we often make the biggest decisions in our lives. We decide to step up. To grow. To get better. And then we work hard to avoid that pain & create new results (which we do want) instead going forward.

Failures are important to shaping our character & so children should be taught *how to deal with failure*, not have it masked for them (like a painkiller).

Raise a child to love failure, to see value in it, to reflect, learn from it, to deal with it optimally & you've done one of the best things you can ever do for their success & happiness in life.

This is how we set up the youth (& ourselves) for a great existence of endless potential. We learn to interpret failure differently. First, for ourselves. Then pass this along to others; culturally making this shift. But, it starts with you, reading this book. Reading these very words...

When failure comes knocking on your door - & it will - how will you answer? Will you give up, or will you keep going?

When a client rejects your proposal, a publisher rejects your book, someone calls you "stupid," your next product launch flops, your service fails, your opponent beats you or you don't qualify for the tournament, remember that each of these failures has learning to them that you just need to uncover.

Chances are, you only failed because there was something you didn't know or something you didn't do incorrectly which caused you to fail to begin with. Learn that, then repeat what you did & you'll get better results next time.

And when you truly get & live all these new understandings about failure - when you truly own that failure is not fighting against you, but actually helping you on your path to success - one of the best ways to achieve anything faster becomes...

| Fail Fast & Fail Often

As Thomas Watson Sr. once said: *"The fastest way to succeed is to double your failure rate."*

Don't just fail once in a while, but fail often. Fail fast. Do more, test more & experiment more; live this way. Sure, as you do more, you'll fail more, but you'll also learn more, get better & achieve anything faster.

You'll mathematically skew your odds of hitting upon a great breakthrough, discovering something amazing & achieving something big in your favor.

In Silicon Valley, for example, this is becoming part of the culture. Startups build failure into their systems. They launch a new feature, product or service with the assumption that it's going to fail. Failure is the expectation. So is learning, tweaking & improving - fast.

From day 1, they are looking for failure (whether that's a glitch, user experience problem, layout issue, etc) that they can fix, solve, improve & optimize. They're looking to *fail fast*.

The idea of a *'minimum viable product'* & a *'lean startup'* (as explained by Eric Ries in his book, *The Lean Startup*) comes from this. Failing small. Failing fast. Learning quick. Being agile & adjusting. Improving. Innovating. Tweaking. Testing. Fast. Creating success by accepting (& learning from) failure.

And it's this methodology that, at the core, lead many of those crazy Silicon Valley startups to go from nothing to million & billion dollar valuations in what seems like no time at all.

At the core, it's their attitude towards failure, learning & growth that turns what seems 'impossible,' into success.

Like a great scientist, we shouldn't get disheartened or disappointed when we fail. Failure is just data - insight into what you're doing well or not so well...

Check that data. Examine it. Ask yourself, *'What created this failure?' 'What could I do better?'* or *'What worked & what didn't?'* Then, onto the next experiment...

You fail, learn from it & move on. Look at it this way - use these *beliefs* to form interpretations when you fail - & failure doesn't sting, but educates.

As Richard Branson once said: *"The best lessons are learned from failure. You mustn't beat yourself up if you fail – just pick yourself up, learn as much as you can from the experience and get on with the next challenge."*

Or in Winston Churchill's wise words: *"Success is stumbling from failure to failure without loss of enthusiasm."*

Nothing more; nothing less. If you go from failure to failure without loss of enthusiasm, with time, success will be yours.

As Johnny Cash once put it: *"You build on failure. You use it as a stepping stone. Close the door on the past. You don't try to forget the mistakes, but you don't dwell on it. You don't let it have any of your energy, or any of your time, or any of your space."*

And as Robert F. Kennedy once said: *"Only those who dare to fail greatly can ever achieve greatly."*

We mustn't be scared of failure & we mustn't fear to dare greatly, falling flat on our faces sometimes & failing big, as that's what will help you not just dream big, but achieve big.

Simply put: we must build up our tolerance, get mentally strong, emotionally unlimited & go after what we truly what; to face any 'fear or failure' face on, remind ourselves that we are strong, that we can handle it & then dream (& play) big.

You may have realized that this part of the book has the most quotes within it. This is because I really want to you get this. To not just understand it at a surface level, but really see how integrating these new beliefs about failure into 'who you are,' can change your life.

And with that, here are just a few more great quotes from great people on how they view failure:

"It's fine to celebrate success but it is more important to heed the lessons of failure." - Bill Gates

"Without failure, there is no achievement." - John C. Maxwell

"You have to be able to accept failure to get better." - LeBron James

"Success is never final, failure is never fatal. It's courage that counts." - John Wooden

"Little minds are tamed and subdued by misfortune, but great minds rise above them." - Washington Irving

"Ever tried, ever failed. No matter. Try again, fail again. Fail better" – Samuel Beckett

Can you see the pattern here yet?

Every one of these quotes here is from a highly successful individual - across dozens of different fields - from business to sport, from science to psychology, from politics to film. And they all view failure in a similar way - which is the opposite of how society tells us to view it. That's the pattern.

In fact, you could probably fill an entire book with quotes of highly successful people talking about the power, value & importance of failing, dealing with challenges & seeing struggle as strength.

What all this means is simple: those who achieve great things in their lives view failure differently than the way that society has conditioned us to see it.

They view it as a stepping stone to where they want to go, looking to learn from it, growing, pivoting, adjust their course & moving forward no matter what the struggle ahead is.

Best part: you can shift your *belief* & view 'failure' in this way too. It's a choice; one you can make right now.

Do not let a 'fear of failure' stop you from dreaming big & pursuing those lofty ambition any longer. Failure will be part of the journey - no doubt - but shouldn't stop you. Rather, you should learn to love, value & cherish failure in your life.

So if anyone tells you (or you think to yourself) you should aim lower as you 'might fail,' reply like this...

"You're right, I might fail. In fact, I might fail dozens, hundreds or even thousands of times along the way. But, I'll learn from my failures. I'll use them as fuel to get better. I'll enjoy them. Embrace them. Utilize them. Plus, it will be worth it in the end, because failing over & over, before going on to achieve my ultimate ambitions will bring me a heck of a lot more growth, happiness & fulfillment than merely settling, being 'realistic' & playing small. And happiness & fulfillment is what we're all really after, don't you think?"

See, how you view failure is a part of the *'beliefs'* that form *'who you are,'* & therefore influence how you view events, situations & circumstances that come into your life.

And you already have certain *'beliefs'* about failure that are part of the present you. What I'm challenging you to do here is merely to put those existing 'beliefs' under the microscope & if you find any of these 'beliefs' shared in this chapter (*e.g. 'failure is a stepping stone to success,' 'failure is beneficial,' 'everybody fails, no need for shame, guilt or embarrassment here,' 'I should learn from my failures,' etc*) as better options, then integrate them into 'who you are.' *(don't worry: we'll talk about how to do this in chapter #7 of this book!)*

Lastly, when you do experience failure, feel free to come back & re-read this chapter. Or, even before you experience your next failure, prepare yourself to respond effectively, by re-reading this many times over.

For example, there are some books, articles or videos I've gone through dozens of times. This is because *'repetition'* is a great tool to condition yourself into new ways of being. And you can do the same here with this (or any other) chapter.

The more you can repeat this information about the failure, the more these positive, optimal *beliefs* about failure will become part of your 'identity.' Which will ensure you interpret incoming information differently & get better results.

Ultimately, this is how you become unstoppable...

Failure or success; it doesn't matter as either way it's a good thing for you...

Failure is learning that leads to success & success is what you aimed for all along. All upside - no downside.

Embrace this & you'll find great strength.

YOUR POTENTIAL HAS BEEN TAMED TOO LONG!

Let me tell you about how baby elephants are tamed & you tell me if you can spot any similarities between this & how human beings are conditioned to think & dream small...

They take elephants while they are still <u>baby</u> elephants (small) & they tie a chain around their necks (or ankles).

They attach this chain to a nearby pole so that when the baby elephant attempts to walk away, the chain stops them.

The baby elephants pull, push & twist attempting to get away, but each time they are held back by the chain. They realize that they aren't strong enough to break free, so they stop resisting & just stand there.

The next time they tie up the baby elephants, again, they attempt to break free. And again, they fail to do so.

This happens a number of times until, at a certain point, the elephants no longer even attempt to break away figuring that it won't work anyway. *They stop resisting & accept their faith.* At which point the chain is often replaced with a small rope.

Even as the elephants grow up, get much bigger & stronger (at which point, they could break free of the chain or rope with total ease), they don't. They don't even attempt to.

That's why, when you walk past a circus, for example, you can see big adult elephants standing passively with a small rope tied around their necks. The adult elephants don't even fight it despite the fact they are now big, strong, grown-up, adult elephants easily capable of break free of the rope.

Sometimes the rope isn't even attached to anything. Merely having the rope around the elephant's neck is enough of a symbol to keep the elephant under control.

We may look at this & consider the elephants 'stupid.' *Why would they give up like that? Once they grow up & are now so much bigger, why don't they attempt to break free again?*

When it's presented objectively like this, it's easy to see that if the elephants just persisted instead of being blocked by their *'mental barriers,'* they could easily regain their freedom.

However, we fail to realize that we - human beings - operate a lot like this as well in our lives.

The 5 reasons we covered here work together & tame us, domesticate our potential & take away our freedom to pursue the big things we're truly capable of - especially when we are still young & learning the ways of the world.

We get told to dream smaller. To settle. To be realistic. That the world is hard & achieving what we want isn't possible. That we should play small because failure is something that should be avoided at all costs.

Before long, we're just like those adult elephants, all grown up, skilled, educated, smart, powerful, yet still being held back from dreaming big & tapping into the infinite possibilities that exist for us. *Not because of we 'can't' but because we simply remain mentally caged by our past & mental limits.*

We don't recognize that the problems which held us back in the past probably don't today *(especially with all the new knowledge, skills & experience we may now have).* Yet we still don't tackle those challenges as we've been conditioned to believe that they're too big for us to handle *(they're not!)*

We grow. We get better. Yet, we are still stuck & reluctant to think bigger because we were conditioned in the past - just like the baby elephants were.

It's the combination of these 5 reasons that slowly lowers our ambitions. It's like quicksand; slowly drag us down to the point that we struggle to even believe that we are capable of achieving anything great than what we have right now.

These reasons become a lifelong doctrine of *'thinking small,'* *'playing small,'* *'being realistic,'* & *'settling for mediocrity'* instead of pursuing what we really want to achieve.

Remember: it doesn't happen overnight, but over many years.

In fact, you may have heard the saying, *'like a chicken in water. The water temperature rises so gradually, that the chicken doesn't know it's boiling until it's too late.'* Well - it's a little bit like that.

So much so that if you ask many people why they think small or consider big ambitions outside their reach, they'll often tell you it's just 'who they are,' 'who they've always been,' how they were born or how the world works. *They've forgotten about their potential, but it's still there...* (it's *not* too late!)

And with that, let me ask you this simple question:

If we can get conditioned to dream small, is it at all possible we too can be conditioned (to train ourselves) to dream big?

Absolutely - the good news is that *conditioning* (or, *training*) works both ways. You can change your *identity* to be one way or another. You can train yourself to dream bigger or to dream smaller. And it starts with a choice, followed by new thinking & feeling new actions & as a result, a new 'you'...

WHY NOT DREAM A LITTLE BIGGER?

'Why?' 'Why would I bother?' 'Why would I push myself?' 'Why would I aim higher when I'm good where I am?'

That's how most people response (or at least start to think to themselves) when a new possibility appears in their life. Their first, automatic response is *'Why would I bother?'*

Instead, to raise your ambitions & start moving beyond these 5 big reasons that keep people playing small, start asking the opposite. Ask yourself what personal development legend, Jim Rohn, used to say: **why not?** *(this question is gold!)*

<u>Why not</u> dream a little bigger? <u>Why not</u> see how good you can get? <u>Why not</u> see how many countries you can visit? Beautiful things you can see through your own eyes?

<u>Why not</u> see how many truly breathtaking experiences you can have in your life? **Why not?**

Why not see how many books you can read? Things you can learn? How knowledgeable you can become? How skilled? How extraordinarily masterful you can get? **Why not?**

Why not see how amazing a relationship you can create with the person you love? With the friends, family members & people you meet? Why not see if you can put a dent in the universe? Change the world for the better? **Why not?**

Not 'why?' but '<u>why not?</u>' **You can, so why not?**

You have plenty of time in your life, so <u>why not</u>?

You can make your life a masterpiece if you want to, choose to & commit to, so why not? You can fill each day with meaning, bliss, gratitude, appreciation & awe, so why not?

While others may look at the same possibility or opportunity & say 'why would I do that when I don't need to?' you ask, 'why not? It's there. You have time. You can. So why not?

Time is going to pass by anyway. You can't spend your life just laying on the couch all day (nor do you probably want to), so why not get up & do something magnificent that you'll look back on with pride, joy & gratitude? **Hey - <u>why not</u>?**

AMBITION | 235

By asking this you start to condition yourself to say 'yes' to great opportunities that you would otherwise have said 'no' to & you begin to tap into new possibilities & create a new life.

So, catch yourself when you find yourself buying into any of these 5 reasons that keep us playing small & start asking 'why not?' to train yourself to play bigger in life.

See, we are far more powerful than we think. We can do more, be more & achieve more than we realize. Not overnight, but with time, everything can change *(if we choose to improve it)*.

Remember: there are infinite possibilities co-existing for your future & it's through your thoughts, feelings, decisions & actions that you're selecting which ones become your reality.

> **EXERCISE: CAN YOU PLAY A BIGGER GAME?**
> Towards the end of the last chapter, there was an exercise designed to get you to think about *clarity* & the direction you want to take in your life in; what you value & truly want.
>
> This exercise, like that one, is a chance for you to stop, to pause, to reflect & think about your ambitions from the point of view of: *how can I play a bigger game?*
>
> You now know the 5 big reasons why we often lower our ambitions in life & you also know that you can condition yourself to play bigger (if you choose!)
>
> Just as you could become physically flexible by stretching your body, you train yourself to dream bigger, by stretching your ambitions & your belief of what's truly possible for you.
>
> So, take another 30 minutes now & explore why you've only aimed so high in the past, which areas you want to play a bigger game in & what specific ambitions you can set for yourself going forward.

Remember: reading is not enough; implementation is key.

First, big picture: *Do you believe, deep down, that there is more you can do, achieve & become in life? Do you want something more in life?* **Key:** Find that voice & listen to it.

Which areas of your life have you lowered your ambitions & played below your true capabilities? And which area of your life are you ready to truly step up in?

Look back at the ambitions & goals you set for yourself & ask yourself: *How can I play bigger here? Is more possible?*

Look back over this chapter - read it over & over if you want - to remind yourself your life is filled with possibilities great than what you may be aware of right now.

See, the more time you spend in this reflection, the more likely you are to truly embody the content in this chapter & start setting bigger ambitions for your life.

Although, once again, it's not about materialism ambitions, but all of them. For example: *is there a bigger, higher level of joy, peace, happiness, connection, love, awe & freedom you can experience?*

Now, let's zoom in: *What is 1 area of your life that you've really been settling & dreaming small in that you can start to really dream big in from now on?*

And what's a big ambition - one that might even scare you a little - that you can pursue in this area of your life?

Start with 1 area of life if that's best for you & then continue to expand from there...

Height of ambition - like *clarity* - is also something you can develop & cultivate by immersing yourself in possibility, stretching yourself & asking *'is there more?'* or *'why not?'*

Take time to complete this exercise now.

In the next section, *'Psychology,'* we talk about 'who you are,' & how to *align* that identity with your ambitions. We talk about beliefs as well as actionable guidance you can use to uninstall limiting beliefs & install empowering ones *(at will)*.

The next section builds on what you learned so far giving you the next pieces to the puzzle & supporting you in creating the life that you freely choose for yourself. *Let's continue...*

3.
PSYCHOLOGY:
MASTERING MINDSET

"Things do not change; we change"
HENRY DAVID THOREAU

Your mind is a powerful tool that can help you create a magnificent existence - filled with freedom, deep bliss & an endless source of joy. However, it can also bring you to your knees, drown you in misery & keep you enslaved to a life you wish to escape. It can create & it can destroy. It can free & it can imprison. It can be your best friend or your worst enemy. And that all depends on how you choose to 'condition' it...

Fortunately, no matter what you've experienced in the past or where you are today, you can choose to shape your psychology to become your greatest asset from now on - a worthwhile act which enables you to tune into great potential in your life...

6 | WHY YOU ARE 'WHO YOU ARE'
3 CATEGORIES OF CONDITIONING

"If you understand others you are smart.
If you understand yourself you are illuminated.
If you overcome others you are powerful.
If you overcome yourself you have strength."

- *LAO TZU*

I've always found the act of 'people watching' to be a deeply fascinating one. I regularly find myself at airports, coffee shops, hotels, or just out in public, watching people...

Not in a creepy way, but in a curious one...

From the barista serving coffee to the flight attendant serving refreshments. From a family eating a meal at a restaurant to hotel staff checking in a new visitor. I find myself wondering what a person might be thinking, feeling, wanting & 'creating.'

Why are they doing what they are doing, who are they & why are they who they are, to begin with?

Why have they tuned into certain possibilities & not others? What brought them to this moment - right here, right now - as well as what are they likely to create in the future?

This passion of mine started at around age 12... I would read books, listen to material & watch videos on the many of the topics that my work draws insights from today (such as personal development, self help, human psychology, positive psychology, performance psychology, neuroscience, human behavior, amongst others...) & I wouldn't be able to stop...

Time would fly by as I flicked through the pages, went from one video to another or attended event after event with my parents, soaking up this knowledge, these insights & practices I could use to better understand myself...

And my fascination only deepened when it really 'clicked' for me just how powerful the brain really is & the link between one's mindset & success in life. *Much of this research is only getting mainstream traction, gaining popularity, nowadays.*

While this research, at first, was fueled more by curiosity than anything else, it quickly turned into more as I saw the results start to show in tangible & intangible ways...

HOW TO CREATE WHAT YOU WANT IN LIFE...

The previous section of this book, *'Ambition,'* was focused on helping you gain true clarity & alignment in what you're really aiming for. That's the 1st step; *knowing what you want.*

Unless you have that, you may just spend your life spinning your wheels - so busy going 'through the motions' & listening to what you 'should' do in life (the 'rules' of society) never truly creating the life you, deep down, desire for yourself.

However, that's just the start. Once you know what you want, it's about living that in your life; *making it happen!*

And that's where this 2nd step comes in: understanding 'who you are,' why you are 'who you are,' discovering how your old ways of being may sometimes be leading you away from what you want, as well as being able to make powerful changes in your life. *That's what this section,* **'Psychology,'** *is about!*

It's help answer questions you may have been seeking some answers to for years (even decades!) It'll help you understand your 'who you are' - your beliefs, thoughts, feelings, decisions & actions - better, ultimately helping you align your identity with your ambitions to create a magnificent existence...

See, if you want feelings of peace, for example, yet you're the first to admit you're currently a 'stressed out' individual easily annoyed & frustrated by many things in life, you're unlikely to create & sustain that ambition & live you want for yourself.

If you're truly committed to what you know you truly want, you must be willing to change (or better put, 'align') 'who you are' with that ambition. Simply put, as the subtitle suggests:

| To Create The Life You Want You Must Become The Person You Want To Be

Well, how do you do this? By exploring & changing your *'Psychology'* (or, *'mindset'*) - *this section right here...*

Specifically, you would usually start by *understanding* why you are 'who you are' & why you do what you do - which is what *this* chapter is about.

And then - if you choose - the final step is changing certain *beliefs, habits & behaviors* you no longer want. And replacing them better, more effective ones you'd rather embody *(which is what the next & last chapter of this book all about...)*

It all comes together - I assure you. And, it starts by getting to know yourself a little better (at a deeper level). See, while 'know thyself' may not be cutting-edge advice, it's the critical. And with that, I introduce to you the...

3 CATEGORIES OF CONDITIONING

If knowledge gives you power, what does a deep knowledge & understanding of yourself give you? I'd suggest it provides an immense, life-changing & success-shaping inner strength...

And that what this chapter - specifically, this groundbreaking new framework you're about to discover, the **'3 Categories of Conditioning'** - will give you: a deep knowledge of 'you.'

In fact, I'd bet that upon the completion of this chapter, you'll know more about why you are who you are, why you make the decisions you make & do what you do - *you'll know more about yourself* - than you probably learned in 4 years of high school & 4+ years of college *(combined!).*

However, I guess we'll only find out if this is the case for you at the end of this chapter. *So, let's begin...*

3 CATEGORIES OF CONDITIONING

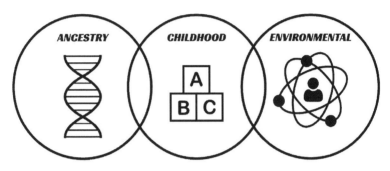

When attempting to understand 'why you are who you are' most people will only touch on 1 of these 3 categories. We're going to touch on all 3 as it's actually a combination of them that has made you 'who you are.' Each has affected your identity *(but perhaps not in the ways that you'd expect...)*

1 | **ANCESTRY:** BIOLOGICAL CONDITIONING

> *"Your genetics load the gun. Your lifestyle pulls the trigger."*
>
> - MEHMET OZ

The first of the 3 core things that shapes 'who we are' (at least at the surface level) is everything that's 'pre-determined' in some way; that which has been passed down to you before birth. *This is the conditioning of biology (or, genetics).*

From the very first moment you showed signs of life, in your mother's womb *(before birth)*, a part of 'you' had formed.

If your parents had certain eye colors, you were more likely to have certain eye color too. If your parents had certain hair colors, you're likely to have a certain hair color as well.

In fact, from the colour of your skin to your height, to your blood type to even your IQ *(estimates place the heritability of IQ between 55% & 77%) - it was all passed along to you by your ancestors (not just parents, but previous generations as well) through your genetics (or, biology.)*

However, I'm sure you know this already; that parts of 'who you are' were pre-determined in this way.

What we're going to explore is the implications of this, as well as where this 'ancestry conditioning' ends. *Is anything else controlled by your genes? And how much? Is your destiny set at birth, or is personal choice a better predictor of success?*

There are 2 big principles you need to really understand (regarding the biological conditioning you received) here to create the life you want. *Firstly...*

THE PRO'S & CON'S OF EVERYTHING (& PLAYING TO YOUR STRENGTHS)

'I'm not pretty enough' 'I'm too short' 'I don't like my nose' 'My eyes are so ugly' 'My body type is awful.' 'I wish I looked a different way... then I would be definitely happy in life.'

Some people spend much of their lives dwelling in the genetic disadvantages they believe that they had received...

In reality, when looking at this more objectively, much of the hate we send to ourselves is unjustified. The disadvantages we perceive are actually only one side of the coin *(& there's a whole 2nd side of huge advantage that you can play too...)*

Like many great thinkers, thought leaders & teachers share (& high achievers would attest to) there are advantages (pro's) & disadvantages (con's) to anything & everything.

Being very tall may give you an advantage in basketball, help you reach high places & look more intimidating in a wrestling ring, but also means you may end up paying more for clothes & shoes, find great hardship in fitting into tight spaces, have to also kneel down in photos & are at a huge disadvantage in sports like gymnastics or horse racing. *Both pro's & con's.*

If you look like a supermodel - beautiful in that way - you may have an advantage on dating sites, can earn money by just standing there, looking pretty & getting photographed (if you choose) & may have more followers on social media, but people may also be less likely to pay attention to your intellect (perhaps completely overlooking your personally too) & you may be less inclined to look inwards & work on your personal growth if you are so beautiful on the outside. Plus: that beauty isn't exactly easy to maintain, so yes, there are downsides.

And, as movies have vividly shown us, we also think the grass is greener on the other side of the fence & that our lives would be so much better if only we were tall instead of short, more beautiful on the outside, were of a different race, yet people who do look exactly like that are ironically wishing they were more like you are. *It's rather paradoxical, but very accurate.*

Ultimately, I've found (& I'm sure you can also recognize too) that there are pro's & con's to everything, so we may as well just accept what we were biologically given & then play to our strengths (maximizing the pro's of what we got).

To not dwell in the disadvantages, but focus on the 'pro's' of the biological aspects of 'who we are.'

Which leads us onto the 2nd principle we must bear in mind...

IS YOUR DESTINY ALREADY SET? (& ARE GENES REALLY AS IMPORTANT AS WE'VE BEEN TOLD?)

'Biological determinism' (or *'genetic determinism'*) is the idea that human behavior (who you are, what you do & what your life ultimately becomes), is controlled exclusively by genetics.

Its an argument is that genetics are the biggest (& perhaps, the only) part that truly matters when it comes to the things we're good at (our abilities), the results we create, as well as the emotional reality that we end up experiencing.

It's this thinking that leads people to have an *'external locus of control'* (as we talked about in chapter 3) feeling that life is happening to them & that they have no control over it.

'I'm not naturally gifted at this…' 'I'm just not this type of person' 'I just wasn't destined for that type of life…'

This is the thinking that arises from the belief that it's our genetics that control our destiny, not our decisions & actions.

And while this view (*biological determinism*) may have been popular back in the day, modern research continues to conclude that, while certain things have an inherent biological link, things such as health, skills, success & happiness aren't strongly linked. *These are the results of choices, not genes.*

The best example of this is identical twins. They are, by definition, identical. *Except, they aren't…*

Biologically, they have the exact same genetic code, but in reality, they're very different people with different 'identities.'

While they look the same (genes, in most part, control your appearance) they have different interests, do thing differently & beyond the surface level of looks, are very different people.

Don't get me wrong... certain things (& certain people's lives especially) are highly shaped by genetics - such as those who are born with a disability - but for most people, the impact our genetics have on our lives, as modern research shows us, is much less than we may initially think...

And it's in the rest of this part right here (this 1st category of conditioning) that we're going to explore when genetics do *(& most importantly, when they don't)* shape 'who we are', what we do & the results we ultimately create in life. Starting with...

GENETICS & HEALTH

For generations, individuals in school & medical professionals at work were taught that illness & health problems were primarily the result of our genetics...

The notion that if your dad went bald at the age of 42, you're going to go bald around that time in your life too. That, if your mum had diabetes, this was passed down to you genetically & you were very likely to have diabetes as well. Or, if your parents, grandparents & grandparents all died around the age of 75, you're likely to die at a similar age too...

That was the common belief about health & for some, remains their way of thinking today. *But, there's just one problem...*

Much of modern health research conclusions go directly again this notion (& society's awareness is slowly catching up too...)

For example, in one study they found that genetics accounted for only about 5% of an individual's health problems, with the other 95% attributed to environment & lifestyle choices *(e.g. diet, exercise, sleep, pollution, stress levels, etc)*.

And as conclusions like this continued to appear, the thinking of people (especially those interested in health & wellbeing) slowly started to change from a genes-first way of attribution to a lifestyle-first way of thinking about health & fitness.

They realized that, while genetics did play a small part, if you make healthy life choices, you could essentially overwrite your supposed genetic destiny, being healthier, living longer & not having the same health issues your ancestors may have had...

I'm sure as you read this now, Mehmet Oz's quote - the one this part of the book here started with - is making more sense: *"Your genetics load the gun. Your lifestyle pulls the trigger."*

But, there's more. As more research was done, one particular field evolved out of it, which challenges our existing way of looking at our biology & genetics altogether. This new science:

The Science Of 'Epigenetics': *the study of changes in organisms caused by modification of gene expression rather than alteration of the genetic code itself.*

This field of study suggests that our genes are actually more like light switches, dimmer switches or Christmas lights, which can metaphorically 'turn on' & 'turned off' depending on how & when they are 'activated' (or, 'expressed.')

This "gene expression" is signaled through stimuli (internal & external), such as the environment, as well as our thinking & feeling. All of which makes it our lifestyle, environment & life choices that essentially signal to the genes what to do & how to affect our bodies, brains & lives *(not the genes themselves).*

Additionally, they found a single gene can be 'expressed' in many ways, depending on, once again, how & when it's activated *(which explains why identical twins <u>aren't</u> identical in character, as well as why they can look a bit different too.)*

If you're interested in this as well as it's vast implications, you can choose to study this exciting new field of 'epigenetics' for yourself, but the short summary & premise is this...

It is not your genes within themselves that affect your health, wellbeing or pretty much anything else, but the way that they are 'expressed' by your choices, lifestyle & environment.

Which means, while you may have very similar genes as your uncle who got cancer, that does <u>not</u> mean you too will get cancer. Far from it. As those same genes can be expressed in different ways. And it's primarily through your life choices that those same genes either express themselves in the same ways (& you follow in your uncle's footsteps) or - thanks to your different life choices - those same genes are 'expressed' differently & you live out a healthy future...

Another area of life in which people often turn to 'genetics' as the explanation for the things they want (or don't want) in their life is *learning, skill & ability*...

GENETICS & ABILITY: 'TALENT' VS 'SKILL'

If you ask many people what is that makes someone 'skillful' 'extraordinary' 'a master' or 'a genius' at what they do, the answers you'll receive often won't be pretty...

They'll likely tell you it's *genetics* (specifically, some sort of genetic superiority or 'innate talent') that makes people great.

If you ask, many people will attempt to tell you that people like Shakespeare, Warren Buffett, Henry Ford, Abraham Lincoln, Richard Branson, or Beethoven, are special. That they have were born with superior genes that made them innately gifted at what they do...

Yet, this old view of *ability* doesn't hold up against modern research either *(which more & more people are recognizing!)*

And it was in my first book, *Skilled Success,* that I first shared this, challenging the notion of *genetics* as the cause of great skill, instead turning to what modern research had to say...

Today, we know it's less about 'talent' (the idea that ability is someone gifted to you genetically at birth) but rather about 'skill' (which is developed through deliberate, intentional & focused learning & training) that creates skill & mastery.

Besides the research, in that book I also shared examples of some of history's most skilled individuals - people considered 'geniuses' or back in the day, or even 'child prodigies' - & what really created their extraordinary ability...

For example, *Mozart* was considered a 'natural born genius.' A 6-year-old kid impressing musicians many decades older than him from stages across Europe & composing his own at the age of 8 was a prime example of someone innately gift. Except, under the microscope, we find a much more likely explanation for his incredible skill.

As Michael Howe shared in his book, *Genius Explained*, after researching it deeper, we find *Mozart* had already clocked upwards of 3500 hours of musical training before his 6th birthday *(which is more training that some musicians put in throughout their entire, lifelong careers...)*

This was largely possible because *Mozart* had a father (who was a reasonably skilled musician himself) teaching him to play before he could even walk or speak.

What he was able to do was compress 3500 hours of training into the first 6 years of his life, making it *seem* like he was born with musical gifts. In reality, it was, more than anything else, his insane training that made him so masterful!

And you find the same story repeats for many people who are considered to be 'geniuses' at what they do (as I also share inside *Skilled Success*.)

However, I think *Michelangelo* (another masterful person in history) put it best when he said this about his own genius:

"If people knew how hard I had to work to gain my mastery, it would not seem so wonderful at all."

"If you knew how much work went into it, you wouldn't call it genius..."

Like many extraordinarily skilled individuals, people on the outside can't see the actual work it takes to get great, so they just pawn it off as genetic superiority or 'innate talent.' It's easier that way & it's a great excuse to take the weight off their own shoulders to do something great themselves...

However, when we take the time to research it, 'patterns' form & our knowledge deepens. Genetics may play a role, but a very small one & there are many much more influential factors at play for both skill & actual success. *Which brings us onto...*

GENES, INTELLIGENCE & SUCCESS (IS 'IQ' AN ACCURATE PREDICTOR OF SUCCESS?)

IQ *(which stands for 'intelligence quotient')* is the metric measure of intellect & intelligence.

And we've been told that 'IQ' is critical to amounting to anything great in life; that those with higher IQ are smarter & have great potential in life, while those with a lower IQ are unfortunate & destined for a life of underachievement. *Or, at least that's what we are sometimes told...*

And because IQ was built up to be so important, plenty of research was done to test this supposed correlation between IQ & success. Which also included the longest psychological, longitudinal study to date on the topic...

It was the year 1921 when a man named *Lewis Terman*, decided to study those with high IQ.

He believed - as he once said - *"There is nothing about an individual as important as IQ, except possibly his morals."*

So, over the next few years, he sorted through the records of over 250,000 students (elementary & high school students) with the goal of finding the top 1000 most gifted students.

He eventually ended up with 1,528 students (856 males & 672 females) with the *highest IQ* (which averaged at over 140 & ranged up to 200). He labeled this group *'Termites.'*

Over the next few decades he - & members of his team - studied this group & this becomes the longest psychological, longitudinal study to date about IQ. The study today is known as the *'Genetic Studies of Genius.'*

During this study, he followed & studied the lives of this 'gifted' group. They were all tracked, tested & analyzed. And he made sure to track everything. Every job. Every promotion. Every marriage. Every illness. He collected everything he could get his hands regarding the lives of his *'Termites'* - news articles, letters, documents - you name it.

When he began to report his findings, at first, they seemed promising. A large portion of his 'gifted' students went to a good school & got good grades. In fact, final schooling results from the study show that over 50% of *'Termites'* finished college, compared to 8% of the general population at that time. A huge difference. And big win for the importance & value of high IQ.

But, over time, his discoveries didn't match his ideas about the importance of IQ & its correlation to one's level of success.

Although some *'Termites'* reached high levels of prominence, skill & achievement in their respected fields, the majority of their lives were more mundane. By the 4th volume of *'Genetic Studies of Genius,'* Terman had noted that as adults, his subjects pursued common occupations *"as humble as those of policeman, seaman, typist and filing clerk"* & concluded his multi-decade study by saying this:

"At any rate, we have seen that intellect and achievement are far from perfectly correlated."

Which is simply a nice way of saying *'There is little correlation between intellect (IQ) & achievement"*

During the study, Terman went as far as to meddle in the 'Termites' lives, giving them letters of recommendation for jobs, which makes the study tainted & biased in some way.

But, even despite the fact that *Terman* went *this* far to give his 'gifted' children an advantage, despite everything, the results still didn't show what he was attempting to prove.

In the book, *Fads, and foibles in modern sociology & related sciences*, sociologist, *Pitirim Sorokin* expands on the findings by showing that Terman's selected group of high IQ children *performed no better* than a random group of children selected from similar family backgrounds.

Since about 90% of the high IQ children in his study were white & the majority came from upper or middle-class families, it's a fair criticism, which only continues to reaffirm how *little* IQ matters in the game of life success.

Now, it may seem sad to hear about a man who spent his entire life studying the importance of high IQ only to find that there was *little correlation between IQ & success*, but his work did actually bring a huge amount of value...

He may have set out to prove that those who were born with high IQ *(which is said to be mostly biologically inherited; estimates placing the heritability of IQ between 55% & 77%)* go on to achieve more, but instead, he proved the opposite, which, if we think about it, is a far more empowering result that gives us far greater control over our own skills & success.

His study showed us that IQ *doesn't* has little correlation to success. So, no matter whether you have an incredibly high IQ or very low IQ, it doesn't really affect your ability to become highly successful at what you do & create an incredible life!

In another study, a group of researchers studied the IQ of chessmasters & found that their IQ was, statistically, no higher than the IQ of other, less successful, chess players.

And since then, other studies have been done to show this same trend across other industries, topics & skills, continuing to re-confirm that higher IQ does *not* lead to higher skill.

Which all means, if you were born with low IQ, you are *not* - by any means - genetically screwed.

And, if you've believed that it's been your *high IQ* that's been giving you the edge in life, it's hasn't. Something else is likely responsible (e.g. your hard work or learning ability) not IQ.

However, as you may have realized in Terman's study, there is 1 thing that high IQ does correlate & link to...

Because of how top universities & colleges assess applicants, IQ *does* correlate strongly to your odds of getting into a top school. As you saw in the study, a staggering 50% of 'Termites' went to college (compared to the national average of 8%).

This may change in the future as colleges catch up to current research, but for now, IQ does matter in this context.

So, if you want to get into a good college, then, yes, IQ *does* matter for that, but if you believe that IQ correlates to skill, business success, relationship success, life satisfaction, or happiness, then, just like *Terman*, you may just go your whole life believing something that *1) the latest research shows is a very inaccurate assumption & 2) may just be holding you back from taking full control of your life & achieving that which you really want to achieve.*

So, if you did an IQ test once & found you have a low IQ, do <u>not</u> base your potential on this, or you may end up living your life based on a faulty premise that does nothing but stop you.

This work is important because it helps explain why some people with low IQ (or undesirable genes overall) go on to become some of the most extraordinarily skilled, successful & joyous people there are *(& hopefully inspires that you can do the same - irrelevant of your IQ or genetics...)*

SUMMARY: DID YOUR GENES SHAPE 'WHO YOU ARE' TODAY & THE FUTURE IN FRONT OF YOU?

The answer: <u>yes</u> & <u>no</u> *(something I really wanted to convey!)*

When it comes to the physical aspects of 'who you are' (looks, eye or hair color, etc) as well as some metrics like IQ, **yes**. Research continues to show us genes are a big influencing factor here, controlling this aspect of your identity.

However, when it comes to the things that, in my personal experience, matter most in life (such as health, relationships, skills, success, impact & emotional wellbeing) then **no** - *genes have little-to-no correlation to each of these things in life.*

And with that, here's something (the 2nd category) which has shown to correlate much more strongly to 'who you truly are', what you believe, your habits, behaviors & life results...

2 | **CHILDHOOD:** PRE-CONSCIOUSNESS

> *"Give me a child until he is 7 and I will show you the man."*
>
> - ARISTOTLE

Over the last few decades, science has shown us some very interesting & eye-opening things about how the start of our lives shapes 'who you are' & what we do later on in life...

Firstly, while one might assume that this *2nd category of conditioning* begins with one's first breath, alive & well, we now know that it can actually start earlier than that...

Scientists have found that a baby, while still in the mother's womb, can already pick up certain information from the environment around it.

Much more research is still to be done about this - as well as its implications - but it's interesting to know *(at least for me personally)* that before you were even 'alive' you were already processing information & experiencing life in some way.

The 2nd interesting & eye-opening thing scientists have found (something we dive deep into here) when examining brain activity is that, during the first few years, a newborn actually operates <u>exclusively</u> at a level below 'consciousness' - known as the *'<u>subconscious.</u>' Specifically, they found the following...*

During the first 2 years of a newborn's life, the brain functions at the lowest level of brain wave activity, known as *'<u>delta.</u>'*

And for simple understanding, *'Delta'* brain waves are what an adult's brain is running on while they are sleeping.

Which means, a newborn (until about 2 years of age) is pretty much asleep with eyes open. Which explains why newborns fall in & out of sleep so frequently & easily...

Then, after the age of about 2, until about 5 or 6 years of age, a child begins to demonstrate slightly higher brain wave patterns; known as *'<u>theta</u>'* (one level up from 'delta').

After the age of about 5, until they are about 8, children will slowly start to step into 'consciousness.' First demonstrating 'alpha' brain wave patterns, ultimately followed by 'beta' - however they still spend a lot of time in 'theta' here too.

PSYCHOLOGY | 257

Only once a child has passed 7 - 8 years of age, does a child no longer primarily function in the brain wave pattern of 'theta'...

'How & why does this matter?' you may be thinking...

Well - it's because *'delta'* & *'theta'* (which, as you now know, children spend almost all their time in for the first 7 - 8 years of life) are the same levels that are present, in adults, during imagination, dream & hypnosis.

Simply put: children, during the few years of their lives, are basically walking around in a constant state of *hypnosis*.

As they don't yet possess full *'consciousness'* - which is the ability to analyze, assess, think about, judge or reason any incoming information from the environment - all new information bypasses this conscious filtration, instead just going straight into the subconscious mind.

Meaning: unlike an adult who hears something & has the mental ability to analyze it, question it, judge it, or reject it, a newborn doesn't. It just accepts it. Critical thinking is absent.

So, during the first 7 - 8 years of *your* life - as you did not yet possess a full sense of consciousness (your 'identity' was still being crafted; not fully functional) - incoming *'information'* & the corresponding *'interpretation'* were the same thing...

What your parents, family & teachers told you, you accepted (you didn't have any other choice; you didn't yet have the ability to analyze it) & stored in your subconscious mind.

And, you likely proceeded to then act out this information...

You were basically being hypnotized (conditioned into a way of believing & being) during the first 7 - 8 years of your life.

'WHY THIS IS?' YOU MAY THINK...

One of the most common & accepted explanations for why we are born without full consciousness - the ability to analyze & reason incoming information - is the idea that before you can consciously think, you must know what to think about...

Essentially, before you can be conscious, you have to have something to actually be conscious of...

The second part of this explanation, of course, is that growing up there are hundreds & thousands of different little things a child must learn to become a functional member of a family, community & society in general.

We may overlook these things, assuming that being a human being is a simple task, as we do these things automatically, but there are actually hundreds & thousands of little things a newborn must learn to be a 'human being' in society.

That's why you operating primarily in 'delta' & 'theta' for the first few years: so you can pick up these basics.

You didn't need to learn these things through some 'being a human being 101' class or textbook, rather, nature just made you operate subconsciously so you can just pick up these things from the environment around you...

You watch your parents & family, you listen to your siblings, teachers & community & it's just a matter of time before the 'rules' & lesson you need to function as a human being - what to do & what _not_ to do, what is acceptable & what is _not_ - are installed into your brain (as you're operating hypnotically...)

You just download the information - which you do naturally because you're operating in 'theta' - & follow along in life...

There's just one problem. And that is that the information you received in these first few years, while useful *(hey, you survived - you're still alive... good job conditioning)* is also very skewed in certain ways...

'LIKE PARENT, LIKE CHILD...'

The people who are around you during these first few years (family, siblings, community & especially so, parents) were not passing along all of the possible views that exist about life, but rather their own subjective 'beliefs.' What they believed, they shared & you were conditioned to believe too growing up.

Which is the main reason children will often become similar to their parents - *'like father like son'*, *'like mother, like daughter'* or a mix - having similar life experiences & results.

Your parents didn't have evil intentions (just as, if you're a parent, you don't have evil intention towards your children), they just simply did the best they can (just as *their* parent).

Unfortunately, as nobody is perfect, nobody parents perfectly either, instead passing along both their good traits as well as their limiting 'beliefs' to their kids. *Perhaps, 'beliefs' like...*

- Life is hard & an endless struggle.
- Love is painful.
- Life is dangerous (you must be scared!)
- There's never enough money for people like us...
- Rich people are bad people.
- People are evil, so watch out...

Then you played out these 'beliefs' during your life, perhaps never even stopping to realize these 'beliefs' were installed into your subconscious in those first few years of your life.

Yet, whether you realize it or not, they impact 'who you are,' the decisions you make, actions you take & results you get.

And, if you continue to follow all of them, you'll likely end up with the same results as your parent & family (*who innocently installed these 'beliefs' into you to start with).* You'll end up creating the same familiar destiny. *Same input, same output.*

And if you find this hard to believe or doubt that those who raised you impacted your life, remember that these 'beliefs' operate subconsciously (a level below consciousness) so you may not even realize how they are affecting your life today. *Yet, they absolutely are - for better or worse...*

CONSCIOUS NOW: NEXT 10 YEARS OF CHILDHOOD

'What about the next 10 years of my childhood & teenage years? How did those affect me?' you may also think...

Firstly, scientists have shown at this point your consciousness has fully formed & you now actively display all brain wave patterns. Which means you're no longer in this hypnotic state, accepting all incoming information without analysis.

Rather, at this point, you're able to fully analyze, reason, think about & consciously challenge any incoming information.

Which is why children at this age are increasing curious to explore the deeper truth behind things. So much so that their parents may hear an endless bombardment of *'why's'*...

Why do I need to go to bed at this time? Why do I need to eat this? Why do I need to be nice to this kid? Why? Why? Why?

It's a good thing. It's *human curiosity* first kicking in - which is a powerful tool for *clarity* in life, as well as gaining wisdom.

Existing information is also being challenged now. Which is why it's usually around these ages that children first learn it's not actually Santa Claus flying around the world in one night giving them (& all the other kids) presents but rather their parents. Or that it's not the tooth fairy giving them money in exchange for their teeth, but their parent sneaking into their rooms at night like skillful ninjas & making that exchange.

Parents can no longer get away with little white lies because the child's conscious mind is now looking for understanding, willing to analyze, reason & challenge anything that it doesn't fully comprehend.

And the gap between incoming information & interpretation now behinds to form. What one hears & sees can now be subjectively perceived very differently for each & every child.

However, this is not to say that we do not get conditioned anymore. We do - just in different ways. Now, other forces are at play now. Especially as children are now being influenced by the education system (& teachers within it), friends, their community, the media & the social norms (or, 'rules') - as we discussed in the *'Ambition'* section.

During these ages between 7+ & adulthood, children are still much more susceptible to new information & 'beliefs' as new information doesn't tend to clash with other information & life experience one already possesses - like it does as we get older). Change is an easier process too, as beliefs, habits & behaviors are still fresh & not lifelong ways of being that are deeply integrated into one's sense of self.

And, all this brings us onto the 3rd category, which will further these understandings.

However, before that, it's important I wrap this part up by reinforcing a very important point...

WHAT NOW? IS YOUR FAITH SEALED YET?

In the 1st part, I shared that no, your future is not genetically & biologically sealed; somehow destined for a destination that you're unable to change course from...

And the same applies here. Sure, you were conditioned in many, many ways growing up, but your future is still very much in your hands.

Think of it like a computer. Just because a friend or family members logs onto your computer while you're away on holiday & installs some 'programs' ('beliefs) onto it, doesn't mean it's going to be on your computer forever.

It could. It could not. You could come back from your time away, become aware of these new 'program' ('belief') that got installed onto your computer & then proceed to 'uninstall' (or 'overwrite') these programs with other ones that you prefer.

Like weeds in a garden, you could walk up & remove that which you do <u>not</u> want, replacing it with what you do want.

The same applies to the 'beliefs' 'habits' & 'behaviors' in our lives. Just because they are installed into you by your parents while we were in that nature-induced hypnotic trance known as 'delta' & 'theta' brain wave patterns during the first 7 - 8 years of your life (or later in childhood) doesn't mean you can't <u>choose</u> to change it. *You absolutely can!*

In fact, I'm sure we all know people who, no matter what their childhood was like, what their parents were like or what they may have been conditioned to believe growing up, ended up become aware of their 'programs' & began changing who they are, as well as what they do...

You have that same choice to change at any moment of your life (if you choose too!)

And, in the last chapter of this book, you'll actually learn a powerful 4-step process you can use to do this; to change any 'belief' 'habit' or 'behavior' in your life, conditioning a new, improved iteration of 'who you are'...

Before we get there though, we have to finish this first journey we're on; the adventure of understanding 'why you are who you are' today. *And that brings us onto the 3rd category...*

THIS BOOK'S DEDICATION...

The 'dedication' & 'acknowledgements' pages in most books are usually written before or after the book is finished. And, are inserted into the book at either the beginning of the book, or the end, as a result.

This is not the case with this book...

A strong urge to write a dedication come to me right here - right after finishing the writing of this bit you just read - & so I decided to write (& insert) the dedication accordingly...

Plus, it's my personal belief that timing & context are very important when sharing something truly meaningful, which is what I hope this rather-randomly-added 'dedication' does.

DEDICATION

I dedicate this book to my amazing parents - my mum & dad - who I know for sure sacrificed, cared & gave more to me & my brother than we could ever even comprehend.

Like all parents, they made mistakes, passing along 'beliefs' that, looking back, they wouldn't have wanted to pass alone (which they are the first to admit; an honesty I really admire...) however for every mistake, there were hundreds & thousands of feats of incredible parenting.

They supported me in all I pursued, supported me, inspired me & helped me become the person I am today *(as well as, through their example, helped me realize the type of parent I want to be to my children in the future...)*

So I want to take this moment to dedicate this book to them, as without them, it never would've been written...

3 | ENVIRONMENTAL: ENDLESS INFLUENCE

> *"Show me a successful individual and I'll show you someone who had real positive influences in his or her life."*
>
> - DENZEL WASHINGTON

You would assume that after the conditioning of childhood, it's over - that adults are no longer conditioned in any way.

However, this is *not* the case. Far from it. In reality...

| As Long As You Are Breathing, The Conditioning Is There. <u>It Never Stops</u>

'Who we are' is endlessly been shaped, changed & adjusted. Our *'beliefs'* are constantly been molded - challenged, changed or strengthened (either consciously or unconsciously).

It's kinda what living is: *engaging in the web of information, opinion, thoughts, feelings & beliefs that co-exist together.*

After childhood, you simply switch primarily to the 3rd category of conditioning: ***environmental.***

The influence comes less from you parents now & more from society, culture & the environment as a whole *(the people you spend time with, the information you consume, things you pay attention to, situations that happen & your response, etc)*. And this all shapes 'who you are' (in the present) as well as 'who you'll become' (in the future).

See, we've already talked about the power of 'culture' & how 'rules' of society lead us to only aim for certain goals in life, however it goes beyond this. Environment influences much more than just the goals you set, but also the way you think about yourself, others, the world around you, what you should do & your view of life in general. *The conditioning is strong.*

But let's not fear. While this may sound bad & the word *'conditioning'* (or, 'programming') can sound scary, it's not. Or, at least, it doesn't have to be. In reality, *conditioning* is neither good nor bad. It just 'is.' And it all depends on the type of conditioning you choose to put yourself in...

Like the human mind in general - or a hammer - *conditioning* is neutral. Our brains suggestibility is neither good or bad within itself. That depends on how you use it.

For example, one can program their mind in an incredibly, positive way that enhances results, improves happiness & elevates your levels of joy & bliss in life. Reading great books, watching inspiring movies, listening to powerful song lyrics, working with mentors or getting advice from wise advisors are all examples of this type of 'conditioning.'

Basically, your programming yourself to think in a certain way by choosing to listen to certain people or engage in certain types of information over others.

When you read, listen or watch something like this, you're actively choosing to be influenced (to be *'conditioned'*) by this incoming information. And that's great. Like conditioning work at the gym, this makes you stronger, fitter & better.

On the flip side, engaging in other types of *'conditioning'* can make people feel totally helpless, powerless, deep in the land of victimhood, sad, miserable, depressed & even suicidal.

Here - in this 3rd category, **environmental** *conditioning* - we're going to explore just how this all works. You'll discover how the world around you affects you, how you sometimes get led to believe certain things because of the things you see, listen to or watch, as well as how you can better choose the type of *'conditioning'* to engage in to create the life you want.

And this *environmental conditioning* can be sub-categorized further into 3 main parts (as it is here in this book). Now, we're going to explore these 3 sub-categories. *Let's continue...*

1. **People:** Those You Spend Time With Influence 'Who You Are' & What You Do.

As Goethe said, *"Tell me who you spend time with and I will tell you who you are."*

As Jim Rohn said, *"You are the average of the five people you spend the most time with."*

Or, as philosopher & great stoic, Seneca, said it almost 2 millenniums previously (before his death in 65 AD): *"Tell me with whom you consort with and I will tell you who you are."*

The impacts of our environment (specifically, people) on our beliefs & behaviors is an understanding & life principle that many of the wisest people have taught & lived for generations.

However, thanks to modern research & scientific study, the impacts of the people one spends time with on their actions aren't merely philosophical talk, but a stellar principle for us to follow with confidence.

For example, based on the data of 12,067 people from 1971 to 2003 (32 years), as part of the Framingham Heart Study (one of the largest, longest-running health studies!), researchers found that if your friends are obese, your risk of obesity is 45% higher than normal (over the next 2 to 4 years.)

And while 45% may seem like a large percentage, it's less than the discovery that you're 61% more likely to become a smoker yourself if you are friends with people who smoke.

The same results also translated into less specific behaviors like happiness in general. The researchers found that if you're friends with people who are happy (those who report high levels of life satisfaction) you're more likely to be happy & experience high levels of life satisfaction yourself.

Meaning: *spent time with people who do certain things or think about the world in a certain way & you're more likely to also engage in those same beliefs & practices. Or...*

| People You Spend Time Influence 'Who You Are' & What You Do

Based on what you now know, this is very logical too. To put this very simply, I often share this example...

If you take someone struggling financially & make them best friends with Jeff Bezos, Bill Gates, Warren Buffett, Carlos Slim & Mark Zuckerberg for the next 12 months, do you think that person will change? You bet!

It's almost irrelevant who it is; lump anyone in with a group of billionaires *for long enough* & their financial results are certain to improve.

They'll likely end up thinking about finances, business, wealth & the world in general very differently after those 12 months. And because their *'beliefs'* about money, wealth, business & the world have changed - *'who they are' changed* - they're likely to make a lot more money after these 12 months.

And the same applies to all areas of your life...

Spend time with people who prioritize health, eat well, work out regularly & have great health in general, & with time, their results are likely to rub off on you. You're likely to be positively affected - *conditioned* - by them to get new results.

Spend time with very wise, smart, intellectual people & you're likely to become even wiser. *I hope you get the point...*

However, the question remains, *'why?'* A lot of people talk about this people phenomenon (as we're done here) but few dig deeper to understand *'why'* this happens. *Let's explore...*

UNDERSTANDING THE 'PEOPLE' PHENOMENON

The first big part of the explanation is that - as both biological studies & psychology studies show - we are a *social species*.

We've evolved & adapted to live with each other - socially - as a method of survival, strength & overall wellbeing.

And, more specifically, it's in smaller social circles that these adaptations are most obvious (easiest to spot.) Whether it's an accent changing when spending time with new people in new countries, the period's between girlfriends syncing or social groups finding common places of preferred dining, we adapt to become like those around us (& vice versa).

People adapt to become similar to those they spend time with as a way of 'fitting in,' being accepted, staying as part of the group & ultimately surviving. However, it goes beyond this...

It's just about surviving, it's also about *belonging*. We want to belong. We want to feel part of something greater. *It's part of the human condition & what really lights us up in life...*

It's one of the biggest reasons we build communities, social circles & peer groups in the first place - to connect & belong.

It's the reason social networks are the most visited websites & apps on the internet, as well as some of the biggest companies in the world. And it's also the reason why cultures & religions exist - they make us feel part of something greater.

We want privacy, but not really (or, at least, not always). We often much prefer the company of people we care about, find interest in & connect with, over the desire for privacy.

And it's this connection & social existence that creates spread of information passed from one person to the next. Which leads us to the next part of the explanation: *information*.

Let's go back to the most foundational visual *once again*:

As you spend time with certain types of people, you receive certain types of information.

So, spend time with people who are unhealthy & overweight, for example, & you receive very different information than you would from people who are fit, healthy & clearly demonstrate great health. They talk about healthy differently. They talk about being physically fit differently. You see them eat different foods & treat their bodies differently *(which are also forms of information - sensory input - which your mind then goes on to interpret).*

And, as you continue to expose yourself to that type of new *information* (by spending time with a certain group of people) you're more primed to form certain *interpretations*, which drive certain decisions, actions & results.

On the contrary, when you spend time with different people - *like the 12 months with the world's richest people example that I shared before* - you hear, see, feel & experience new things (*information*) than you wouldn't normally do so.

They think about, view, deal with & talk about money, wealth & business very differently than an average person, which is passed along to you as you spend time with them.

Simply put: *When you spend time with certain people, you are exposed to certain types of information, which have the potential to challenge or strength your old 'beliefs' ('who you are') to make you act differently & get different results.*

Plus, those who you spend time with also set the expectations, baselines & standards for what is acceptable & what is not.

Go to a vegetarian or vegan party with a bucket of chicken & you may feel bad about this. Judged. Out of place. *Why?* It's not the bucket of chicken within itself, but the untold, yet well-known 'rules' of that certain social group - the standards & expectations they follow *(like a silent list of 'do's & don'ts.')*

On the flip side, going into a chicken shop & ordering a salad can give you a similar feeling (even though it's well known that the salad is much better for your health than chicken).

Again, it's because of the social standards & expectations that exist among these individuals in this particular environment...

Healthy people have higher standards for themselves in the area of health, just as wealth people demand more from themselves in their careers & businesses.

They've raised their expectations of themselves in these areas & believe more is possible for them here. And so, by spending time with these people, you're going to think & feel different...

And these standards, baselines & expectations are also forms of *information* which we receive from these people around us that influence us. And, even if we don't see or hear this information, we sense it...

IT'S NOT MEDICAL; IT'S PSYCHOLOGICAL

Weight, smoking, levels of life satisfaction (as in the research examples shared before), wealth, health & other areas of life are not 'diseases' that you 'catch' from those you spend time with. It doesn't work that way. It's not the flu.

Rather, it's the combination of doing things to 'fit in' - to survive & belong - as well as the *information* coming in from those you spend time with, which creates the strong influence those we spend time with have on 'who we are' & what we do.

The results themselves aren't necessarily passed along, but rather the underlying seeds ('beliefs') that form those results.

For example, those who spend time with others who are poor don't suddenly lose all their savings (the fruits; the effects), but rather 'catch' the underlying *'beliefs'* (the roots; causes) about money that make people poor in the first place. Beliefs such as, *'money is the root of all evil,' 'making money is just too hard'* or *'it's just impossible for me to make more money.'*

As Benjamin Franklin once said, *"He that lieth down with dogs shall rise up with fleas."*

Meaning: *spend time with those who are living lives you <u>don't</u> want to live (in this metaphor, 'dogs') & you'll end up getting results that you <u>don't</u> want to get ('fleas.')*

That said, like actual fleas, you can get them removed. You can override the *'beliefs'* that don't support you in your life with more positive, empowering ones *(which, we'll talk about later in this section.)*

However, if given the choice, it's easier to just avoid getting fleas (the result that you <u>don't</u> want) altogether surrounding yourself with great people to begin with...

WARNING: THE INFLUENCE IS SNEAKY

Some of your friends might be complaining about how hard it is to lose weight & be healthy; how they've been on all these diets but none of them have worked & so they gave up. *"It's just too hard,"* they said & because you don't want to be left out, you start to nod along. You don't agree with them. You're healthy & fit yourself. You know it's possible (it just takes some self-discipline). However, you unconsciously nod along or go along with the conversation just to 'fit in.' You just became a member of this social group so you don't share your true opinion as that might offend them. *Frankly, at times, our desire for belonging is stronger than our common sense...*

See, the effects of those you spend time with start small. *The influence is sneaky.* So much so that you don't even realize that you're being influenced by these people (yet, you are!)

Then, because your friends regularly eat at a certain restaurant (a place that probably contributed to their obesity in the first place), you go along. *'You're not going to eat alone while all your friends are eating at that steak house'* you tell yourself, before proceeding to tag along. That restaurant is unlikely to serve much that's truly healthy so you make small compromises as to what you eat - trade-offs just small enough for you to rationalize them without feeling bad about yourself.

You eat what you *wouldn't* normally eat. Then you skip days at the gym as your new friends *'don't feel like it today.'* You take the elevator instead of the stairs too. See, *each trade-off is so small that individually they don't make a difference.*

However, one small trade-off after another &, like a snowball, you're rolling down a hill, in a downward momentum spiral which is leading you to a known destiny: *the same health & fitness results as your friends (those you spend time with).*

However, it doesn't have to be this way as firstly, you can choose who you spend time with, as well as, secondly, you can choose whether you want to be influenced by them or whether you want to influence them & bring them up - *it's said that it's the person or group that are the most certain & committed that influence the others.* And thirdly, each trade-off is a choice that instead of discarding as insignificant, you can treat differently to create different results.

WHO DO YOU SPEND YOUR TIME WITH?

Knowing that almost everything in our lives is being influenced by the people we spend time with - from wealth to health, from our risk of obesity to our self-esteem, from our happiness to our likelihood of engaging in drugs or criminal behavior ('peer pressure') - we must be more aware of who we choose to spend our time with. *Once again, we must harness the power of intention & choose wisely here as well...*

And yes, it's a *choice*. And not just any choice, but one of the most important ones that you're actively making in your life.

Hence, spend time with people like yourself (like-minded people) who are going to support you & lift you up, as well as people who have achieved what you want to achieve (people you can learn a lot from very, very quickly). These people will inspire you, support you in forging new *'beliefs'* & help you achieve extraordinary things. *Do this & your life will change!*

If you want to achieve more financially, for example, spend time with people who are doing well in this area. Engage in money-related conversations with these people over others. Learn from them. Ask questions. Seek out their guidance.

People love to learn, but they also love to pass along what they've learned, so ask them questions about their journey. And see how you can help them (to add value to them) as well.

Spend time with people who display the values that you find important; those you can learn from or trade value with.

This doesn't mean you have to abandon or 'cut' your existing friends (although, as you grow, you may no longer connect with your old friends like you used to - unless they grow too), it just means you must become aware of who your spending time with & the influence they are having on you.

Ultimately, you now know how much the people you spend time with influence your future. And what you choose to do with this information is up to you *(although, I do recommend you use it wisely to create the life you truly want...)*

PROXIMITY MATTERS

As you're about to learn *(coming up)* it's not just the people who you spend the most time with that influence your behavior as others do too. However, those you spend the most time with - whose in closest proximity - that influence you the most. Or simply put, *'Proximity Matters.'*

Your partner, your close friends, family, co-workers & others *(those you spend many hours per day or week with)* are the people who influence you most.

Knowing this, we can choose to, not just be intentional in who we spend time with, but also in the proximity we create.

If you have a mentor, for example, spending more time with them each day will raise the influence they will have on you.

Historically, apprentices would leave their old environment when getting mentored. They would leave their homes & live with (or close by to, the mentor). They would spend all the time in a day together - *total focus*. And they would interact directly with the mentor - 1-to-1. *Not a class of students, but personal, 1-to-1 mentoring*. And that's the core methodology of training that created many of the great artists, painters, writers, thought leaders (amongst others) throughout history.

While that's an extreme example of *proximity*, the premise is what can give you power: ***proximity***. If you want to learn & get positively influenced by someone a lot, get into proximity. Spend lots of time together (as much as possible.) Be truly engaged in conversations you have together.

Be intentional about who you spend time with, but also how much or little time you spend with these people & how they this is also influencing you...

META-STRATEGY: ENVIRONMENT (PEOPLE)

Environment is a 'meta-strategy' as, like throwing a pebble into a pond, this 1 thing - focusing on who you spend time with - ripples out to form positive influence on almost all areas of your life simultaneously (areas such as health & fitness, wealth, family & relationships, happiness & overall life satisfaction. *And that's incredible leverage!*

However, people always say, *'Well, I don't know people like that to spend time with...' 'How can I surround myself with new people then?'* or *'But, I can't reach successful people - I don't have access to them"* Here are some practices for you...

ACTIONABLE STEPS TO TAKE:

1. **Audit Your Circle** (& It's Influence On You)

The first (& easiest) step you can take is to simply audit your circle (those you know & spend time with), become more aware of how different people you spend time are either positively or negatively influencing you in various areas of your life, as well as how you can spend your time differently amongst just your existing friends.

You probably have existing connections that you've been overlooking - great people you haven't reached out to in a while that you can easily re-connect with.

2. Become Aware Of The Influence

If you can't do anything else, at least *become more aware* of when people are unconsciously influencing you.

For example, if your uncle is the total opposite of the type of person you want to be, you don't have to 'cut' him from your life, but simply become more aware of the influence he may be unconsciously having on you to reduce its effects...

Love him. Care for him. Connect with him. Talk to him. However, <u>intentionally</u> decide to yourself that you *don't* want to be influenced by him. Then listen more carefully to each word, knowing that you can choose to form better *interpretations* to the incoming *information*.

3. Spend Time With New People (Reach Out)

The next & most obvious one is to meet, connect with & spend time with new people who you can learn from. *This starts by <u>reaching out</u>* - finding those you want to spend time with & striking up a connection with them.

This may be on a forum somewhere, in some group on social media, at a networking event or just a connection passed along to you by a friend - whatever the channel, be willing to put yourself out there & connect with new people!

4. Work For Less (With Better People!)

Earning $67,000 per year working with a great group of people whose values align with yours, who are very happy, joyous, fulfilled & support you, is ultimately a better choice than earning $74,000/yr but working with people who you don't like & don't want to be like.

In that same way, earning less from clients that you love working with (& positively influence you) is usually a better choice than earning more from clients that bring you down.

The 4th actionable step you can take is to choose to work in a different environment - even being willing to work for less if it enables you to work alongside great people.

Instead of just focusing on maximizing your short-term income, focus on creating the *life* you want (short-term & long-term). And spending the majority of your day working with people who you *don't* want to spend time with isn't going to do that for you. Be intentional & select your work not just for the short-term income, but long-term influence.

5. Find Work That Literally 'Forces' You To Spend Time With Amazing People

When I was 15 years old, I began a 3-year apprenticeship with an early mentor of my mine, *Clinton Swaine*. During this, the majority of my time was spent with people who had paid USD$30,000 as part of a training package to come to these events (& be part of this business community).

A large percentage of these people were business owners, entrepreneurs & speakers. And many were already doing very well in their lives - coming here to do *even* better.

I observed these people. I watched what they did, how they behaved & learned from them. I modeled them. And they largely influenced who I am today - as did my mentor who I was traveling with during this time.

It was an apprenticeship & I didn't make a dime from those 3 years of time there (no salary), but that didn't matter as the influence on who I am today was worth much more than any paycheck would have been. *Immeasurably more!*

In this same way, you can choose to work for less (or for free - part-time if you can't do full-time) but in work that literally 'forces' you to spend time with amazing people you can watch, observe & learn from...

If health & fitness is important to you, go work at a gym. You'll literally be 'forced' to spend time with people who are, *not* saying *'I'll workout tomorrow'* but those who are working on their health today. You can observe them. Listen to their conversations & absorb their outlook on health. You can learn how these people who actually go to the gym think about their fitness differently than those who *don't* show up for exercise daily (& model these differences in mindset.)

Or, go work at a luxury 5-star hotel, a golf course, high-end tailor or at a fancy restaurant, as there you'll get something much more financially rewarding than just your immediate paycheck: *the ability to learn, listen to, observe & model the actions, behaviors & habits of highly wealthy individuals* (assuming finances are what you want; it's all about *total alignment* between your actions & ambitions.)

Or, even better - like in my experience - find an opportunity which enables you to both work with amazing people & in a field that's linked to what you want to do long-term...

6. Get A Mentor (Or A Coach)

As I shared in my first book, **Skilled Success**:

> *Oprah Winfrey was mentored by Maya Angelou. Henry David Thoreau was mentored by Ralph Waldo Emerson. Mark Zuckerberg was mentored by Steve Jobs. Leonardo Da Vinci was mentored by Andrea del Verrocchio. Raphael was mentored by Leonardo Da Vinci. The list goes on & on.*

> *An incredibly high percentage of those who have reached a world-class level had mentors.*
>
> *This doesn't mean you can't succeed without a mentor, but research continues to show how positively mentoring (or coaching) can impact learning speed & one's progress to mastery.*
>
> *And clearly for all the people above, based on their results, as well as their comments in interviews or in their works, mentoring was of huge benefit.*

If you can, find mentors & coaches (*yes, you can have more than 1!*) in the areas you want to thrive in as the right mentors (& coaching) are some of the best investments of time, energy, attention & money one can possibly make.

And if you can't get mentoring from someone in person, you can - as I also shared in my book *Skilled Success* - get a mentor from afar or a 'virtual mentor.'

See, many very successful post content, documenting their experiences & life lessons, which you can treat as mentoring. Do this repeatedly & it's like having a group of mentors you're constantly learning from.

Mentoring & coaching are great tools that were massively beneficial for me, for each of the individuals listed above, countless others & could be great tools to get you around an incredible person (or people) who positively influence you & propelling you to higher levels of success & fulfillment.

7. Build A Platform

Start a blog. Launch a podcast. Create a fan page. Start a video channel. Build a 'platform' on which you can invite great people to share their wisdom - usually in the form of an interview between you & then.

Successful people want to share. They want to express & many care deeply about their impact & legacy.

So, create a platform which allows them to do that & it will allow you to spend tons of quality time learning from them.

I mean, just look at what Larry King, Ellen DeGeneres, Oprah Winfrey or Tim Ferriss have done. They created a *platform* - a 'show' of sorts - which they invite people onto.

Today, they are at a point where they can invite, hang out with & ask questions to almost anybody they want on the planet - thanks to their 'platforms.'

It's a great way to engage in amazing conversation with people you wouldn't normally be able to call up & chat to.

Although, from an educational standpoint, few examples compare to that of Napoleon Hill, who was hired by Andrew Carnegie (a business owner, worth, in today's dollars, $372 billion) to go through the people in his Rolodex, interview them all & compile their 'keys to success.'

Plus, this was in the 1900's (the industrial age) - long before the internet & the widespread availability of information as we have it today.

He interviewed the wealthiest people in the world as part of this mission (which later turned into the book, *Think & Grow Rich*.) And in that book lays another profound strategy for spending time with amazing people...

8. The 'Master Mind'

Napoleon Hill defined a 'Master Mind' as a *"Coordination of knowledge and effort, in a spirit of harmony, between two or more people, for the attainment of a definite purpose."*

The idea is to, not just surround yourself with great people, but have them actually work together,, in harmony, to brainstorm, plan & support each other.

And the idea of a *'Master Mind'* is even more applicable today than it was back during its introduction as today we are more connected. *You can create your own mastermind (or find & join an existing one) easier than ever before.*

In the book *Principles*, Ray Dalio (one of the most successful hedge-fund managers of all time) starts by saying that his success has more to do with his ability to deal with his 'not-knowing of things' than anything that he knows.

And one of the things Ray Dalio would repeatedly do was put all his investment speculations, assumptions & predictions under the scrutiny of smart people around him *(a 'Master Mind' of sorts - similar to Andrew Carnegie.)*

Create or join a 'Master Mind' & meetup regularly to exchange ideas, advise & suggestions - which *you can even do it through the internet so no travel is required.*

9. The <u>Virtual</u> 'Master Mind'

There are brilliant people who you would probably love to learn from who, 1) unfortunately have passed away, or 2) who are alive, but you *don't* have access to. *I mean...*

Just imagine how awesome would it be to get business, career or financial advice from people like Henry Ford, J.D. Rockefeller, Julius Caesar, Cleopatra, Queen Victoria, Steve Jobs, Coco Chanel or Abraham Lincoln?

Or, what if you could get life advice from Socrates, Plato, Sun Tzu, Marcus Aurelius, Michelangelo, Amelia Earhart, Wright Brothers, Mother Teresa, Gandhi, Martin Luther King Jr, Friedrich Nietzsche or Sun Tzu?

What if you were part of a 'Master Mind' group with all of these incredible world leaders who were giving you ideas, advise & suggestions for your life?

Well, it's possible *(if you're willing to get creative)*. And it's though this idea of a *'Virtual Master Mind...'*

Just as some people get help making key decisions in life by asking themselves things like, *'What would my grandma do?'* & feel as if their grandma is actually giving them suggestions *(because they know exactly what grandma would say if she was sitting right in front of them)*. Well - you can do the same with the life of anyone else you want...

If you learn about certain people enough - read biographies, research their life story, watch documentaries, etc - at a certain point, you begin to know what they would say in a given moment *(almost as if they were right in front of you.)*

Simply put: as you get to know their past, their beliefs & what they would do in given situations, you can then close your eyes, ask yourself *'What would this person do here?'* & have great answers flood to you as if they came directly from these great individuals.

Now, repeat this with several individuals you look up to, really getting to know as much as you possibly can about them & you have your *'Virtual Master Mind'* - *a group of people you know or don't, dead or alive, giving you advice as if they were sitting around your dinner table in person!*

So, if you don't have people in person you can be positively influenced by, that's not an excuse either. Instead, learn about people you look up to, get to know what they would advise & use this strategy of a *'Virtual Master Mind.'*

> Use these 9 actionable steps to spend time with people who are going to bring you up, support you & positively influence you to make better decisions & get better results.

However, the 'people' phenomenon goes even further than this. It's not just the people who you spend time with that influence your 'who you are' & what you do, but also those who you <u>don't</u> spend time with as well...

I know this may sound strange, but it's actually one of the most profound insights one could ever learn. And that's exactly what's coming up right now...

3 (PROVEN) DEGREES OF INFLUENCE

You already know that the researchers found if you're friends with people who are obese (or go on to become obese), you're 45% more likely to become obese yourself - but that's not even the most shocking part. *Not even close!*

The researchers also found that if the friend of your friend is (or becomes) obese, you are between 20% & 25% more likely to become obese yourself - *even if you've never met this friend's friend before!*

But, it doesn't stop there. They also found the if your friend's friend's friend is (or becomes obese) you're about 10% more likely (than average) to become obese yourself!

Your friend may not even know this person. And, both you & your friend may have never met, seen or interacted with this person in your life, yet you are still about 10% more likely than average to become obese because of their influence...

So, the influence of people on your behavior isn't just about the 1st degree (those you personally spend time with), but, as the research says, also about the 2nd & 3rd degrees...

3 (PROVEN) DEGREES OF INFLUENCE

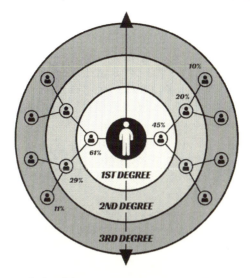

Nicholas A. Christakis & James H. Fowler proposed this theory of *'3 degrees of influence'* back in 2007 & considerable proof has been shared to show that this is the case. Plus, they (amongst other researchers) didn't just stop at examining the risk of obesity but went further...

You already know from before, if your friend smokes (or starts smoking) you're about 61% more likely than average to smoke yourself. But it goes beyond this. If the friend of your friend smokes, you're 29% more likely to smoke yourself. And if the friend of your friend of your friend (3rd degree) smokes (or starts smoking), you're still 11% more likely to smoke yourself.

On the flip side, the researchers found the same applies to happiness & life satisfaction. And new research is constantly being conducting, finding similar patterns in many, many different areas of life (& specific behaviors of individuals).

Jim Rohn may have said, "you are the average of the *5 people you spend the most time with*" & while the premise is spot on, research has proven we can't take the number '5' too literally.

The people who spend the most time with, or look up to & respect most are more likely to shape your behavior, but there are *varying levels of influence* people (even those you don't personally know) have on you or me.

Specifically, it's not just your friends (the people you know & spend time with) that influence you, but also the friends of your friends, as well as the friend's friend's friends.

Meaning: it's not just the individuals you spend time with but also who *they* spend time time with. It's not just a *'people phenomenon,'* but a *'network & community phenomenon...'*

Of course, while each degree away shows a lower level of influence, it's not so small that we should dismiss it...

THE 'NETWORK & COMMUNITY' PHENOMENON

While it's easy to look at each person - you, me, anyone - as merely single individuals living their own individual lives, the reality is all 7+ billion of us are like an interconnected web of energy, frequency, thought, feeling, decision, action & results. We all part of one global network - all connected in some way.

A good comparison here is of the internet itself. Realize it or not, all websites & web pages are all interconnected in some way. Nobody owns the internet & no website is isolated on its own - it's all connected.

Also, the internet as it is today was not created by 1 person. Vinton Cerf & Robert Kahn may have been the first 2 people to create the basic technology of the 'internet,' however, they *couldn't* have created the internet as it is today. Nobody could. The internet is like a big canvas on which billions of unique people express themselves & contribute to the experience. T*he same applies to us: human beings.*

No single person creates the human experience as it is today, but we are all contributing to it in our own way. Every single one of us with each & every action we take.

For example, if you start to smoke, it doesn't just negatively affect your health, but as you now know, increases the risk of everybody *within 3 degrees of you* to also start smoking as well. This includes your friends (& people you spend time with), their friends & their friends too. *3 degrees.*

And, as statistics show the average adult has an average of 40 friends, of which, 9 are 'close friends,' that's a big influence.

Of course, these are averages & some have many more friends (as well as 'close friends') than this, while others have a lot less, but these are statistical averages.) **Which means...**

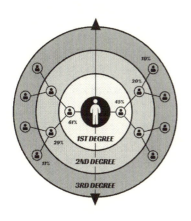

At the 1st degree, because you started smoking, an average of 9 'close friends' & a total of about 40 friends are now 61% more likely to smoke as well.

At the 2nd degree, if each of your 40 friends also has 40 friends (based on the statistical averages), that's 1600 people now 29% more likely to smoke *(just because you started to).*

At the 3rd degree, if each of those 1600 also has around 40 friends, now 64000 people are 11% more likely to smoke *(all because of the ripple effect you created by smoking yourself).*

Now, if you encourage one of those close friends, your spouse or your family to smoke - either knowingly or unknowingly - their influence spread too.

Since they started, they're also statistically influencing around 64000 people across their 3 degrees of influence to smoke.

And this also only assumes that our influences spread across the 3 degrees as the research has shown as of right now.

See, while researchers haven't yet found a 4th degree or 5th degree of influence (friend of a friend of a friend of a friend of a friend) on an individual's behaviors, I'm sure this too will be discovered in the future, as we are all connected in some way.

And, if they did find a 4th degree of influence, cross-reference this with the number of average friends a person has (like we've done here) & 2,560,000 people (yes, over 2.5 million people!) would be about 1% - 3% more likely to smoke *(just because of your influence when you started smoking!)*

A more clearly-visible example of this is that of how & why things go 'viral' on the internet. How a video, post or meme from someone pretty much unknown on the internet can go viral, reaching many millions of views in just days (with $0 in ad spend) & near-instantly propel someone to fame.

Think of 'Charlie Bit My Finger,' PSY with 'Gangnam Style,' a man questioning what a fox says in this viral music video, that dress that's simultaneously blue & black as well as white & gold or 'The Annoying Orange.'

Virality is the result of a lot of people doing a small thing - 'liking' 'sharing' & 'showing their friends' - that, like a snowball, builds & builds to a point of total 'virality' *(where everybody seems to be talking about it.)*

It's the result of people telling *their* friends (or sharing with their friends on social media), who then share it with *their* friends, who in turn, share it with *their* friends.

Quickly, your 1 share of that video can ripple into an indirect influence on hundreds & thousands of people in some way…

And just as videos or memes go viral, so do *ways of thinking, feeling, beliefs & behaviors* (as in the smoking example.)

So, if you've ever done something, reasoning to yourself that it *'doesn't matter,' 'your actions don't matter,'* or that *'your decisions don't have any impact'* on others or the world in general, you may be a little surprised right now to learn just how much each & every one of us, with each & every small decision, impacts the human experience as a whole.

What you do, what I do & what anybody does matters (big time) as it's what shapes the human experience.

And, not to get political, but ultimately, it is *not* the politicians that are going to change a country (or the world), but the collective intention, motivation, courage, commitment & accountability of people coming together in this way.

Which means, you, me & everybody is helping to influence not just our lives, but the world as a whole with all that we do.

Plus, when you bare in mind that we are not only all connected energetically, but also physically & relationally to each other, do you really recognize just how important you are in this process of creating the world as it is today...

As originally found by Frigyes Karinthy in 1929 & popularized in 1990 by John Guare, **'6 Degrees Of Separation'** is the idea that we are all connected to each other within 6 degrees.

6 degrees: *all people are 6 (or fewer) social connections away from anyone else on the planet.*

Meaning: in a ongoing chain of 'a friend of a friend of a friend' statements, any 2 people on the planet today can be connected within a maximum of 6 steps *(6 degrees).*

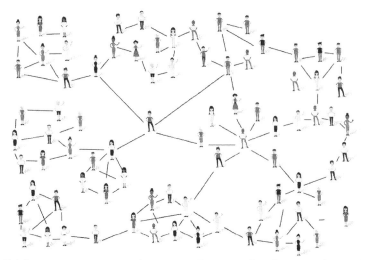

Which means, yes, you're a maximum of 6 degrees (6 social connection) from Bill Gates, Jeff Bezos, Elon Musk, Roger Federer, Michael Jordan, Serena Williams, Cristiano Ronaldo, Beyoncé, Meryl Streep, Leonardo DiCaprio or anyone else.

And if we're 6 (or less) degrees away from everyone else on the planet & our behaviors have (so far) shown to influence people across 3 of those degrees, I hope you can really get just how massive an influence what you do has on the world!

BIG-PICTURE: EVERYTHING COUNTS

One of the reasons I become a vegan when I was 14 years old - beside the well-documented health benefits & seeing my parents completely transform their health & fitness thanks to this way of eating - was the moral implications...

Early on, I learned the actual 'behind-the-scenes' of what happens to produce the meat, fish & dairy we have been taught ('rules' of society) to crave, want & eat. *I realized how this 'belief' wasn't serving me or the planet as a whole...*

I had also been studying business & entrepreneurship since I was about 12 years old, so I was well aware of basic economic principles such as the law of supply & demand & how this can be used to help create the change that most doubt is possible.

Put very single, the law of supply & demand explains that supply (availability), as well as price, will rise or fall, settling at a point where the quantity demanded (at the current price) will equal the quantity supplied (at the current price).

Or even more simply put, if there are people wanting to buy something, it will be produced & sold to meet that demand. In this case, animals will continue to be slaughtered to produce meat as long as people want to buy meat.

If demand rises, people will produce more. If demand falls through, so does supply *(as, if you produce too much, it just goes to waste & doesn't provide any economic benefit.)*

And when it comes to moral side of veganism, where animals *(in my personal opinion)* should be treated very differently than they are being treated today, it is each & every one of us that contributes to the problem by contributing to *'demand.'*

When I first mention this reason for being vegan, people often quickly ask, *"Do you really think, just because you don't eat this steak, all slaughter & abuse of animals is going to stop?"*

"Of course not," I reply, *"Not initially - but with time, it's possible."* All I know is with each & every decision what I'm doing is lowering 'demand' for animal products *(plus, based on what we talked about before, my decision is influencing those around me to also put their own beliefs about food under the microscope & be more conscious going further...)*

As I no longer eat animal products, for example, demand falls by 1 person. Which means less meat (supply) is produced as 1 fewer person want to buy. When the next person challenges this social norm & stops eating meat, demand falls again. And supply drops to match. Over & over again. *The cycle repeats...*

Continue this trajectory until, hypothetically, nobody wants to buy animal products anymore & supply stops altogether...

Also, over the years I've grown to understand the humanity, decency & goodness of even people who run slaughterhouses. They are not bad people. They are just like you & me, looking to, first & foremost, meet their basic needs (to survive) before focusing on anything else. They are just making a living. They want to provide for their families. Hence, they work there...

However, if demand no longer exists (nobody wants to buy animal products anymore) they won't just continue to produce meat needlessly. They'll be no money there anymore.

In another example, if people challenged *beliefs* like *'I must wear makeup to look good & impress those around me'* things would begin to shift there too.

In fact, the companies behind these ads telling you that you're not beautiful unless you have buckets full of makeup covering your face, won't have the incentive to push these messages anymore or produce full supermarket aisles worth of makeup as people don't want to buy. *As demand drops so does supply.*

Or, if most people didn't follow the *belief* that you need some fancy college degree to amount to anything in life, things in the education system would change. Education as we know it would adapt or die off (making room for something better...)

The reason that college tuitions keep rising is more & more people want to go to these top school, as they believe it's their key to a good life. *And as demand rises here, so does price.*

However, as we collectively begin to realize there are more effective methods of education & that the primary purpose of education should be actual practical skills & not some piece of paper (a diploma) that people believe they are completely hopeless without, education would change. The world would.

However, it starts with each & every one of us (& this is what we must keep in mind, both personally & if we want to help influence any new change in the world - it happens with each seemingly-insignificant decision from each & every person.

Let's go back to the quote from Einstein shared in chapter #3:

"The world will not be destroyed by those who do evil, but by those who watch them without doing anything"

Fundamentally, it's our *'belief'* that what we do doesn't matter that at the end of the day lead the biggest global issues.

And, as I share with my clients, *it all challenges with each & every decision & action, from each & every person.* That what causes problems as well as creates solutions. Simply put...

| Everything Counts

As William James once said, *"Act as if what you do makes a difference. It does."*

Your actions are not insignificant; they matter. And they have weight to them. Like pebbles dropped into a pond, they create ripples in your life, influence others (across many degrees) & the world as a whole (contributing to the human experience.)

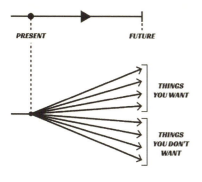

Plus, as we talked about back at the beginning, the future is nothing more than an infinite set of *'possibility streams'* which coexist at any moment.

And it's through our daily thoughts, feelings, decisions & actions that we tune these into possibilities in our lives...

PSYCHOLOGY | 293

On a global scale, it's the decisions & actions of everybody that create the world we live in - we all co-create this world with everything we do (or don't do.)

See, Martin Luther King Jr may have been the figurehead of the Civil Rights Movement, but that change (that new gained freedom) was actually the result of the collective actions - the day-in, day-out decisions & choices - of each & every person. I'm sure that Martin Luther King Jr, were he were alive today, would be the first to say the same. And this same principle applies to every great change ever created, as well as every great shift we (humanity) will create in the future...

BECOME AWARE OF THE INFLUENCE

To continue this journey, we must become more mindful of how the past influence of those you spend time with shaped your *identity* - *'who you are'* - today, as well as how you're being influenced (or influencing others) going forward.

Do this & you'll tap into great personal power. And repeat this on a bigger - communal, national or global - scale & now you're contributing to a greater human existence.

That's the 1st form of **'*environmental* conditioning'** - people - now, let's explore the next...

2. **Surroundings:** That Which Is Around You Impacts What You Think & Do

In criminology (the study of crime, order & criminal justice), there's a concept called, *'the broken windows theory'* & it can help us understand how our physical environment impacts, not just crime, but 'who we are' & the decisions we make.

The 'broken windows theory' states, *"visible signs of crime, anti-social behavior and civil disorder create an urban environment that encourages further crime and disorder, including serious crimes."*

The reason it's called *'broken windows'* is because, in the publication, the following example is provided:

> *Consider a building with a few broken windows. If the windows are not repaired, the tendency is for vandals to break a few more windows. Eventually, they may even break into the building, and if it's unoccupied, perhaps become squatters or light fires inside.*
>
> *Or consider the pavement. Some litter accumulates. Soon, more litter accumulates. Eventually, people even start leaving bags of refuse from take-out restaurants there or even break into cars.*

And this not just affects one part of our lives, but all parts. In different physical environments, we are primed & conditioned to make different decisions & take different actions.

Think about it: *do you act the same way in a bar or club as you would in an office, or are different parts of 'who you are' expressed because to the physical environment around you?*

Part of it is about the people you're spending time with, but it's also about the physical environment around you *(note: these 3rd categories of conditioning will often go together.)*

I was recently in India when I had a discussion regarding this very topic with an amazing person I had been recently introduced to. He said it brilliantly: *'people wouldn't even think about spitting on the floor in a 5-star hotel, yet they would do it as soon as they step out into the streets of India.'*

These 2 areas could literally be a few steps apart - inside the hotel vs outside in the streets of India - yet that 1 behavior (spitting on the floor) is deemed completely inappropriate in one environment, but seemingly acceptable in the other.

I've seen this play out in my own life - you probably have too...

If the room is a mess, I'll tend to care about its tidiness less, & the mess will pile up until it's eventually cleaned (later on). If a sink is piled up with dishes, I'm more likely to leave another dirty dish in there than if the sink is empty. If, while I'm traveling, the clothes in my suitcase are a mess, I'm more likely to just throw something in there (instead of folding it).

In one physical environment, you're primed to express what, at the time, is your 'worst self,' while in another you're set up to express your 'best self' - optimized for a result you want, which supports your thinking, feeling & decision making.

But, this goes far beyond crime or cleanliness into everything:

| What's Around You (Your Physical Environment) Impacts What You Do

It's the reason spiritual cultures & religions around the world have places of joint sharing & worship, as well as the reason great companies build amazing offices. Rarely is it just about making things look nice, but rather about creating a physical environment that people find empowering.

In the case of offices, this turns into better work satisfaction, less conflict, better productivity, creativity & overall results.

Some companies even need to 'force' their employees to actually go home at night & sleep as they just want to stay & work, largely because of the environment *(both in terms of people & the physical world created within the office walls)*.

It's the reason people prefer to go to a gym than to workout at home - the *physical environment* of a gym impacts their thinking, feeling & sets them up for better results.

It's the reason companies that provide co-working spaces have multi-billion dollar valuations. Sure, people could work at home, but prefer to go to a co-working space because of both the people & the physical environment they create there.

People may make fun of screenwriters flocking to coffee shops every morning to write their screenplays from there, but the environment of a coffee shop is often much better for work & productivity than working from your bed, bedroom or kitchen table (which tends to encourage relaxation, play & fun over productivity, making it optimal for some things & not others).

Like it or not, beyond the people around us, what's physically around us forms the 2nd layer of *environment conditioning* which impacts the sides of ourselves we express, the choices we make & behaviors we display. *And, knowing this, once again, allows us to be more mindful & intentionally in setting ourselves up for the results we truly want...*

HOW TO APPLY THIS IN YOUR LIFE...

What's your desk, workspace or office like? What stuff do you have lying around your house? What's in your fridge? Are alcohol or cigarettes in your house or in your immediate environment? How close or far the closest gym is to your home or office? What restaurants are closest to where you live? Where to do you live - community, place - in general?

All of these are great questions for us to explore as their answers affect what we do. If your fridge is stuffed with things you know aren't good for you (or alcohol is plentiful in your home) it becomes easier for you to engage in those behaviors.

If you live in a place where the closest gym is a long drive away, you're less likely to go there than if the gym is close by. And the same applies to nearby restaurants & shops.

What's the culture - assumed rules, standards & expectations - of the country, state, city & local community you live in?

You're more likely to follow those cultural beliefs & standards if you're living in a place where that influence is strong. On the flip side, if you live in a place where the culture perfectly aligns with the life you want, you're actively setting yourself up for better results & enhanced life satisfaction.

| The Physical Environment Helps Form Standards & Expectations, Which Influence Our Behavior

Live in a more health-conscious community where, beyond the people, the physical environment is supportive - gyms & sports clubs are everywhere, healthy restaurants are on every corner, yoga & meditation centers are close by, etc - & that *physical environment* will make it very easy for you to make decisions that are aligned with what you truly want...

CHOOSING GREAT PHYSICAL ENVIRONMENTS

Which means, when you're moving house, choosing where to work, picking the location of your new office or going on holiday somewhere, you may want to consider, not just the basics you normally would, but also how it's going to impact your psychology, thinking, feeling & life in general.

If health is a top priority, you may want to choose a location that has a healthy restaurant & gym close by as now you'll be more inclined to eat healthier & exercise regularly. Long term, look out for weather, pollution rates, healthcare as well as life expectancy rates of people in that country, as these are much better metrics for you to make decisions on than other things.

In fact, you could probably add an extra 5 - 10 years (if not more) to your lifespan by simply living in one country, city & community (physical environment) compared to another!

If you want to hang around with millionaires & have their influence rub off on you (people), you may want to consider spending time in places like New York, Monaco, Singapore or London *(& physical environment helps here too.)*

New York, for example, is the most, not millionaire, but billionaire filled city in the world, with over 1,000 billionaires living there. Monaco, on the other hand, has a population in which 1 / 3 have a net worth of over a million dollars.

You may be paying more to live in these places, but the intangible influence of your environment is something that can give you a great return on your investment.

It's not that you can't meet highly-wealthy people anywhere else - *you can* - but these are the places in which your odds of that happening are the highest. *People congregate together & these are places healthy or wealthy people congregate...*

And, if you're building a big business, while you can do it from anywhere, it tends to be easier to go to a big city in which things you need (yet you don't know you need) are available.

Suddenly need overnight printing or shipping or something? Need something repaired as soon as possible? Need a big venue for something? Need to buy this very specific, niche item quickly? Big cities will tend to help you solve these needs much quicker than living somewhere in the countryside.

Just as you can add to your lifespan with the physical environment you're spending most of your time in, start (or move) your business to a new location &, for a big business, you could probably add an extra 6 or 7 figures in revenue (accumulated over a couple of years) doing this alone.

On the flip side, if want to get relaxed, a countryside, beach resort or beautiful island are *physical environments* that will prime you for your desired states of relaxation & bliss much better than the environment or a busy city or loud household.

By matching up the <u>physical environments</u> you're spending time in with the things you truly want in life, you're actively setting yourself up for success...

YOU CAN TRANSCEND THE ENVIRONMENT

> *"Man is not the creature of circumstances, circumstances are the creatures of men. We are free agents, and man is more powerful than matter"*
>
> - BENJAMIN DISRAELI

The people we spend with & physical environments around us have the power & potential to influence us. No doubt!

But, this does <u>not</u> mean you're a victim to your environment & conditioning from the things around you!

Firstly, just as you can choose those you do (or do not) spend time with, you can choose what physical environments you're going to be surrounded by.

But, beyond even that, understand you can always transcend your environment (both people & physical surroundings).

You can absolutely be relaxed & peaceful in a busy city, build a big business from the countryside, write a hit screenplay from your bed instead of the local coffee shop or be healthy where no gyms or healthy restaurants are close by. <u>*No doubt!*</u>

In fact, you can also choose to influence your environment, instead of being influenced by your environment. It's definitely not easy, but it is possible…

What important to really 'get' here is that you are going to be skimming upstream if you do this, so you better become a well-trained swimmer to make it *(without falling under the influence of your environment.)*

On the flip side, you can always use your internal will to set yourself up for success from the beginning & make things as easy as possible by aligning your physical environment with your values & ambitions. *You have a lot of <u>choices</u> here!*

3. **News & Media:** The Information We Consume Makes Us 'Who We Are.'

If food feeds our bodies, *information* is the food that feeds our minds. And just as we can eat junk food or healthy food, we can feed our minds with food (*information*) that either conditions us into the future we want or the future we don't.

And while shops & restaurants mainly provide the food we use to feed our bodies, outside of conversations with people we spend time with, it's the news & media of various sorts that feed us the *information* we consume.

For example, as Malcolm X once said...

"The media's the most powerful entity on earth. They have the power to make the innocent guilty and to make the guilty innocent, and that's power. Because they control the minds of the masses"

The *information* we consume - whether that the newspaper, the news, articles on the internet, videos, radio, podcasts, books, our Facebook feed, etc - is one of the biggest factors that control us, shaping 'who we are.'

What we consume is who we become, hence we must be very mindful of the information we consume.

In this part, we're going to explore how new's & media outlets operate & how they may be sabotaging your potential. After which, we'll look at methods you can use to better manage your attention & condition yourself for success. *Let's start...*

UNDERSTANDING THE 'NEWS'

The news, *which forms the main source of information for many people about the world we live in* - whether that's the local newspaper, the online news site or news you listen to on the radio - actually come from *for-profit entities* (companies).

Realize it or not, however most news comes from 'news companies' whose job primarily objective is to make money. For them, the more money they make the better; *it's business.*

'How do they make money?' you may think. It's a good question as news companies don't sell product or services like other businesses. *So, how do these companies become billion dollar companies? What do they sell? What's the product?*

The answer: *you.* The people who consume news are actually the product of the news outlets - it's *their attention* they sell in the form of advertising opportunities. *To who?* Advertisers.

The advertisers are the actual customers of most new sites, channels, blogs & outlets (the real source of their revenue) while the consumers are actually the product they sell.

And the more people's attention they have - the more readers, listeners & watchers - the more advertising they can sell (at higher prices) & the more money they make. *Making their first goal to maximize eyeballs (readers, listeners, viewers.)*

Now, what you're reading here isn't, within itself, bad. You're simply paying with your attention (which is turned into ad dollars by these companies) instead of paying money. It's the reason why things these outlets are 'free.' *What makes this trade either effective or largely ineffective for you or me is the tactics they use to get our attention in the first place.*

See, you may assume that to get people to 'pay attention' you would want to share as many positive, happy & empowering news stories - that people really 'want to' pay attention to - as possible, right? Well, that's <u>not</u> quite the case...

New companies are smarter than that. They understand what most *do not* - that there is a better way to get our attention.

That method is to tickle our survival instincts & make people, not just 'want to,' but feel like they 'have to' pay attention...

WHY FEAR & SCANDAL RUNS THE MEDIA?

In his book, *Thinking Fast & Slow,* Nobel prize-winning psychologist, *Daniel Kahneman* introduces us to the concept of *"loss aversion,"* which refers to our tendency to prefer avoiding losses than acquiring gains

He found, researched & documented that we (human beings) are more motivated to avoid losing something that we already have than we are to gain something new. Simply summarized: *we prefer not to lose $5 than to gain $5.*

And to figure out just how much more motivated we are by one than the other, Daniel Kahneman & this research partner Amos Tversky, conducted an experiment...

In it, the people were asked, *"I'm going to flip a coin & if it comes up 'tails,' you lose $100. How much would you have to win if it's comes up 'heads' in order to take this gamble?"*

Tails: you lose $100. Heads: *what's the minimum you would you need to take on the gamble?*

For example... Tails, you lose $100. Heads, you win $140.

If you're like most people who participated in the experiment, you would actually reject this. As Kahneman says, *"the fear of losing $100 is more intense than the hope of winning $140."*

In fact, most people responded they needed a minimum of between $150 & $250 *(average: $200)* if it lands on *heads* in order to take on this gamble. Not $120. Not $140. But, $200!

Logically or mathematically, any number above $100 skews the advantage in your favor. Let's say it was $120. Repeat that gamble 10 times, or 50, or 100 & you're likely to win a lot of money. But, psychologically, the fear of loss is stronger than the prospect of gain, so most didn't take this initial gamble.

Only once heads gain them back a 1.5 to 2.5 return *(average: a 2:1 ratio between the prospect of gain vs the fear of loss)* did the *majority* of people in the experiment take the gamble.

Of course, you'll get people who are more risk-tolerance, or more risk-averse, but this simple experiment showed that we are approximately 2 times more motivated by the *fear of loss* than we are by the *prospect of gain.*

This understanding was then dubbed, *"Prospect Theory"* & outlined in detail in their research paper, *"Prospect Theory: An Analysis of Decision under Risk."*

Now, why is this being shared? It's because news & media outlets or sources knows this. Either through research or just years of pattern recognition, data analysis & adaptation *(doing more of what worked in the past)*, but they know this!

Hence to maximize viewership (& as a result, boost revenue) news & media outlets put out more fear-driven, fear-inducing & often scandalous, news stories than anything else.

They know that those are the stories that will get us to not just 'want to' pay attention, but feel like we 'have to' pay attention.

They are the ones that best knock on the doors of our reptilian brain - our 'survival instincts' - tune into our deep-seated evolutionary fears (such as the fear of the death or the unknown) & best motivate us to pay attention to them.

In fact, in studies where subjects are shown negative video footage (a war, an airplane crash, an execution, a natural disaster), they have shown to pay more attention, their brains become more aroused, can better recall what happened & overall engage more cognitive resources to consume the media than for non-negative footage.

In my work studying marketing, I've often heard this advice for writing headlines, titles & email subject lines, *'if all else fails, go negative.'* And that's how the media operates - except they skip the *'if all else fails...'* part & just go straight to *'go negative'* part in order to maximize consumption & revenue.

They filter reality, discard the stories that won't get attention *(even if people need to, or at least should hear them)* & instead opt for those that will give them the most of people's attention - usually, *the negative ones*. That's how they make the most money - which is their primary goal to start with.

They are not bad people, but acting in according to the best interest of the model & system they work within; *one that if you continue to follow will continue to dominate.* Check this:

1) the media's first & main priority is to make money.

2) Fear, sensationalism & extremism is a better, more effective way for news & media to get our attention.

And it's this combination of understandings that explains why the media is filled with articles, headlines & stories that are primarily negative (or even completely scandalous).

A 'SKEWED' VIEW OF THE WORLD

Because of all of this, the news provides a 'skewed' view of the world. Biased. Tainted. Not accurate, but exaggerated.

The information we receive from news & typical media is largely clouded or diluted; skewed towards fear as that's what brings in readers, listeners, viewers, ad dollars & revenue for these news & media outlets.

Fear is a strong motivator. A lethal one. They know that & they use it - day in, day out. The unfortunate by-product of this is that, for those who consume typical news & media, their mindset is far more attune to fear & survival that to abundance & the infinite possibilities that co-exist for them.

For example: watch plane crashes, train's derailing or wars erupting on the news every single day & it's not before long your mind is strongly conditioned into a reality in which you fear flying, travel, leaving the house or any other fear in life.

Logically, we know flying is safe. Real-world statistics show we only have a 0.000014% chance of dying flying. It isn't just safe, but the safest mode of travel in the world today.

In fact, it's shown it's 19 times more dangerous to drive than to fly. And some stats show that you're more likely to die from a bee sting (estimated odds: 1 in 5.5 million) or from being struck by lighting (estimated odds of death: 1 in 1.9 million) than from flying (estimated odds of death: 1 in 7 million).

Yet, we don't act in accordance with this. Despite these statistics proving how safe flying is, if you watch enough plane crashes - *which they news will undoubtedly show* - you may end up irrationally fearing flying (or anything else in life.)

It's nothing more than conditioning; either train yourself (or be trained by others; the news, the media, etc) how to think.

Watch enough news stories about terrorism, crime in other countries & how inferior other cultures supposedly are & you may just end up terrified, distrusting or very judgemental of other people who, at the deepest level, belong to the exact same species as you (your fellow 'human beings.')

In my own life, I've seen this most with my grandparents & great-grandparents. They watch the news every single day & as you could predict, they are terrified. They live their lives that way: filled with constant, never-ending fear.

They don't fly. They rarely leave the house. They believe that they're going to get robbed - stolen from - all the time. They are terrified of most of what happens in life.

Fear has become their reality. I love them, but in my personal opinion, they live very limited & emotionally-draining lives.

Why? Largely because of the conditioning - the doctrine - that they have chosen to feed their minds with.

As we talked about in the last section, take something, repeat it enough times & your mind becomes more & more likely to believe it (& act in accordance with it). *That's conditioning.*

Hence, if you want to live an unlimited life; one filled with abundance instead of fear & joy instead of terror, you must consume the type of information that aligns *(condition 'you'.)*

This doesn't mean you can't read the newspaper once in a while, research sad topics, read about the war or watch horror movies - you can - but don't live & get addicted to that world. If you have to, make that a very small part of the *information* you consume about the world compared to everything else.

Ultimately: make choices to <u>actively condition yourself</u> *for the life you want (rather than the life you don't.)*

EXTREMISM: SUCCESS HAPPENS OVERNIGHT?

"But Bogdan, the media covers positive things too" you may say. And it does. It covers it - a lot!

In fact, research shows us that after fear, anger & destruction, the 2nd category which gets covered most by news & media is the polar opposite: *complete joy, pride & celebration.*

Why? It's because while fear is the strongest motivator to get people to pay attention, emotions of joy, pride & celebration are the 2nd strongest motivators.

And, anything in the middle - the journey, everyday life & growth - doesn't usually get covered as it's considered boring or 'not newsworthy.' *Polarity & extremism are their tools.*

Now, while this may seem to counteract & solve the initial issue of fear-driven media, it doesn't. In fact, it only makes it worse. When the media isn't covering fear-driven stories that induce fear into the public, it's covering the other extreme of what seems like 'overnight successes' - omitting the journey.

The news might report (create a story) on the gymnast that can do the gymnastic routine that no one else could do, but not cover the years & years of hard work, training, blood, sweat & tears that it took her to get there.

The 102-year-old blind man who, despite his lack of sight, learned to play the violin extraordinarily is going to get a news story on him, but his years of hard work when those around him thought he was crazy - that his ambition was 'impossible' - will likely be omitted because of the format. *Hard work, training & learning just aren't so 'newsworthy.'*

So, even when the news does report on joyous, cheerful, inspirational & abundance situations like these ones, because of the *'breaking news'* format they use, what's truly valuable in that story is omitted & only the triumph is shown.

This has it's upside - it brings us spikes of joy & inspiration. However, in the long-term it can be very damaging. It causes the same way of thinking I've worked with clients around the world to help them overcome: *the idea of 'overnight success.'*

The triumph is shared on the news, but the years or decades of work *(the journey)* are omitted, misleading us to believe in 'overnight success' 'overnight fame' & 'instant riches.'

For example, people see Kobe Bryant, Roger Federer, David Copperfield or Madonna at their best, but never see the years of early wake-ups, tireless nights, hours of hard work & years of struggle that it took to help them get there in the first place.

"Headlines, in a way, are what mislead you because bad news is a headline, and gradual improvement is not," Bill Gates said. *Gradual improvement just isn't newsworthy.*

We get conditioned to believe this is how the world works (& that this will also happen to us.) All of which makes us very susceptible to 'get rich quick schemes' 'magic transformation pills,' instant gratification & shortcuts that often backfire.

It makes us impatience, more likely to quit when success doesn't come instantly, get discouraged by little things that get in the way or *not* willing to do what it takes to start with.

But, while these first 2 reasons should be enough to make many people (especially those in this work) avoid the news like the plague (as it's unconsciously sabotaging their life), *the 3rd reason is arguably even worse than the first 2...*

IS THE NEWS EVEN 'REAL'?

I tell people all of the above & all that remains is this 1 excuse: *"Bogdan, but I need to be informed. I need to know the truth; the reality about what's going on in this world." "I want to be in the know; that's why I read, listen to & watch the news."*

I respect that. I appreciate it. In fact, I value it. I too am curious & want to know what's going on. The challenge: *is the news really 'real'? Does it actually represent the 'real' world?*

As we know, the media runs public perception. The media can make good people bad & bad people good. What the media believes to be true is what the average individual will often go on to believe is true as well.

And if public opinion is so strongly shaped by it, I believe it's important then to find out what truly runs the news & media.

Most rarely stop to ask this question of, *"what runs the media then?" "Is the source of their content even credible? & "Does it accurately represent the world around us..."*

That's what Ryan Holiday explored & challenged in his book, *Trust Me, I'm Lying: Confessions Of A Media Manipulator.*

Firstly, as you learn about the 'behind-the-scenes' of the news & media - such as in this book - the facade of news & media acting in the best interest of keeping you informed about the world *(as the vision statement may say)* quickly fades away...

Secondly, after many years of working in these fields, Ryan shares about just how information makes it into the news in the first place. Just take a look at these stats:

- In a media monitoring study done by Cision & George Washington University, 89% of journalists reported using blogs for their research for stories.

- 50% reported using Twitter as research for stories.

- More than 66% reported using other social media networks, such as Facebook or LinkedIn as research for their stories.

Yes - that means that a lot of the stories you read on top news sites, read in magazines, in newspapers & even watch on news channels, are sourced, based on & researched from social media or blogs on the internet.

And there are various case studies in which the initial posts or blogs these particular news stories are based on, get largely discredited by the very same people who wrote those posts or blogs in the first place.

Some kid could have written some fake post on social media (or on a blog) & it forms the basis - *without verification* - for a big blog story or even a national news story seen by millions.

You know how in court, one may be asked about the source - the origin - of the information, argument or evidence they are sharing with the court, well in the case of the news, it's often like *"Yeah, that article I wrote for national news was based on a few tweets & blog entries I found on the internet."*

And this happens hundreds & thousands of times every day. Not because of the writer's evil intentions, but largely due to the economics of the system they work within.

Specifically, the **time pressure** writers are under to produce new stories *(when working for top digital news blogs, online journalists are expected to produce between 5 & 10 fresh, new articles per day!)* & the **type of compensation** they receive *(they are often paid 'per article,' which incentives quantity over quality, or 'per article view' which incentives writers to just focus on writing catchy headlines that get clicks & not great, well-researched & valuable articles.)*

And because of this *time pressure* & *type of compensation*, every second spent on writing great, educational articles is actually a moment wasted; *not spent on writing more short articles with catchy headlines people clicks & make money.*

Dive a little deeper into this world & you'll find that because of how the economies of these industries work, most top news sites & blogs don't go out and source their own news at all, but rather just pull from what's already out there - irrelevant of whether it's been verified or not.

They don't fact check as it's not in their best interest to do so; that just slows them down from writing more stories, getting more attention & making more ad revenue. So they take shortcuts that sacrifice quality.

Research - go down the rabbit hole - & you'll see for yourself.

Lastly, even if it is 'real,' it's rarely helpful as the time frame of 'breaking news!' reporting is far too short for real value...

HOW TO *REALLY* 'GET INFORMED'...

As Pulitzer Prize-winning author, *Will Durant*, once wrote, *"Most of us spend too much time on the last 24 hours and too little on the last 6000 years."*

Little value can be gained from just observing the last 24 hours *(the news)* without exploring from a higher perspective.

Sure, you can learn about what someone did, how they did it or, sometimes, even why they did it, but you won't learn what truly drove that behavior. Nor will you see many case studies of how this similar behavior played out in other situations.

As the saying goes, *"once is chance, twice is coincidence, third time's a pattern."* Single events (as shared in news stories), in the case of learning & true understanding, are like single pieces of data in a scientific experiment; *it's not enough data to form any real & accurate conclusions about anything.*

Like a scientist, if you really want to gain information that's most valuable to you, you must observe the same thinking, feeling, decisions & actions across many, various situations, until you see 'patterns' - not just 'chances' or 'coincidences.'

So, if you truly want to learn about the world, to be informed, as well as know what's likely to happen in the future, *study history* (not the last 24 hours of history - the news - but the past years, decades, centuries & millennium.)

You may have heard the saying *"history repeats itself,"* - well, it does. While things are new & ever-changing, at their core, they follow the same fundamental 'patterns' of humanity, society & nature. These are the 'patterns' - the insights about the world - that give the greatest knowledge, wisdom & power. However, they can't be learned from a single event, but only from a more complete study of many similar events over time.

For example, while you won't be able to learn much about the latest economic crash, what's *really* happening, why it's *really* happening or what's going to happen next by consuming news stories, you can definitely learn plenty about this *(& even be able to predict what's going to happen next)* by looking into the past, studying past economic crashes, learning economic principles & finding 'patterns' you can use going forward.

A great example of this is the hit video by one of the world's greatest investors, Ray Dalio, titled, *"How The Economic Machine Works - In 30 Minutes"*. It's an incredible video that breaks down complex economics into simple understandings.

Within 30 minutes anybody who watches it will have a basic understanding of economics, as well as how & why economies crash. In his book, *Big Debt Crises*, he builds on this, sharing case studies of the 2008 financial crisis, the 1930's Great Depression & the 1920's inflationary depression of Germany's Weimar Republic. He's a man who's truly 'informed' - *really 'in the know'* - about *economics, economic crashes & what's likely to happen next, yet he'll likely to be the 1st to attest that his knowledge did <u>not</u> come from consuming typical news.*

Frankly, this level of deep understanding of any topic cannot be obtained from the 'breaking news' format of information.

It's actually a little ironic - the very thing people consume so they can 'be informed' & 'know what's happening in the world' - is actually the very same thing that could never truly give you these things *(but only a very surface level of it)*

It's only by zooming out & looking for 'patterns' *(as Will Durant or Ray Dalio have done)* can you truly 'be informed.'

PUTTING IT TOGETHER: **REASON THIS WITH ME...**

News companies are usually for-profit entities & their #1 priority is to make money; to get your attention so they can sell it to advertisers. *That's their product: your attention.*

And to get your attention, they often put out very extreme messages they know people are biologically & psychologically more likely to consume *(either because they feel they 'have to' or they really 'want to.')*

The most popular category is that of fear-driven new stories, as these are the ones that best get our attention. They filter reality, sharing the most of that which will induce fear *(as when you're 'scared,' you're paying the most attention.)*

The more bad, tragic & shocking stories they share, the more your reptilian brain - *your 'survival instincts'* - are going to make you feel like you 'have to' pay attention. And the more attention you give them, they more ad revenue they make.

And because of this skewed, biased, showcasing of the world, we get conditioned into a certain thinking, feeling & being. We get programmed for stress, high alert & fight-or-flight.

When you're seeing all the bad things in this world - day-in, day-out - without a balanced outlook, you are not being conditioned for acceptance, knowledge, abundance, success, freedom or living a great life. No. *You're being programmed for survival, fear & the lowest levels of human consciousness.*

Think about it: *if you had some stranger sending you a message every single day with some new thing that's wrong with this world & telling you why you should live a life filled with fear... would you keep reading his messages every day?*

Secondly, they put out the opposite: joy, pride & celebration (but because of the 'breaking news' format of the news, they omit all the value, detail & insight within the stories) usually creating perceptions of 'overnight success.'

You pay attention, making them more ad revenue, however the by-product is, in this case, you get conditioned to be more impatience, more likely to buy into instant gratification, get discouraged easily & more likely to give up when success doesn't show up immediately.

And it's this mismatch between one's expectations ('instant success') & reality (success doesn't happen overnight) that can be a big catalyst for the loss of hope, feelings of helplessness, sadness, anger & even depression.

If one continues to jump from one shiny object to another (labeled 'shiny object syndrome), thinking that with the next opportunity they are going to 'get rich quick' or 'gain instant fame,' & their expectations continue to crash into the rocks of reality, this mismatch can be really lethal.

In summary: *most news outlets are less 'news' & more just a curation of things designed to get you to pay attention (that come with big, unwanted, psychological consequences.)*

MENTAL BREAKDOWN & DYSFUNCTION

Just as when you consume enough bad food (like the guy in the hit documentary, *Super Size Me,* who ate McDonald's every single meal for 30 days) & your body begins to break down, gets dysfunctional & you gain weight, the same actually happens to your mind.

Spend enough of your mental capacity in fear, stress, terror, extremism & ideas of 'overnight success' & soon enough 'who you are,' begins to changes. You become a different person & often not in the ways you'd want.

You become more cynical. You feel more helpless, shifting from an internal locus of control to an external one. You feel like a victim of life. More doubtful. More pessimistic.

You don't see the opportunities around you because you're *Reticular Activating System* has been primed to pay attention to very different things now.

Your mind begins to break down, moving further & further away from the kind of thinking & feeling required to create that life that you truly want...

However, it doesn't have to be this way as you choose the conditioning & information you consume, as well as the interpretations you form from it. *It's your choice...*

Remember: at any moment, you can choose to reason with this logic (as well as conduct your own research if you want), *stop* consuming typical news stories & instead focus on really 'getting informed' through various other means *(like books, courses, valuable conversation, documentaries & research).*

EXERCISE: 30 DAY NEWS DETOX
Do you really need to know what's going on in the White House right now, updates on overseas wars or who crashed on the motorway today? *Do you really need to see all of that every single day?*

Especially bearing in mind that it's often, 1) skewed & 2) programming you for lower & lower levels of consciousness - for fear, for greed & for stress.

If you're open to something new, support yourself with this exercise. *For the next 30 days, go on a '*<u>***news detox.***</u>*'*

That's right... for the next 30 days, don't watch the news, don't read the morning newspaper & don't check news sites during your lunch break. When the news starts on the radio, simply turn off the radio until the music comes back on.

You can still consume information & many forms of media, but don't consume typical news outlets during this detox.

Stick with it & only assess after 30 days. See for yourself how much more abundant, powerful, prosperous, clear-headed, energized & motivated you'll feel after this time. *Just test it!*

> And no risk... if after the 30 days, you don't feel the benefits, just go back. However, reserve your judgment for after you complete this exercise & test it for yourself.
>
> Ultimately, words can only say so much. As can other people else's experiences. Or even facts & statistics. Beyond all of these, the most powerful realization comes from personal experience & testing something out in your own life.
>
> *Take this 'news detox' for a 30 day test-drive & then assess the results. Be strong. Be committed. You can do it!*

However, this isn't just about 'news' - *it's bigger than that.*

Big picture: it's about being more aware & intentional with all the *information* that you choose to consume in your life...

From the movies you watch to the websites you visit, from the TV shows you watch to the apps you use, from the music you listen to through to the ads you pay attention to, from magazines you look through to the gossip you engage in (or the complaining you listen to.) All of this falls into this 3rd sub-category of *'environmental conditioning.'* In big ways...

| What You Consume Is Who You Become

So, it's important you surround yourself with, not just people, but *information* truly aligned with your values & ambitions.

Plus, if we truly believe in how your life is being shaped by the information & influence of things around you, why would you ever want to let a destructive, sabotaging, distracting or disempowering piece of information (or, interpretation) into your mind anyway? If you truly believe that, you must...

| Guard Your Mind

Just how exclusive clubs, galleries, hotels or restaurants will have a bouncer to stop certain people from entering without verification, or how in an airport there are multiple levels of security (check-in, baggage drop, passport control, security, boarding gates) to protect people, as well as ensure only the right people (those on flights) enter the airport & are able to board a flight - *well, you must do the same with your mind...*

You must put *information* around you under scrutiny. You must check it. Don't let that which doesn't support you get into your mind, hijack it & fly you to a life of misery. Rather, be like a bouncer at a club or security at an airport, *'guarding your mind'* against information that doesn't support you.

Decide that from now on, all information doesn't just get an open pass into your mind (the operating system of your life). *No.* Now, it gets screened & checked to ensure your mind is being fed the right way. Threats are not allowed in (or are escorted out quickly if they manage to sneak in) while guests *('information' you want)* are treated like 1st-class passengers.

'Guarding your mind' is about both, minimizing that which doesn't support you ('the news', complaining, gossip, etc) while maximizing what serves you *(education, knowledge, books, educational videos, inspiring stories, messages from role models, appreciation, fun-filled conversations, etc).*

While great health is the result of treating your body like a temple, creating the life you want is the result of treating your mind like a temple too. Take care of it, support it & feed it what will give it the required nutrition for real growth!

EXERCISE: FLOOD YOUR FEED
See, it's one thing to 'guard your mind' by turning off the TV in the morning while the news are on or to mute the radio during the advertisements (that's very controllable & easy to do), but it's another thing when it comes to social media &

ads online. Here, people often feel like this is completely outside of their control; that they can't do anything about it.

However, this is not the case. Like it or not, you can change the type of information that shows up on your social media feeds & even the kind of ads you see online. *Here's how...*

Big companies - especially social media giants like Facebook or Youtube (owned by Google) spend millions of dollars (& hours) tracking, gathering data & optimizing algorithms to show you <u>exactly</u> what you're most likely to engage with, watch & react to (*based on your <u>previous viewing habits</u>*).

Which means, your social media feed is a lot like a *'self-fulfilling prophecy.'*

The more you consume a certain type of information (e.g. 'tennis' content), the more that platforms will show you posts, videos, articles (& even ads) about it. In their system, you're now a *'tennis fan,'* so they'll show you content (& advertisers will run ads to you, through the platform) about tennis.

And the more you continue to engage with tennis content, the more of it you'll see on your feeds. *The cycle continues...*

As you consume more stuff about tennis, you show interest more. As you show interest & engagement, you get shown more content about it as these platforms show you more of that to keep you engaged & using their platforms.

Once again: *this is neither good nor bad, but depends on how you use it...*

For example, when I'm scrolling my social media feeds nowadays, I can't go a few seconds without seeing something inspiring, motivating or educational on my feed.

My social media feeds are filled with information that truly feeds my mind & guides me to the life I want. *This wasn't accidental; it was intentional.* And, you can do the same...

You can turn your social media into a flood of inspiration that supports you in creating the life you want. And, you can even <u>indirectly</u> change the types of ads you see to ones that support you in achieving your goals. *It's possible now that you know the basics of how social media algorithms work...*

Imagine if... instead of a bombardment of distracting cat videos, ads for junk food & videos about things you now consider a 'waste of time,' your social media feeds now just showed you content & ads that you really want to see!

This exercise - ***flood your feed*** - is about making this happen. It's not complex & doesn't take too long. It's a small change that can have profound benefit for you... *(especially when you factor in that statistics show the average young person spends 4 hours a day on social media!)*

Once you've defined the type of person you want to become & the ambitions you want to create in your life, go & **'flood your feed'** with these steps...

ACTIONABLE STEPS TO TAKE:

  1. **What You 'Like' & 'Follow'**

The first big thing that affects the type of content (& ads) you see on your feed is based on that which you've indicated you want to see through the things you 'like' or 'follow.'

By changing this, you change what shows up on your feed.

Hence, I urge you to take a few minutes to 'unlike' or 'unfollow' that which doesn't support you, while beginning to 'like' & 'follow' the types of pages, profiles, people, businesses & brands that'll show you the types of content that'll support you in achieving your ambitions.

Simply put: *'like' & 'follow' things according to what the best, future version of yourself would 'like' & 'follow' instead of what your past self may have been indulging in.*

As you start to indicate to the social media platforms that you are no longer interested in certain things, but interested in others (by what you 'like' & 'follow') you'll see new things.

For example, when you stop 'liking' & 'following' your local pizza store, a tobacco company or some of your favorite childhood sweets companies, those types of contents (& ads) are less likely to show up on your feed, distracting you from the type of health you may want to create.

When you combine this with the 2nd part: indicating to the social media platforms what you are actively interested in seeing going forward *(by engaging accordingly)* your feed will be transformed & any time you spend on social media will be positively conditioning you for the life you want...

2. What You Actively Engaging With

Beyond your list of 'likes' & 'follows,' algorithms respond to what which you actively engage with; *posts, ads & content that you like, things you comment on, share, heart, retweet, thumbs up, etc.*

So, if you want new things (things aligned with the life you want) showing up on your feed, that's what you must engage with *(while engaging less with what you don't want.)*

And be mindful as clicking on a post, link, article or ad for something which you *don't* truly, deep down, want not only wastes your time once but also makes those type of things show up on your feed more in the future (likely to waste your time again later on.)

It's a perpetual cycle that either supports you or distracts you - *you choose how you use it!*

If you want, you can even start to tap into positive forward momentum right now by taking 5 - 10 mins & intentionally engaging with things you want to start seeing more of...

3. Websites That You Visit

Lastly, the websites you visit on the internet *(even when you're not on a social media site)* also affect what shows up on your social media feeds.

This is because a lot of websites are now hooked up with these social media platforms (through their ad platforms) so that business can better advertise to you.

You may have seen this before... You go to some website somewhere on the internet. And, when you go back to your social media feed, you see an ad from that same person or business showing you the exact product you were looking at, asking you if you *'forgot Something?'* suggesting you click, return to the site & complete your order.

Beyond just this, a lot of the ads you'll see will come from the people, businesses & brands who you've shown interest in all over the internet.

Knowing all of this, the 3rd way you can skew what shows up on your social media feeds is by visiting websites & apps that align with what you want to see going forward.

Use this simple, yet powerful, exercise to turn social media into a great conditioning tool for the life you want!

INTERPRETATION OVER INFORMATION

Earlier in this chapter, I shared that you can *transcend your environment*. That, while your environment has the potential to influence you, you are not a victim to it & have a choice.

The same applies here with this 3rd form of conditioning. It's not the incoming information that shapes your 'beliefs' & results (although you want to skew this in your favor so you don't want to have to swim upstream) but the *interpretations* you form based on that *incoming information*.

I added this quick note here to make sure you (or others who read this chapter), don't start to use environment & incoming information as an excuse to be victims in their existence. You can choose to interpret things differently & make different decisions to get different results.

I suggest you re-read chapter #3 of this book (back in part #1) if you find yourself not living this foundational principle.

THERE IS ABUNDANCE

One of the things the news & media often do is make us feel that there is not enough. That there's *lack* & *scarcity* in life.

Why? Because scarcity invokes f*ear*, which as you know, is the best way to get people to feel they 'have to' pay attention.

In reality, there's much greater *abundance* than you may have been conditioned to believe there is in this world.

Once again, in the book *Abundance*, Peter Diamandis & Steven Kotler show, mathematically, scientifically & logically, just how much brighter the future is that we may think today.

They dive into many fields of advancement to show how the world is getting better in so many critical metrics & just how *abundant* it is & will be in the future.

However, to see the *abundance* in this world you must prime & condition yourself to see it. It must become a part of 'who you are' - else you'll likely miss it. *Once you do this, life becomes, in my personal experience, a lot more magical...*

But, don't worry, as we'll talk about exactly how you can condition yourself into a new state of consciousness (any new way of being) in the last chapter *(it's a must-read chapter that a lot of this book so far has been preparing you for...)*

THERE IS <u>ONENESS</u>

And the last big by-product of the news & media are the views of separation, difference & division we are conditioned into.

I've had the privilege of traveling all around the world from a very young age, getting to meet people from many different nations, races, cultures, religions & communities...

And, when I first started traveling, I would go into a country with many assumptions & stereotypes in mind (based on what I saw in news & various forms of media.)

Almost as if these fellow human beings were from a different species & we had nothing in common. Separated & divided; no feelings of oneness & unity. That's how I thought & felt.

I went to many countries in Asia, India, Australia & many countries in Europe with these instilled judgments.

Some of it was a little bit accurate, but a lot was inaccurate or wildly exaggerated, with key foundational parts omitted.

However, as I met, interacted with & connected with fellow human beings from different countries, cultures & groups around the world, I realized there was much more *oneness* than I had realized back when I was making assumptions based on the information from the news & media.

I recognized my past view wasn't what I wanted & decided to change it, replacing it with a greater sense of oneness *(as you'll learn how to do - shift 'beliefs' - in the next chapter.)*

Since then, I've also interacted with countless people who I've seen have a similar view to what I used to have. They see other nations, groups & communities as inferior, 'weird' or as enemies *(based on the conditioning of the news & media.)*

They do not see oneness & unity but see division & separation between themselves & other people in other countries, cities, religions, races & cultures.

And it just happens to be one of the core psychological reasons why we have armies, wars & global power struggles.

'No mother would kill her own child' it's said, but a mother (or even more so, a father) would go out on a battlefield & kill someone else's child without thinking twice about it. *Why?*

Because we get conditioned into an 'us vs them' paradigm; into division & separation compared to oneness & unity.

On the flip side, once you realize we are all connected, you can start to think, make decisions & do things differently.

This repeated amongst society & peace can become the result now - *as can greater connection & compassion.*

In reality, you, me & the person on the other side of the world in some poor 3rd world country are very, very similar.

In fact, you, me & every other human being on this planet, genetically speaking, are almost identical.

See, if you take your DNA & compare it to that of a monkey, you'll find (as researchers have confirmed) it's 99% the same.

PSYCHOLOGY | 325

And if your DNA is 99% the same as the DNA of a monkey, how similar to do you think it is to any & every other fellow human being on this planet? Almost identical.

Sure, there are small nuances that form different skin colors, body types, different height, hair color or eye color, etc, but we are almost completely identical when we are born. They are very small differences in the grand scheme of things.

I challenge you to also put this conditioning - the 'belief' that we are divided & separate (just as the 'beliefs' of fear, scarcity & lack) - under the microscope & think about them.

Ultimately, as Albert Einstein put it...

> *"A human being is part of the whole, called by us 'Universe'; a part limited in time and space. He experiences himself, his thoughts and feelings as something separated from the rest - a kind of optical delusion of his consciousness.*
>
> *This delusion is a kind of prison for us, restricting us to our personal desires and affection for a few persons nearest us. Our task must be to free ourselves from this prison by widening our circle of compassion to embrace all living creatures and the whole of nature in its beauty."*

There is abundance. There is a oneness. And there is a choice.

FREELY CHOOSING THE EXISTENCE YOU WANT

The '**3 categories of conditioning**' is a framework for understanding what made you 'who you are' today, but more importantly, it's a framework for becoming the type of person you want to become (& create the life with your freely choose.)

And it's a critical framework that aids the next part of this journey, which is shifting some of your *'beliefs'* to create a new *'you'* that aligns with the future you freely choice for yourself.

As we talked about in chapter 2, *'who you are'* (your identity) filters the possibilities & opportunities you seize in your life & the future that you create, however now *(in the very next & last chapter)* I'll go to reveal a powerful process for changing any 'belief' 'habit' or 'behavior' you want.

Much of what we've covered so far (while it can be profound & life-changing within itself) is the lead-up & pre-work required to get you ready for what's coming up in the next chapter...

Now - *you are ready! So, let's begin...*

7 | CONDITIONING A NEW 'YOU'
A NEW 'YOU' FOR A NEW LIFE...

"Everyone thinks of changing the world, but no one thinks of changing himself."

- LEO TOLSTOY

Everything in this book up until now brings us to this special last chapter - *this one; right here & now* - in which we bring practicality to the big-picture understandings we've covered...

See, you already know your identity creates your subjective view of reality & it's only by changing yourself that you change your life. You also know many of the foundational principles required to make a change in yourself as well.

And, this last chapter builds on all of this, sharing a powerful process you can use to change any 'belief' 'habit' or 'behavior' you want, through your own conscious effort.

As Henry David Thoreau once said, *"I know of no more encouraging fact than the unquestionable ability of man to elevate his life by conscious endeavor."* Now, let's begin...

CHANGING 'WHO YOU ARE': A 4-STEP PROCESS FOR CHANGING 'BELIEFS,' 'HABITS' & 'BEHAVIORS'

It was back in chapter #2 that I first challenged the common advise of *'be yourself'* as rather incomplete, sharing that life isn't about 'being yourself' but about 'creating yourself...'

Also sharing that 'who you are' has already changed countless times in your life already (whether you realize it or not...)

Hey, think about it... you're probably a very different person today than you were when you were 5, 10, 12, 18, 25 or perhaps 32 or 51 years of age - you changed as you grew up & went through your adult life. You changed beliefs, formed new habits & adapted your behaviors.

What this means is that *change is possible for you*. If you've already changed countless times in your life (& you have) it means you can change parts of 'who you are' going forward as well (if you choose to of course.)

See, people often assume change is impossible, failing to truly recognize that they've changed so many times before; they believed things were impossible, yet become real for them...

Plus, as it turns out, that's what *'self-mastery'* is actually all about: being will to change parts of 'who you are' to become a better & better version of yourself. It's all about transforming & transcending the past 'you' & constantly becoming a better person today than you were yesterday...

However, the difference between what you've probably done in the past & what you're going to learn here is **intention.**

In the past, you probably changed unconsciously or without much intention. You changed to adapt to the environment or to survive. You changed (for better or worse) without really planning on it & consciously choosing to do so.

Often, it was something new that came into your life *(a new person, job, teacher or mentor, a new piece of advice, new situation, etc)* that <u>stimulated</u> a change in beingness within you. *Chances are, you didn't stimulate that identity, habit or behavior change from within, but it came from outside.*

And that is one way to change your identity & your life: for something new to come into your life. It's a rather random & unpredictable approach - waiting for things from outside to help you improve yourself - but it is one way to do it.

The other (much more controllable & predictable) way is to consciously <u>stimulate</u> an identity, habit or behavior change *from within* - using the power of *intention & choice*.

See, as you know, we change *'beliefs,' 'habits'* & *'behaviors'* all the time. *That's what the human animal is wired to do: to change, adapt & evolve.* But, for most people, this change always comes from outside of them. Rarely (if ever) do people actually stop, pause, reflect & consciously design who they truly want to be (& change accordingly.) *Yet, this is perhaps the most powerful thing you can ever learn to do...*

When you learn to create change in your beliefs, habits & behaviors *from within* - at will; without having to rely on anything outside of you - that's when you truly tap into the power to shape your life as you want it (at any time!)

'Who you are' shapes your life. By changing your identity, you change your life. So, when new things come into your life, seize them. That's one level. *That's giving someone fish...*

However, when you learn to change 'who you are' at will first, *that's learning to fish...* (an ability that leads to an endless amount of metaphorical fish - new results - at will...)

Master this & you can tap into much more potential than you may have even believed was possible before this book...

Ultimately, you can consciously & intentionally choose to change part of your identity to create the person you want to be & live the life you want to live. You can stimulate change from within; through your own intention. *That's what this 4 step process in this last chapter here is about! Let's begin...*

1. **Clarity & Disassociation:** Recognize The Potential For A New 'You' & Select Changes You Want To Make.

To make a conscious & intentional shift, you must first be aware of where you are right now & where you want to be.

You must see this clear gap between your current, present-day beliefs, habits & behaviors, as well as know what you prefer instead *(as we covered in the 'Ambition' section)* before you can cross this bridge & make any change you want to make.

What 'beliefs' 'habits' & 'behaviors' have you identified during this book (& your entire life experience before it) that you would like to change? Which ones don't fit the person you want to become? Think about it. Ideally, write it down...

EXERCISE: OLD VS NEW SELF
What beliefs, habits & behaviors does your 'old self' have, which you would like to replace as part of your 'new self...'

Take 15 - 30 mins (minimum) to journal on this, as this is the 1st step to any change.

Here are some examples:

OLD Way: Smoking / Drinking / Drugs / Self-Abuse
NEW Way: I want to stop these destructive habits.

OLD Way: Phobia of... snakes / spiders / heights / etc
NEW Way: I don't want to have these phobias anymore.

OLD Way: Nail-biting / Hair-pulling / Issues sleeping
NEW Way: I want to get rid of these irritating behaviors.

OLD Way: Eat / drink too much... pizza / sugar / coffee
NEW Way: I want to free myself of this overconsumption.

OLD Way: I lack confidence & self-esteem (always fearful)
NEW Way: I want to be a confident, courageous person.

OLD Way: I still believe, 'money is the root of all evil'
NEW Way: I know this isn't true, but unconsciously I'm still holding onto these beliefs. I want to replace them so I can stop self-sabotage myself financially & achieve more.

Your goal here is to get very clear on the changes you want to make (or at least have 1 small change in mind just so you can go through this process). All change begins here...

Next, you must disassociate from that <u>old</u> 'belief' 'habit' or 'behavior' you want to change. *You can <u>no longer</u> see this as the only version of you; the only potential that exists for you.*

You must 'disassociate' because as long as you are clinging to a certain way of doing or being (& it remains an integrated part of 'who you are') you <u>won't</u> change...

You won't even believe that change is possible for you (or if you do, you'll be so closed-minded that you won't be able to see this change as something real that is worthwhile for you).

Or as J.P. Morgan eloquently put it, "The first step towards getting somewhere is to decide that you are not going to stay where you are."

By *dissociating* - stepping back to realize change is, in fact, possible & other paths are also available to you - you open yourself up to a better version of yourself. *It's the first step...*

YOU LEARNED TO BE 'WHO YOU ARE' TODAY (& YOU CAN 'LEARN' TO BE YOUR BEST SELF AS WELL...)

> *"The only way that we can live, is if we grow. The only way that we can grow is if we change. The only way that we can change is if we learn. The only way we can learn is if we are exposed. And the only way that we can become exposed is if we throw ourselves out into the open. Do it. Throw yourself."*
>
> - C. JOYBELL C.

You were born a mostly blank slate, with nothing but certain parts of your biology decided for you...

You weren't born with fear, greed or distrust. You weren't born with opinions, judgments or conditioned behaviors. You didn't have a favorite food, drink or ice-cream flavor. You didn't have any things you liked or hated.

At birth, you were like that blank canvas. And everything after that, you 'learned...'

The reason you are *'who you are'* today (beyond your biology, body & basics such as breathing, eating or sleeping) is you *learned* to be that way. You <u>learned</u> those ways of thinking, feeling & doing. That's what 'conditioning' (which we covered in detail in the last chapter) really is...

| Conditioning Is Nothing More Than 'Learning' To Be A Certain Way

If you live in a state of constant fear, for example, it's because you were conditioned to be that way. You choose to accept that conditioning & integrate it as part of *'who you are.'*

Or simply put: *you 'learned' how to be scared.*

You learned it very well. You learned how to think, feel, move & see life as a scared person does excellently. You learned that behavior (conditioning) & got really, really got at it; very good at finding the worst-case scenario in everything in life.

So good in fact, that you no longer even need to consciously think about it. You've gotten so incredibly skilled at being terrified that you do it automatically (like brushing your teeth or driving your car.)

It's an integrated part of your identity because you learned & trained it so many times...

And, whether we realize it or not, this is who we think we are. We think we are our behaviors, decisions, actions & results, but those are usually just conditioned things & we are so much greater than that *(as we talked about in chapter 2)*.

CHOOSE TO 'LEARN' SOMETHING NEW...

If you were born like a blank canvas - not in a constant state of fear for life - & you merely 'learned' to be a scared person living in fear, is it possible that you 'learn' how to be a more calm, blissful or courageous person instead?

You 'learned' (were conditioned) to be one way, so is it at all possible you also 'learn' (condition yourself) to be a different way? **Remember:** you were not born that way...

You weren't born shy, bad-tempered, jealous, evil, a drinker, a smoker or drug user. You weren't born with a requirement to follow all of the 'rules' of society.

Rather, you 'learned' all of that...

You were not born with it, you were conditioned into it.

Hence, with new information & new input can you condition your mind to think differently, change & become a new 'you?'

My work with customers & clients all around the world, the work of countless great people who came before me & the latest scientific research all point to the answer: **YES!**

You can change your 'beliefs' & condition yourself into a new, better version of 'who you are' - a version of you which doesn't smoke, drink, do drugs, get angry, jealous or stressed easily, isn't scared of flights, public speaking or spiders & doesn't lack self-esteem & courage.

You can condition that 'new' & 'improved' version of yourself, that loves learning, is smart, courageous & confidence, finds great bliss & peace in daily life, lives fully, loves completely & lives a magnificence existence! *It's possible.*

YOU MUST BELIEVE CHANGE IS <u>POSSIBLE</u>...

This big-picture outlook on life (which just happen to align which modern-day psychological research) shared above is just one way for you to 'disassociate' from one way of looking at the world & open yourself up to change. Another way is to look for <u>*inspiration*</u> in the journey of others...

Want to make the change to stop smoking, drinking, taking drugs, fearing heights, biting your nails or drinking gallons of coffee or soda every single day?

If you don't fully believe this change is possible, you can start by reading, listening to & watching others share their stories of change. Research the topic & spend time talking to others who have done what you want to do. Talk to friends & family who have gone through the same thing & changed.

All of this will help you build up the belief that you can do it too. It'll likely lead you to think... *'If they can do it, so can I!'*

The more you believe change is possible for you (which it is) & you can make it quickly & easily (without going through 12 years of therapy) the more likely you are to change!

In reality, it's possible to change in mind-blowingly short periods of time if you take the right steps & you're open. By *disassociating* from one particular path as the only version of 'who you are,' you're acknowledging change is, in fact, a possibility for you... (which is critical to any change!)

'*Yes, I can change; it's possible for me*' is this 1st belief you need in place to change. The 2nd is, '*I must change...*'

 2. **Big Enough <u>Why</u>:** Getting Leverage On Yourself By Associating <u>Pain</u> To The Old & <u>Pleasure</u> To The New...

As Friedrich Nietzsche said, *"He who has a way to live for can bear almost any how."* This original quote also inspired more recent adaptations such as, *"If you have a big enough why for anything, you can bear almost any how..."*

Like it or not, people don't change unless they have a strong enough reason to do so *('leverage' on themselves.)*

It why, once you believe change is a possibility (belief #1), the 2nd belief you must have in place is that 'change is a must.'

A lot of people want to change, but find it hard to get themselves to fully commit to it & follow through. They only dabble with it because their desire to change is only so strong.

People will often say, *'hey, I could really do this'* or *'I should really do this'* but these are usually just code for: *'I want it, but not strong enough; I'm not fully committed to it.'*

So they never make a change in the first place (even though they know they should) or if they do, it doesn't last. They end up staying the same - even though a part of them wants more.

To change, you must really want it. It must feel, not like something you 'could' do or should do, but something you are truly 'must' do. That's the 'leverage' you must get on yourself.

Fortunately, you can make change a 'must' (get leverage) by...

CHANGING YOUR 'ASSOCIATIONS'

"Nature has placed mankind under the governance of two sovereign masters, pain and pleasure. It is for them alone to point out what we ought to do, as well as to determine what we shall do. On the one hand, the standard of right and wrong, on the other the chain of causes and effects, are fastened to their throne. They govern us in all we do, in all we say, in all we think," philosopher Jeremy Bentham once said. And, like it or not, he was spot on...

There are 2 guiding forces that control our lives:

- **Pleasure** (good, right)
- **Pain** (bad, wrong)

However, within themselves, they have little-to-no impact on us. What really matters & shapes our lives is the *'associations'* we formed between things in life & these 2 guiding forces.

See, as we go through our lives, we form *'associations'* ('links' - connections) between certain beliefs, habits, behaviors & these 2 guiding forces (pleasure & pain.)

We link *this* with 'pain' or *that* with 'pleasure.' We link 'pleasure' to *that* & 'pain' to *this*. And it's these *'associations'* that ultimately control our decisions, our actions & whether or not we follow through with what we set out to in life.

There just 1 problem: we often form these 'associations' *unconsciously* - often without even realizing it.

And we end up unconsciously linking 'pleasure' to things we don't really want (like alcohol, drugs or smoking, because they get us out of some pain & into pleasure in that moment) or 'pain' to things we truly desire, want & even need (like work ethic, trust, physical exercise, learning or willingness to fully commitment in a relationship).

And, as long as these limiting *'associations'* (ones which go against what is truly aligned with your highest, best self) are present, we're unlikely to follow through & change.

Sure, you may want to be fit & healthy, as well as logically know that physical exercise is good for you, however as long as you unconsciously link ('associate') 'exercise' with 'pain' you're unlikely to follow through & get the results you want.

The same applies to all beliefs, habits & behaviors in our lives!

WHICH ASSOCIATIONS HAVE <u>YOU</u> FORMED?

Don't worry: you don't need to cut your brain open or hire a team of world-class psychologists to learn which *unconscious associations* you have that positively or negatively guide you.

This is because you can learn this, very simple, by just looking at your past & the present day. Do this with intention & the associations become very obvious…

For example, if you exercise regularly, it's usually because you see exercise as 'pleasurable' & worthwhile or you see the act of not exercising as very 'painful' or leading to a 'painful' reality.

Sure, your muscles may feel fatigued afterward (short-term pain), but in the big picture, you have a generally positive *association* with exercise & fitness. If you didn't & you linked more 'pain' to it than 'pleasure', you would instead find a way <u>not</u> to exercise regularly (as many do…)

You may even suddenly become 'sooooo busy' that you 'don't have time' to fit exercise in anymore. Which, as we know, is just one of many excuses people use & isn't really justified.

Plenty of very busy people finds time to exercise. It's not time that's a problem, but the *unconscious associations* you have towards exercise & fitness.

To aid understanding, imagine 'associations' (like all 'beliefs' in your life) like the roots of trees or plants.

They may operate unconsciously (under the surface) but you can learn more than enough about them by looking at the trees & plants that have grown out of them.

Which means, if you want to quickly learn the things that you unconsciously link 'pleasure' or 'pain' to (your 'associations') just look at what you consistently do (or <u>don't</u> do) in life…

WE **DO** THAT WHICH WE LINK 'PLEASURE' TO...

Whether or not you logically believe alcohol, cigarettes, drugs, pulling your hair, biting your fingernails or showcasing your aggression are things that bring you 'pleasure,' the reality is if you consistently do these things in your life, it's because you do, in fact, link some type of 'pleasure' to these behaviors.

To further support understanding, think of 'associations' like lines of computer code (or math equations):

- Smoking = Pleasure
- Drinking = Pleasure
- Drugs = Pleasure
- Self-Abuse = Pleasure
- Nail Biting = Pleasure
- Aggression = Pleasure
- Fast Food = Pleasure
- Coffee = Pleasure

Now, as you read this, a part of you may get a little defensive...

'Pleasure? I don't think that about drinking or smoking. Yes, I smoke, but I don't like it. I hate it. I wish I didn't do it!'

And you're totally spot on. A part of you does believe that, wants to change. It's what make people consider changing something in the first place...

Yet, at the same time, a part of you (usually your subconscious mind) has *associated* things like 'drinking' or 'smoking' with 'pleasure.' *It's why you do it (even if you know better)...*

And this associated 'pleasure' can come in many ways...

It may be a sense of *relief* you get when you're drunk, not having to think about the pain of a bad day, week or month.

Or a sense of *relaxation* you get whenever you smoke (which lowers your stress or nervousness).

Or the sense of *lower inhibitions & a quick, short-term boost of confidence* you get from the alcohol...

Sure, logically, you know there are many ways to relax or gain confidence (that don't harm your health), but as long as these *associations* are there, you're unlikely to change.

You may question some of these other things too, like *'There is no way someone can link 'self-abuse' with 'pleasure!'*

Many years ago, I would've thought the same & would be outraged by this notion. Today, my knowledge has deepened.

Like it or not, self-sabotage & self-abuse do often come from an association to 'pleasure' of some sort; *a feeling it's a 'good' thing to do, or at the very least the 'right' thing to do.*

The 'pleasure' isn't physical or logical, but emotional...

People will feel they deserve to suffer because of something they did or some part of themselves they're ashamed off & so will *self-sabotage* or *self-abuse* themselves to get a feeling of *'justice' 'relief' 'fairness'* or *'balanced karma.'* (all different forms of <u>*'pleasure'*</u> *that relieve emotional conflict...*)

This also leads us to the second side of the coin...

WE <u>AVOID</u> THAT WHICH WE LINK '<u>PAIN</u>' TO...

Beside our associations with 'pleasure,' it's also our links with 'pain' that keep us from changing. Here are some examples...

- Hard work & discipline = Pain
- Relationships = Pain
- Healthy food = Pain
- Exercise = Pain

- Learning = Pain
- Rest, relaxation & time-off = Pain
- People = Pain

You may know something is important (like exercise or social interaction), yet if you've unconsciously 'associated' it with 'pain' in your life, you're unlikely to follow through & get the results you want in this area.

For example, a part of you may want a relationship, but if you are scared of fully committing to one *(an association between 'commitment' & 'pain' or 'Commitment to a partner = pain')* you're likely to do highly irrational things that completely go against what you know you want & self-sabotage you in your relationships. *That's until you change your 'associations'...*

It's also the reason people fear flying or to talk to strangers.

As I've shared a few times now, flying is the safest mode of transportation, however if you've *unconsciously 'associated'* huge 'pain' to the idea of getting into a metal bird & being hurled across the skies in it *(as your unconscious mind may describe it...)* you're going to fear it.

The same applies to social situations & meeting new people you haven't met before (a.k.a talking to strangers!). If you link this idea with 'pain' you're going to resist it...

And, now you know all of this, the 2nd step to making any change in your life (& making it last) is to change your 'associations' until you feel change is a 'must.'

HOW TO MAKE CHANGE A 'MUST' FOR YOU...

Most people link 'pleasure' to the idea of staying the same & 'not changing' (they feel comfortable right now) & 'pain' to the idea of changing (it's unknown, scary & life-threatening; at least that how their subconscious views it.)

Is it any wonder then that most change attempts fail? Not at all. Not with that type of thinking...

Meanwhile, to make change a 'must' for you *(& set yourself up to follow through & get results)* you must do the opposite...

1. **Pleasure:** link enough 'pleasure' to the idea of changing & the results you'll get after this change...
2. **Pain:** link enough 'pain' to the idea of staying the same (not changing) now & in the future...
3. **Both** of the above together *(recommended)*.

Right now, you may be unconsciously linking lots of 'pleasure' to drinking or smoking & 'pain' to the thought of never being able to drink or smoke ever again, however to change you must do the opposite...

You must instead link much more 'pleasure' to the idea of not drinking or smoking while linking lots of 'pain' to the idea of staying the same. That's how you change. *And again, the same applies to any & every change you want to make...*

However, we must bear in mind that 'pleasure' & 'pain' is also different for different people (so we must personalize it to us.)

For one person, being admitted into the hospital with lung cancer is enough 'pain' for them to change & never smoke again. For someone else, they'll keep smoking anyway...

However, if their 5-year-old granddaughter tells them to stop, *'you're not allowed to die grandpa, so stop smoking right this moment as that's what the doctor says caused this'* you may change in an instant. Or maybe not...

It may be the realization a week later that if they don't stop smoking, that may cut down their lifespan further & so the charity work they've spent the last 2 decades doing may never have the impact it truly can. That realization about a purpose bigger than themselves may make it feel like a 'must' for someone & they'll find a way to quit smoking no matter what!

Or, it may be a combination of different reasons that finally gets you (or anyone else) to finally feel they 'must' change. It really depends on the individual here...

What remains the same though is that when you do finally form these new associations - *linking enough 'pain' to staying the same & 'pleasure' to the idea of the new 'you'* - you'll have the 'leverage' you need to change...

From there, actually making the change you want to make (the next 2 steps) becomes much, much easier...

EXERCISE: 'WHY' TO CHANGE (GET LEVERAGE)
What's your 'leverage' -your big 'why' & new associations - that are going make change a must for you...

Start by taking a few minutes to journal on everything that comes to mind on why you need to change. Then start this:

'OLD' WAY:
(copy from step #1)

_____

'NEW' WAY:
(copy from step #1)

_____

LINK PAIN TO 'NOT CHANGING':
What has 'not changing' cost you in the past, or is costing you in the present? If you continue not to change, what will it cost you mentally & emotionally - in your health, wealth, love & happiness - over the next 1, 3, 5, 10, 20 or

50 years? Journal on those questions & then write down **5 big ways** 'not changing' will cause you massive pain...

_____
_____
_____
_____
_____

TAKE TIME TO FEEL IT

Once you wrote down your *5 big reasons*, linking 'pain' to the idea of 'not changing,' take time now to *feel it*!

Close your eyes (for 5 minutes) & feel it fully & deeply...

1. Feel all the pain this belief, habit or behavior has caused you in the PAST...

2. Feel the pain it's costing you in the PRESENT...

3. Feel the pain this will continue to cause you into the FUTURE. See yourself 6 months, then 1 year, then 3 years, then 5, 10 or 20 years from now & even at the end of your life! *Feel all the pain continue this way will cause you for the rest of your life all in this 1 moment.*

Really take time to feel the 5 reasons you wrote above!

LINK <u>PLEASURE</u> TO 'CHANGING':

What pleasure, good & bliss will make this change bring you in your life? How will it make life better, mentally & emotionally - in your health, wealth, love & happiness? - right away & in the future, if you finally make the change? Write **5 big ways** 'changing' will bring massive pleasure..

_____

_____

_____

_____

_____

_____

TAKE TIME TO FEEL IT

Once you wrote down your 5 reasons, linking 'pleasure' to the idea of 'changing,' take a moment now to feel it!

Close your eyes (for 5 minutes) & feel it fully & deeply...

1. Feel the pleasure it'll will bring you if you make this change right here & now - in the <u>PRESENT.</u>

2. Feel the pleasure it will continue to bring you into the <u>FUTURE</u>. See yourself 6 months, then 1 year, then 3 years, then 5, 10 or 20 years from now & even at the end of your life, feeling all the pleasure this will bring you throughout life.

Really take time to feel the 5 reasons you wrote above!

> **SUMMARY: WHY 'MUST' YOU CHANGE NOW**
> Once you've taken the time to write down (& most importantly, feel) everything above, in 1 - 2 sentences write down why you absolutely 'must' change now.
>
> _____
> _____
> _____

3. **Breaking Old 'Patterns':** Interrupting & Snapping Yourself Out Of Old Ways Of Being & Doing...

You now know change is possible & with new *'associations'* you've made it feel like a total 'must' for you *(if not, go back, re-read & implement the first 2 steps before continuing)*...

This 3rd step is about 'interrupting' & eventually 'breaking' old 'patterns' of behavior.

See, something may be a 'must' for you & as a result, both your conscious & unconscious associations are pulling you into a new version of 'who you are,' but at the same time, there's still one thing clinging to the past & holding you back...

This is the 2, 5, 12, 21, 43 or 67 years old of doing something the exact same way; strong, ingrained habits (or, 'patterns').

Without breaking these old 'patterns' you may start making some huge steps forward, but every so often something will 'trigger' you & you'll end up playing out old 'patterns.' Step 3 is all about changing this so the change actually lasts...

'OFF & RUNNING...'

The importance of this 3rd step really clicked for me when I was helping a client of mine edit a book she wrote...

Her book (titled: *I Don't Want To Be Me Anymore*) is a personal story of her tough journey through life. As well as sharing how, when she was about 65 years old, she finally started to turn her life around, getting out of a lifetime of alcohol & drug addiction, stopping her problems with the law & moving past her sense of destruction into great healing...

Personally, I found her story (that's shared in that book) very inspiring as it shares something I've always believed very strongly: *that age really doesn't matter when it comes to changing, improving & bettering yourself!*

I began my journey of self-mastery (& started to see the results from it) when I was about 13 or 14 years old. For her, she was in her mid 60's. And there are also others reading books like this one in there 80's, 90s or beyond. Simply put...

| It's Never Too Late (Or Too Early) To Change & Become The Person You Truly Want To Be

However, this inspiration is not the reason why I'm sharing this example here. It's about something very different...

See, in her book *(which I realized while I was helping with editing)*, when sharing about past situations which included alcohol or drug, she would often use the phrase *'And I was off & running...'* One of the subtitles in the book is, in fact, 'OFF & RUNNING. AGAIN.')

At first, this phrase seemed a little bizarre to me. *'A weird choice of words'* I thought to myself...

However, after reading it a number of times, it really 'clicked' for me - it was like one of those epiphany moments you might see in some movie somewhere...

I realized that this description was actually spot on & a great example of how we play out old 'patterns' in our lives...

In the book, she would describe a situation that triggered her (e.g. when someone said something which she got stressed or angry about) which caused bad habits she wanted to change (e.g. alcohol, drugs, etc) to be set *'off & running...'*

And then the description of what happened afterward became rather vague in the book (which I also realized during the editing, as well as through follow up conversations with her).

Before, she remembered plenty of details of these situations, but as soon as she was 'triggered' & acted based on those same old 'patterns' of alcohol or drugs (even crime sometimes) she struggled to remember very much. It become a blur after that.

She knew that she doing these things & spiraling downwards, but it was hard for her to even be able to rationalize these choices, explain them or feel she could stop this particular nightmare from continuing. She felt completely out of control at those moments; as if some inner demon had taken over the steering wheel & was now controlling her decisions...

Which, as it turns out, is actually partially true.

After she got 'triggered' in some way & her bad habits (which she wanted to change) were set *'off & running...'* she *didn't* make the bad decisions after that herself. Instead, it was those old 'patterns' (those 'inner demons) playing out. *That's until the next morning when this was replaced with massive conscious confusion & regret...*

I'm sure you can relate in some way...

Have you wanted to change (e.g. 'I'm going to be a calm person today', 'I'm going to be understanding & empathetic instead of getting angry at people today' or 'I'm <u>not</u> going to drink tonight'), but you ended up completely forgetting this

& engaging in perhaps an even more extreme version of the very same belief, habit or behavior you wanted to change?

You were able to remain calm (even in seemingly 'stressful' situations) for a few days, but then you just 'snapped' & went on an angry, fearful & pissed off streak like never before...

Or, you hadn't drunk any alcohol for a few days, weeks or months, then suddenly one night, something 'triggered' you (maybe you had a bad day at work, had a small sip of some brand new alcohol you hadn't tasted before or someone said that you're not a 'real man' now that you don't drink, etc) & you drank more in that one night than you remember ever drinking before?

Whatever the change; one moment you were perfectly fine & in control, the next, your old 'patterns' were 'off & running...'

This is because the old 'pattern' was never fully broken (or overwritten), but merely covered up or suppressed (under the surface, waiting for a chance to run rampage - if 'triggered...')

'PATTERNS' YOU PLAY OUT...

That's what we do when it comes to strong habits & consistent behaviors in our lives (or 'patterns.') We get 'triggered' & our subconscious mind (which runs these old 'patterns') just completely takes over...

And the longer you've repeated a habit or behavior (e.g. you've smoked every day for 12 years), the stronger it's wired into your subconscious mind & likely to get 'triggered...'

However, like many things we've talked about in this book, unconscious ways of being or doing (referred to as 'patterns' here) are not good or bad within themselves.

Brushing your teeth, showering or driving are also 'patterns' you play out unconscious. Except: they are supportive ones.

You get in a car as you go to work in the morning via the same route you've taken every day for the past 8 months & your driving 'pattern' is 'off & running...' It's automatic. You don't need to consciously think about turning on the car, pressing the gas pedal or even the turns that you take on the route as you've done it the exact same way so many times that the unconscious 'pattern' just does this for you. *Deeply habitual!*

The same neurons have 'fired & wired' together so many times, that they are almost inseparable...

That's the power of the subconscious mind: you're able to do, without having to consciously think about it, something that during your first driving lesson may have seemed difficult (& required a lot of your conscious focus & effort to do...)

And just as this is an incredibly positive thing in some areas of our lives *(just imagine the hardship if every drive required the same conscious engagement as your first driving lesson; having to think about each & every small thing you do in the car)* but at other times this can really work against us...

Our old 'patterns' can get 'triggered' & be set 'off & running...' long before you can even catch up to them.

You could be halfway through your 2nd pack of cigarettes for the week (or the day!) feeling completely powerless to change it at that moment. *You're playing out an old 'pattern...'*

Fortunately, just as you created these 'patterns' in your life, you can also break them, making room for more empowering ones instead. *How?* Simply...

YOU MUST 'INTERRUPT' THE OLD 'PATTERN'...

Have you ever interrupted someone while they were speaking (or seen someone else do this) so many times in a short period of time that the person attempting to speak just gets quiet or says something like, *'Fine. I just won't tell you my story if you just keep interrupting me...'*

Well, that's what you want to do with your subconscious mind regarding the beliefs, habits & behaviors you want to change...

You must *'interrupt'* the old *'pattern'* (that your subconscious mind normally plays out without any interruption at all) until it gives up on attempting to play out that *'pattern.'* *Or better yet, interrupt it so much it's <u>unable to ever play it again</u>...*

To support understanding, *let's go back a bit...*

A *'pattern'* (in this context) is nothing more than a series of steps (usually done very unconsciously; on autopilot) that you play out one after another...

For example, the 'driving to work pattern' might be this:

- Get into car.
- Turn on the engine.
- Close the car door.
- Drive out of the driveway.
- Get onto the main road.
- Drive for 1km on the main road (until roundabout).
- Take 2nd exit on the roundabout.
- Drive straight for 400m..
- Park by the office.
- Turn off engine.
- Close, get out & lock car doors.

This, of course, is a simplified example as in actuality, there could be hundreds or thousands of little steps required.

Yet, someone can do all of these steps without really thinking about any of them. And sometimes while on a phone, talking to a friend, drinking morning coffee or doing their makeup. *It's a deeply ingrained 'pattern' drivers play out...*

In this same way, someone with a snake or sniper phobia is also playing out a 'pattern' (a series of unconscious steps done automatically one after another)... They focus on the same things, playing the same mental images in their minds, often tensing up their bodies in the same way.

And by 'interrupt the pattern' I'm simply referring to the idea of adding some type of wedge or distraction (something that brings you back to <u>conscious</u> thought & shifts your focus) between the unconscious steps in the sequence.

Instead of letting the steps play through unconsciously, one after another (like you normally do) when you 'interrupt' it, you're intentionally doing something different than that.

<u>HOW TO</u> 'INTERRUPT' AN OLD 'PATTERN?'

As soon as you even get the thought of alcohol, a cigarette, a drug, going to a casino & gambling), a spider or a snake, instead of letting your mind *'off & running'*- playing out the same thoughts, feelings, decisions & actions as it usually does, you must 'interrupt' this *pattern* by doing something very different. And, the weirder the better here. **Some examples:**

- Drop down & do 20 pushups
- Scream something out loud
- Put your finger up your nose
- Jump up & down like a maniac
- Do an evil laugh
- Meditate or strike (& hold) a yoga pose
- Read some jokes on the internet
- Imagine you had a tail & chase it like a dog
- Pour a glass of water (or a drink nearby) on your head

What you do doesn't really matter as long as it's something that's going to 'interrupt' - to interfere with - the 'pattern' that you would normally play out without any interruption.

Each of these little, random & weird things, whether you believe it or not, bring you back to a more conscious, aware state of mind, changes your focus & interferes with the series of steps you would normally play out unconsciously.

Through repetition - constantly 'interrupting' this old 'pattern' & not letting your mind go down the black hole of the same familiar steps that are part of the 'pattern' - you begin to 'break' down old 'patterns,' create progress & making room for new, empowering alternatives to form instead.

Just as 'patterns' are built through repetition, they are also broken in the same way: through repeated 'interruption.'

GETTING OTHERS TO HELP...

In the inspirational novel & movie, *Peaceful Warrior*, there's a scene in which the mentor & the student meet on a bridge.

The student, *Dan Millman*, is in a hurry so he ask to make sure that today's lesson can be completely quickly...

"Sure" the mentor replies. And then pushes him over the edge of the bridge & into the water!

Soaked & frustrated, Dan, gets out of the water & hurriedly catches up to the mentor as he walks away.

"HEY! HEY! I'm talking to you! What the hell is wrong with you?!" he shouts.

"You said you were on a hurry..." the mentor replied, before getting interrupted, *"So you pushed me off the bridge?"*

Calmly, the mentor replied... *"I emptied your mind."*

The mentor continues... *"And while you were falling, tell me, Dan, what were you thinking about? Thinking about school? Grocery shopping? This thing you had to hurry off to?'*

After a series of 'no' responses, he says to Dan... *"You were present. Devoted 100% to the experience you were having. You even had a word for it... Arggghhhhh!"*

When Dan finally says, *"You're out of your mind, you know that?"* the mentor replies, *'It's taken a lifetime of practice."*

While I usually share this great example from this must-read novel (or must-watch movie) to talk about *presence* (being conscious & aware in the present moment - right here & now) or how quickly we can change how we feel in a given moment, it's also a great example of a 'pattern interrupt' *(which is why I'm sharing this example here in this chapter...)*

I also share this to bring up the point that you don't need to do this alone. You can ask others to help you 'interrupt' your old 'patterns' repeatedly as well...

For example, if you're want to stop a finger-nail-biting habit, you can ask friends or family something like: *'If you ever see me even looking at my fingernails in a way that suggests I'm feeling compelled to bite then, can you please interrupt my 'pattern' in some way?'*

You can be creative here; just make sure you follow through in constantly 'interrupting' those old 'patterns'...

And this brings us onto the 4th & last step...

4. **Wiring New 'Patterns':** 'Repetition' To 'Overwrite' The Old With The New (Making Change <u>Last</u>!)...

Once you've 'interrupt' & 'break' an old pattern, most of the work of creating a change is done. But, it's not complete yet; not if you want the best results that'll serve you best in life!

See, as one 'pattern' falls away, another must form...

And unless you consciously create this new 'pattern' you may unconsciously create another one that doesn't help you either.

See, your old 'patterns' while destructive were not completely useless. They actually served a purpose; you linked some type of 'pleasure' or 'pain' to them for a reason after all…

For example, smoking may have been helping you cope with stress. Sure, it was killing you, but it was also helping you relax in particularly stressful moments you experienced…

Perhaps alcohol helped you feel more confident, while also helping you forget your problems when you really wanted to.

Lashing out at people with anger helped you feel in control, instantly giving you a strong sense of power & certainty.

These old 'patterns' didn't serve you at the highest level, but you did them for a reason…

Now that you have 'interrupted' those old 'pattern' you had (through the first 3 steps in this process) a new one has to form to help you deal with those same situations & emotions.

In times of stress, if you're not going to play out your past 'pattern' of smoking, what are you going to do now? *What 'pattern' are you going to play out instead?*

Or in times where you feel out of control & you're not going to get angry & aggressive, what are you going to do instead to regain a sense of certainty & power? *What are you doing to do instead of that?*

Some people stop drinking & start smoking (because it helps them meet that same underlying need). Or stop smoking & start overeating. Or stop overeating & get more aggressive. Or stop that & start whining & complaining all the time…

Either you conscious create an empowering alternative which more constructively helps you fulfill your needs *(which is what this step is here to help you do)* or you may end up with another destructive 'pattern' you're playing out instead...

Instead of using smoking as a way to deal with stress - to calm yourself down - don't switch to aggression or nail-biting, but consider wiring new (& more empowering) 'patterns' such as deep breathing, meditation, exercise or conversation.

Before, when you came back home angry, wanting to forget about the day you had at work, it 'triggered' your old pattern of reaching for alcohol. *Now that you broke this old 'pattern' what are you going to do instead to feel great at home?*

Perhaps, you'll play out a new 'pattern' of taking 3 deep breaths & focusing on being the best wife or husband you can be? Perhaps hitting the gym to get in great shape? Or taking some time to think about what you're grateful for in life?

Those are suggestions; you can choose. *But choose something.*

HOW TO 'WIRE' A NEW 'PATTERN'

Once you've selected the new things you want to do instead that meet the underlying needs your old 'pattern' used to meet, the last part is to train (or 'wire') this new 'pattern.'

This is really the easy part though. You do this just like you built any habit in your life: <u>*repetition*</u>.

You do it over & over again, as well as acknowledge yourself for the great progress you're making along the way.

Don't wait until day 42 to celebrate that your old 'pattern' of alcohol or drugs has been replaced with deep breathing, yoga, gratitude, meditation, or whatever you choose.

Rather, celebrate each day; each & every win. Give yourself a pat on the back, reflect on the great progress you're making & reinforce your belief in yourself.

Ultimately, like anything unmaintained, your old 'pattern' will weaken (until it's gone), while your new empowering 'pattern' (like a muscle) will strengthen. *That's how we change!*

WHEN MOST PEOPLE CHANGE… (& WHY WAIT?)

As you've probably realized yourself, most people don't make any real change until they reach rock bottom in a particular area of their life…

It's only when their company files for bankruptcy, the family abandons them because of their alcohol addiction or they are laying in a hospital bed with a life-threatening illness, do most people consciously & unconsciously feel change is enough of a 'must' for them to follow through. *That's when most change…*

One of the core messages I want to share is… **'*why wait?*'**

Why wait before something gets seriously bad before finally making a change when you can make it today?

It's possible to change out of a desire for something greater, so **why wait?** *Why wait until your health deteriorates to start taking care of it? Why wait until you have relationships issues to start working on improving your relationship?*

Why wait? Let's be <u>preventive</u> & <u>proactive</u> instead!

I've always believed in prevention, as well as anticipation.

As the quote by Benjamin Franklin, which today is often used in the health space, says, *"An ounce of prevention is worth a pound of cure."*

Work on preventing, changing & resolving potential problems before they occur, instead of 'curing' them later when they get really bad. *And this applies to all areas of your life...*

Don't wait; create change now *(especially, now that you know what you need to do to begin...)*

COMING TOGETHER: USING THIS PROCESS

> *"Knowing is not enough; we must apply. Willing is not enough; we must do."*
>
> \- JOHANN WOLFGANG VON GOETHE

Combined, these 4 steps hold tremendous power to help you change any *belief, habit or behavior* you want to change.

However, they do not work unless you work.

As Pablo Picasso said, *"Action is the foundational key to all success."* As Napoleon Hill once shared, *"Action is the real measure of intelligence"*

Or, as Mark Twain once put it, *"The secret of getting ahead is getting started."*

Ultimately, you must be truly willing & then proceed to follow through with this process to make a given change last.

Then, once you do, not only will one area of your life get better, but you'll additionally & automatically, gain a greater belief that you can change other areas of your life as well...

You may then choose to use this process *(as well as all the contents, understandings, strategies & exercises in this book)* to improve other parts of 'who you are' & areas of your life.

This, of course, further reinforces your belief in yourself & the possibilities available to you *(as shared in chapter #1)...*

Before long, you are in *massive positive momentum* (as we also first talked about back in chapter #1).

You're becoming the person you want to be; better with each & every day...

Challenging your limitations...

Stepping into greater & greater potential available to you...

And, as a result, creating the life you truly want to live...

It's possible! And it all starts with the little (yet powerful) thoughts, feelings, decisions & actions you make *(like your choice to get your copy of this book in the first place & even more so your decision to follow through & read it.)*

Once again, as Vincent Van Gogh said, *"Great things are done by a series of small things brought together."*

You now have the understandings, strategies & tools you need *to create the life you want by becoming the person you truly want to be.*

It's been a pleasure writing this book for you. I hope it over-delivered on your expectations & you got tremendous value from it. Now, go see what potential you can tune into...

Talk soon,
Bogdan Juncewicz

ABOUT THE AUTHOR

Bogdan believes human potential is infinite, with an endless stream of possibilities we can tune into through our thoughts, feelings, decisions & actions. It's why he has dedicated his life to his mission of *elevating, improving & evolving human education, achievement & life experience.*

His work is in decoding, demystifying, as well as explaining simply the principles & strategies one needs to become the person they want to be & create the life they truly want. His focus is on that which is proven to work & will continue to produce results for anyone *(irrelevant of age, gender, race or upbringing)* over the long term.

He made a choice to drop out of high school at age 14 in the interest of pursuing something greater (& looks back on this as the best decision he's ever made professionally.)

Today, **Bogdan Juncewicz** is the author of multiple books & international speaker who has spoken on stages across 3 continents, teaching & coaching thousands of people worldwide. Including multi-millionaires, TEDx speakers, musicians, teachers, ex-addicts, TV producers, entrepreneurs, gym owners & more.

He's also the founder & CEO of 2 businesses, which serve fans, readers, customers & clients spanning 6 continents.

He has more than 6 years of real-world, regular 100-hour work weeks, experience, researching, studying & teaching topics, such as accelerated learning, skill development, motivation, productivity & overall self-mastery. His teachings are grounded in years of study in the fields of neuroscience, psychology & human behavior.

And he's also the man behind the content & marketing of other top influencers, businesses & brands teaching wellness, self-improvement, business, finance & more.

Author. International Speaker. CEO. *High School Dropout.*

You can learn more about his mission & work over at **BogdanJuncewicz.com**

WANT MORE? CHECK OUT...

NOTES

NOTES

NOTES

NOTES

NOTES

NOTES

NOTES

NOTES

NOTES

Made in the USA
Middletown, DE
05 November 2023